SCOUTING FOR BOYS

SCOUTING FOR BOYS

A Handbook for Instruction in Good Citizenship

By

ROBERT BADEN-POWELL

(*first Baron Baden-Powell of Gilwell*)

Founder of the World Scout Movement

and

CHIEF SCOUT OF THE WORLD

"Scouts of the World—Brothers Together"

THE SCOUT ASSOCIATION
25 BUCKINGHAM PALACE ROAD
LONDON SW1W 0PY

© THE SCOUT ASSOCIATION

SBN 85165 091 0

Thirty-fourth Edition
Reprinted 1967
Reprinted with revised Appendix 1974

Printed in Great Britain by
Fletcher & Son Ltd, Norwich

CONTENTS

Illustrations by
B-P.

INTRODUCTION

SCOUTING FOR BOYS is a book for all time, and in his own lifetime our Founder saw it in use in almost every country in the world.

Details of programmes and activities must always change with circumstances and conditions, but in its spirit and essentials his book is timeless and universal, and it is for us who come after him to act as its guardians and to see that the whole essence of Scouting is preserved therein, whatever may be the adaptations or allowances to meet varying conditions or needs.

You will find that many of the suggestions for games and practices are still capable of use even to-day, fifty-six years after they were originally written. But perhaps more important is the imaginative presentation of a particular subject which lies behind the suggested activity. We must always remember that the secret of the success which the Movement has achieved is the way in which ideas are presented and not merely the detail of the activities.

Every word that our Founder wrote had truth behind it, and truth is not limited to any single generation or nation.

SCOUTING FOR BOYS is the Handbook showing us how to use, care for, preserve, and hand down, the tool which his genius devised and which he bequeathed to us. If we learn to use this tool in its purity, its simplicity, and its spirit, we shall find that it meets the needs of every place and of each succeeding generation of boys.

Olave Baden-Powell

February, 1963.   World Chief Guide.

FOREWORD

written by B-P. in 1932

I WAS A BOY ONCE.

The best time I had as a boy was when I went about as a sea scout with my four brothers on the sea round the coasts of England. Not that we were real Sea Scouts, because Sea Scouts weren't invented in those days. But we had a sailing boat of our own on which we lived and cruised about, at all seasons and in all weathers, and we had a jolly good time—taking the rough with the smooth.

Then in my spare time as a schoolboy I did a good lot of scouting in the woods in the way of catching rabbits and cooking them, observing birds and tracking animals, and so on. Later on, when I got into the Army, I had endless fun big-game hunting in the jungles in India and Africa and living among the backwoodsmen in Canada. Then I got real scouting in South African campaigns.

Well, I enjoyed all this kind of life so much that I thought, "Why should not boys at home get some taste of it too?" I knew that every true red-blooded boy is keen for adventure and open-air life, and so I wrote this book to show you how it could be done.

And you fellows have taken it up so readily that now there are not only hundreds of thousands of Boy Scouts but millions about the world!

Of course, a chap can't expect to become a thorough backwoodsman all at once without learning some of the difficult arts and practices that the backwoodsman uses. If you study this book you will find tips in it showing you how to do them—and in this way you can learn for yourself instead of having a teacher to show you how.

Then you will find that the object of becoming an able and efficient Boy Scout is not merely to give you fun and adventure but that, like the backwoodsmen, explorers, and frontiersmen whom you are following, you will be fitting yourself to help your country and to be of service to other people who may be in need of help. That is what the best men are out to do.

A true Scout is looked up to by other boys and by grown-ups as a fellow who can be *trusted*, a fellow who will not fail to do his duty however risky and dangerous it may be, a fellow who is jolly and cheery no matter how great the difficulty before him.

I've put into this book all that is needed to make you a good Scout of that kind. So, go ahead, read the book, practise all that it teaches you, and I hope you will have half as good a time as I have had as a Scout.

Baden Powell of Gilwell

Chief Scout of the World.

RESOLUTION PASSED BY THE BIENNIAL INTERNATIONAL SCOUT CONFERENCE HELD AT COPENHAGEN IN AUGUST 1924

The Boy Scouts International Conference declares that the Boy Scout Movement is a Movement of national, international, and universal character, the object of which is to endow each separate nation and the whole world with a youth which is physically, morally and spiritually strong.

It is NATIONAL, in that it aims through national organizations, at endowing every nation with useful and healthy citizens.

It is INTERNATIONAL in that it recognizes no national barrier in the comradeship of the Scouts.

It is UNIVERSAL in that it insists upon universal fraternity between all Scouts of every nation, class or creed. The Scout Movement has no tendency to weaken but, on the contrary, to strengthen individual religious belief. The Scout Law requires that a Scout shall truly and sincerely practise his religion, and the policy of the Movement forbids any kind of sectarian propaganda at mixed gatherings.

THE SCOUT PROMISE

On my honour I promise that I will do my best—
  To do my duty to God, and the Queen,
  To help other people at all times,
  To obey the Scout Law,

THE SCOUT LAW

1. **A Scout's honour is to be trusted.**

   If a Scout says "On my honour it is so", that means that it *is* so, just as if he had made a most solemn promise.

   Similarly, if a Scouter says to a Scout, "I trust you on your honour to do this", the Scout is bound to carry out the order to the very best of his ability, and to let nothing interfere with his doing so.

   If a Scout were to break his honour by telling a lie, or by not carrying out an order exactly when trusted on his honour to do so, he may be directed to hand over his Scout Badge, and never to wear it again. He may also be directed to cease to be a Scout.

2. **A Scout is loyal to the Queen, his country, his Scouters, his parents, his employers and to those under him.**

   He must stick to them through thick and thin against anyone who is their enemy or who even talks badly of them.

3. **A Scout's duty is to be useful and to help others.**

   And he is to do his duty before anything else, even though he gives up his own pleasure, or comfort, or safety to do it. When in difficulty to know which of two things to do, he must ask himself, "Which is my duty?" that is, "Which is best for other people?"—and do that one. He must *Be Prepared* at any time to save life, or to help injured persons. And he *must try his best to do at least one Good Turn* to somebody every day.

4. **A Scout is a friend to all, and a brother to every other Scout, no matter to what country, class or creed the other may belong.**

Thus if a Scout meets another Scout, even though a stranger to him, he must speak to him, and help him in any way that he can, either to carry out the duty he is then doing, or by giving him food, or, as far as possible, anything that he may be in want of. A Scout must never be a SNOB. A snob is one who looks down upon another because he is poorer, or who is poor and resents another because he is rich. A Scout accepts the other man as he finds him, and makes the best of him.

"Kim" was called "Little friend of all the world", and that is the name that every Scout should earn for himself.

5. **A Scout is courteous.**

That is, he is polite to all—but especially to women and children, and old people and invalids, cripples, etc. And he must not take any reward for being helpful or courteous.

6. **A Scout is a friend to animals.**

He should save them as far as possible from pain, and should not kill any animal unnecessarily, for it is one of God's creatures. Killing an animal for food or an animal which is harmful is allowable.

7. **A Scout obeys orders of his parents, Patrol Leader, or Scoutmaster without question.**

Even if he gets an order he does not like he must do as soldiers ✳ and sailors do, and as he would do for his captain in a football team, he must carry it out all the same *because it is his duty;* and after he has done it he can come and state any reasons against it: but he must carry out the order at once. That is discipline.

8. **A Scout smiles and whistles under all difficulties.**

When he gets an order he should obey it cheerily and readily, not in a slow, hang-dog sort of way.

Scouts never grouse at hardships, nor whine at each other, nor grumble when put out, but go on whistling and smiling. When you just miss a train, or someone treads on your favourite corn—not that a Scout ought to have such things as corns—or under any annoying circumstances, you should force yourself to smile at once, and then whistle a tune, and you will be all right.

9. **A Scout is thrifty.**

   That is, he saves every penny he can, and puts it into the bank, so that he may have money to keep himself when out of work, and thus not make himself a burden to others; or that he may have money to give away to others when they need it.

10. **A Scout is clean in thought, word, and deed.**

    That is, he looks down upon a silly youth who talks dirt, and he does not let himself give way to temptation either to talk it or to think, or to do anything dirty.

    A Scout is pure and clean-minded and manly.

---

x ...

2 ... INTER... ...
PONENT ...

3. SCIENCE, VOCATION, HOUS... ... OF ... ...

4. COMMUNICATION OF... ... NATIONIONALISM ... ...

5. ... ... — CENSORSHIP (

7. NATION ... ... SCE. ... LANCS?)

9. REACTION TO ... ...

10. ...

11. REL... / SPIRIT ... ...
   *D... ... DEATH / ... DEVELOPMENT.
   DES... AND ... AND ...

13. ... ... EVIDENCE ... ...
   PHYS... ...

... ... MISSION

SCOUTCRAFT

Camp Fire Yarn
No. 1

WHAT SCOUTS ARE

Peace Scouts · Kim
Boys of Mafeking

I SUPPOSE EVERY BOY wants to help his country in some way or other.

There is a way by which he can so do easily, and that is by becoming a Boy Scout.

A scout in the army, as you know, is generally a soldier who is chosen for his cleverness and pluck to go out in front to find out where the enemy is, and report to the commander all about him.

But, besides war scouts, there are also peace scouts—men who in peace time carry out work which requires the same kind of pluck and resourcefulness.

These are the frontiersmen of the world.

The pioneers and trappers of North and South America, the hunters of Central Africa, the explorers and missionaries in all parts of the world, the bushmen and drovers of Australia—all these are peace scouts, real *men* in every sense of the word, and good at scoutcraft. They understand how to live out in the jungle. They can find their way anywhere, and are able to read meanings from the smallest signs and foot tracks. They know how to look after their health when far away from doctors. They are strong and plucky, ready to face danger, and always keen to help each other. They are accustomed to take their lives in their hands, and to risk them without hesitation if they can help their country by doing so.

They give up everything, their personal comforts and desires, in order to get their work done. They do it because it is their duty.

1

The life of the frontiersman is a grand life, but it cannot suddenly be taken up by any man who thinks he would like it, unless he has prepared himself for it. Those who succeed best are those who learned Scouting while they were boys.

The colonists, hunters, and explorers all over the world are all scouts. They must know how to take care of themselves.

Scouting is useful in any kind of life you like to take up. A famous scientist has said that it is valuable for a man who goes in for science. And a noted physician pointed out how necessary it is for a doctor or a surgeon to notice small signs as a Scout does, and know their meaning.

So I am going to show you how you can learn scoutcraft for yourself, and how you can put it into practice at home. It is very easy to learn and very interesting when you get into it.

You can best learn by joining the Boy Scouts.

The life of a frontiersman is a grand life, but to live it, you must prepare yourself in advance for difficulties that may arise.

THE ADVENTURES OF KIM

A good example of what a Boy Scout can do is found in Rudyard Kipling's story of *Kim*.

Kim, or, to give him his full name, Kimball O'Hara, was the son of a sergeant of an Irish regiment in India. His father and mother died while he was a child, and he was left to the care of an aunt.

His playmates were all local boys, so he learned to talk their language and to know their ways. He became great friends with an old wandering priest and travelled with him all over northern India.

One day he chanced to meet his father's old regiment on the march, but on visiting the camp he was arrested on suspicion of being a thief. His birth certificate and other papers were found on him, and the regiment, seeing that he had belonged to them, took charge of him, and started to educate him. But whenever he could get away for holidays, Kim dressed himself in Indian clothes, and went among the people as one of them.

After a time he became acquainted with a Mr. Lurgan, a dealer in old jewelry and curiosities, who, owing to his knowledge of the people, was also a member of the Government Intelligence Department.

This man, finding that Kim had such special knowledge of native habits and customs, saw that he could make a useful agent for

3

Government Intelligence work. He therefore gave Kim lessons at noticing and remembering small details, which is an important point in the training of a Scout.

Kim's Training

Lurgan began by showing Kim a tray full of precious stones of different kinds. He let him look at it for a minute, then covered it with a cloth, and asked him to state how many stones and what sorts were there. At first Kim could remember only a few, and could not describe them very accurately, but with a little practice he soon was able to remember them all quite well. And so, also, with many other kinds of articles which were shown to him in the same way.

At last, after much other training, Kim was made a member of the Secret Service, and was given a secret sign—namely, a locket or badge to wear round his neck and a certain sentence, which, if said in a special way, meant he was one of the Service.

Kim in Secret Service

Once when Kim was travelling in a train he met an Indian, who was rather badly cut about the head and arms. He explained to the other passengers that he had fallen from a cart when driving to the station. But Kim, like a good Scout, noticed that the cuts were sharp, and not grazes such as you would get by falling from a cart, and so did not believe him.

Kim disguised the man as a beggar, with a mixture of flour and ashes.

4

While the man was tying a bandage over his head, Kim noticed that he was wearing a locket like his own, so Kim showed him his. Immediately the man brought into the conversation some of the secret words, and Kim answered with the proper ones in reply. Then the stranger got into a corner with Kim and explained to him that he was carrying out some Secret Service work, and had been found out and was hunted by some enemies who had nearly killed him. They probably knew he was in the train and would therefore telegraph down the line to their friends that he was coming. He wanted to get his message to a certain police officer without being caught by the enemy, but he did not know how to do it if they were already warned of his coming. Kim hit upon the solution.

In India there are a number of holy beggars who travel about the country. They are considered very holy, and people always help them with food and money. They wear next to no clothing, smear themselves with ashes, and paint certain marks on their faces. So Kim set about disguising the man as a beggar. He made a mixture of flour and ashes, which he took from the bowl of a pipe, undressed his friend and smeared the mixture all over him. He also smeared the man's wounds so that they did not show. Finally, with the aid of a little paint-box which he carried, he painted the proper face marks on the man's forehead and brushed his hair down to look wild and shaggy like that of a beggar, and covered it with dust, so that the man's own mother would not have known him.

Soon afterwards they arrived at a big station. Here, on the platform, they found the police officer to whom the report was to be made. The imitation beggar pushed up against the officer and got scolded by him in English. The beggar replied with a string of native abuse into which he mixed the secret words. The police officer at once realized from the secret words that this beggar was an agent. He pretended to arrest him and marched him off to the police station where he could talk to him quietly and receive his report.

Later Kim became acquainted with another agent of the Department—an Indian University graduate—and was able to give him great assistance in capturing two officers acting as spies.

These and other adventures of Kim are well worth reading because they illustrate the kind of valuable work a Boy Scout can do for his country in times of emergency if he is sufficiently trained and sufficiently intelligent.

BOYS OF MAFEKING

We had an example of how useful boys can be on active service,

Here is a map of South Africa. If you look carefully, you will find Mafeking and many other places mentioned in this book.

when a corps of boys was formed in the defence of Mafeking, 1899–1900, during the South African War.

Mafeking, you may know, was a small, ordinary country town out on the open plains of South Africa. Nobody ever thought of it being attacked by an enemy. It just shows you how, in war, you must be prepared for what is *possible*, not only what is *probable*.

When we found we were to be attacked at Mafeking, we ordered our garrison to the points they were to protect—some 700 trained men, police, and volunteers. Then we armed the townsmen, of whom there were some 300. Some of them were old frontiersmen, and quite equal to the occasion. But many of them were young shopmen, clerks, and others, who had never handled a rifle before.

Altogether, then, we only had about a thousand men to defend the place, which was about five miles round and contained 600 white women and children and about 7000 Africans and local inhabitants.

Every man was of value, and as the weeks passed by and many were killed and wounded, the duties of fighting and keeping watch at night became harder for the rest.

The Mafeking Cadet Corps

It was then that Lord Edward Cecil, the chief staff officer, gathered together the boys of Mafeking and made them into a cadet corps. He put them in uniform and drilled them. And a jolly smart and useful lot they were. Previously, we had used a large number of men for carrying orders and messages, keeping lookout and acting as orderlies, and so on. These duties were now handed over to the boy cadets, and the men were released to strengthen the firing-line.

The cadets, under their sergeant-major, a boy named Goodyear, did good work, and well deserved the medals they got at the end of the war.

Many of them rode bicycles, and we were thus able to establish a post by which people could send letters to their friends in the

The boys of Mafeking did excellent service. They were gathered together into a cadet corps, put into uniform and drilled.

different forts, or about the town, without going out under fire themselves. For these letters we made postage stamps which had on them a picture of a cadet bicycle orderly.

I said to one of these boys on one occasion, when he came in through a rather heavy fire:

"You will get hit one of these days riding about like that when shells are flying."

"I pedal so quick, sir, they'll never catch me!" he replied.

These boys didn't seem to mind the bullets one bit. They were always ready to carry out orders, though it meant risking their lives every time.

7

Would You Do It?

Would any of you do that? If an enemy were firing down this street, and you had to take a message across to a house on the other side, would you do it? I am sure you would—although probably you wouldn't much like doing it.

But you want to prepare yourself for such things beforehand. It's just like taking a header into cold water. A fellow who is accustomed to diving thinks nothing of it—he has practised it over and over again. But ask a fellow who has never done it, and he will be afraid.

So, too, with a boy who has been accustomed to obey orders at once, whether there is risk about it or not. The moment he has to do a thing he does it, no matter how great the danger is to him, while another chap who has never cared to obey would hesitate, and would then be despised even by his former friends.

But you need not have a war in order to be useful as a scout. As a peace scout there is lots for you to do—any day, wherever you may be.

Camp Fire Yarn

No. 2

WHAT SCOUTS DO

Living in the Open · Woodcraft
Chivalry · Saving Life · Endurance
Love of Country

THE FOLLOWING THINGS are what you have to know about to become a good Scout:

LIVING IN THE OPEN

Camping is the joyous part of a Scout's life. Living out in God's open air, among the hills and the trees, and the birds and the beasts, and the sea and the rivers—that is, living with nature, having your own little canvas home, doing your own cooking and exploration—all this brings health and happiness such as you can never get among the bricks and smoke of the town.

Hiking, too, where you go farther afield, exploring new places every day, is a glorious adventure. It strengthens you and hardens you so that you won't mind wind and rain, heat and cold. You take them all as they come, feeling that sense of fitness that enables you to face any old trouble with a smile, knowing that you will conquer in the end.

But, of course, to enjoy camping and hiking, you must know how to do it properly.

You have to know how to put up a tent or a hut for yourself; how to lay and light a fire; how to cook your food; how to tie logs together to make a bridge or a raft; how to find your way by night, as well as by day, in a strange country, and many other things.

9

Very few fellows learn these things when they are living in civilised places, because they have comfortable houses, and soft beds to sleep in. Their food is prepared for them, and when they want to know the way, they just ask a policeman.

Well, when those fellows try to go scouting or exploring, they find themselves quite helpless.

Take even your sports "hero" and put him down in the wilderness, alongside a fellow trained in camping, and see which can look after himself. High batting averages are not much good to him there. He is only a "tenderfoot".

WOODCRAFT

Woodcraft is the knowledge of animals and nature.

You learn about different kinds of animals by following their tracks and creeping up to them so that you can watch them in their natural state and study their habits.

The whole sport of hunting animals lies in the woodcraft of stalking them, not in killing them. No Scout wilfully kills an animal for the mere sake of killing but only when in want of food—unless it is harmful. By continually watching animals in the open, one gets to like them too well to shoot them.

Woodcraft includes, besides being able to see the tracks and other small signs, the power to read their meaning, such as at what pace the animal was going, whether he was frightened or unsuspicious, and so on. It enables the hunter also to find his way in the jungle or desert. It teaches him which are the best wild fruits and roots for his own food, or which are favourite food for animals, and, therefore, likely to attract them.

In the same way in inhabited places you read the tracks of men, horses, bicycles, motor cars, and find out from these what has been going on. You learn to notice, by small signs, such as birds suddenly starting up, that someone is moving near, though you cannot see him.

By noticing the behaviour or dress of people, and putting this and that together, you can sometimes see that they are up to no good. Or you can tell when they are in distress and need help or sympathy— and you can then do what is one of the chief duties of a Scout, namely, help those in distress in any possible way you can.

Remember that it is a disgrace to a Scout, when he is with other people, if they see anything big or little, near or far, high or low, that he has not already seen for himself.

CHIVALRY

In the old days the Knights were the real Scouts and their rules were very much like the Scout Law which we have now.

The Knights considered their honour their most sacred possession.

Just like Saint George of old, the Boy Scouts of today fight against everything evil and unclean.

They would not do a dishonourable thing, such as telling a lie or stealing. They would rather die than do it. They were always ready to fight and to be killed in upholding their king, or their religion, or their honour.

Each Knight had a small following of a squire and some men-at-arms, just as our Patrol Leader has his Second (or Assistant) and four or five Scouts.

The Code of the Knights

The Knight's patrol used to stick to him through thick and thin, and all carried out the same idea as their leader—namely:

Their honour was sacred.

They were loyal to God, their king, and their country.

They were particularly courteous and polite to all women and children, and weak people.

They were helpful to everybody.

They gave money and food where it was needed, and saved up their money to do so.

They taught themselves the use of arms in order to protect their religion and their country against enemies.

They kept themselves strong and healthy and active to be able to do these things well.

You Scouts cannot do better than follow the example of the Knights.

As a Scout, you are obliged to do at least one Good Turn every day.

One great point about them was that every day they had to do a Good Turn to somebody, and that is one of our rules.

When you get up in the morning, remember that you have to do a Good Turn for someone during the day. Tie a knot in your handkerchief or Scout scarf to remind yourself of it.

If you should ever find that you had forgotten to do your daily Good Turn, you must do two the next day. Remember that by your Scout Promise you are on *your honour* to do it. But do not think that Scouts need do only one Good Turn a day. They must do one, but if they can do fifty, so much the better.

A Good Turn need only be a very small one. It is a Good Turn even if it is only putting a coin into a poor-box, or helping an old woman to cross the street, or making room on a seat for someone, or giving water to a thirsty horse, or removing a bit of banana skin off the pavement. But one must be done every day, and it only counts when you do not accept any reward in return.

SAVING LIFE

The man who saves the life of a fellow-being, as he may do in the ✳
sudden appalling accidents which occur in big cities, mines, and
factories, in everyday life, is no less a hero than the soldier who
rushes into the thick of the fight to rescue a comrade amid all the
excitement of battle.

Thousands of Boy Scouts have won medals for life-saving, and I
hope that many more will do the same.

It is certain that many of you will, at one time or another, get a
chance to save a life. But you must BE PREPARED for it. You
should know what to do the moment an accident occurs—and do it
then and there.

It is not enough to read about it in a book and think that you
know what to do. You must actually practise, and practise often,
the things to be done, such as how to cover your mouth and nose
with a wet handkerchief to enable you to breathe in smoke; how to
tear a sheet into strips and make a rope for escaping from a fire; how
to open a manhole to let air into a gassy sewer; how to lift and carry
an insensible person; how to save and revive apparently drowned
people, and so on.

When you have learned all these things you will have confidence in
yourself, so that when an accident happens and everybody is in a
state of fluster, not knowing what to do, you can quietly step out and
do the right thing.

ENDURANCE

To carry out all the duties and work of a Scout, a fellow has to be
strong, healthy, and active. He can make himself so if he takes a little
care about it.

It means a lot of exercise, like playing games, running, walking,
cycling, and so on.

A Scout should sleep much in the open. A boy who is accustomed
to sleep with his window shut may catch cold when he first tries
sleeping out. The thing is always to sleep with your windows open,
summer and winter, and you will not catch cold. Personally I cannot
sleep with my window shut or with blinds down, and when I stay in
the country I like to sleep outside the house.

A short go of exercises every morning and evening is a grand
thing for keeping you fit—not so much for making showy muscle
as to work all your internal organs, and to work up the circulation of
the blood in every part of you.

Every real Scout takes a bath whenever it is possible. If he cannot get a bath, he takes a good rub down daily with a wet rough towel.

Scouts breathe through the nose, not through the mouth. In this way they don't get thirsty. They don't get out of breath so quickly. They don't breathe all sorts of disease germs that are in the air, and they don't snore at night.

Deep breathing exercises are of great value for developing the lungs, and for putting fresh air (oxygen) into the blood, provided that they are carried out in the open air, and are not overdone. For deep breathing the breath must be taken in slowly and deeply through the nose, not through the mouth, till it opens out the ribs to the greatest extent. Then, after a time, it should be slowly and steadily breathed out again without strain. But the best deep breathing after all is that which comes naturally from plenty of running exercise.

LOVE YOUR COUNTRY

My country and your country did not grow of itself out of nothing. It was made by men and women by dint of hard work and hard fighting, often at the sacrifice of their lives—that is, by their whole-hearted patriotism.

In all you do, think of your country first. Don't spend the whole of your time and money merely to amuse *yourself*, but think first how you can be of use to the common good. When you have done that, you can justly and honestly enjoy yourself in your own way.

Scouts learn endurance in the open. Like explorers, they carry their own burdens and "paddle their own canoes".

14

NEEDLING

Perhaps you don't see how a mere small boy can be of use to his country, but by becoming a Scout and carrying out the Scout Law every boy can be of use.

"My country before myself", should be your aim. Probably, if you ask yourself truly, you will find you have at present got them just the other way about. I hope, if it is so, that you will from this moment put yourself right and remain so always. Don't be content, like the Romans were, and some people now are, to pay other people to play your football or to fight your battles for you. Do something yourself to help keep the Flag flying.

If you take up Scouting in that spirit, you will be doing something. Take it up, not merely because it is good fun, but because by doing so you will be preparing yourself to be a good citizen not only of your country but of the whole world.

Then you will have in you the truest spirit of patriotism, which every boy ought to have if he is worth his salt.

THE ELSDON MURDER

A brutal murder took place many years ago in the North of England. The murderer was caught, convicted, and hanged chiefly through the scoutcraft of a shepherd boy.

Woodcraft—The boy, Robert Hindmarsh, had been up on the moor tending his sheep, and was finding his way home over a wild out-of-the way part of the hills, when he passed a tramp sitting on the ground with his legs stretched out in front of him eating some food.

Observation—The boy in passing noticed the tramp's appearance, and especially the peculiar nails in the soles of his boots.

Concealment—He did not stop and stare, but just took in these details at a glance as he went by without attracting much attention from the man, who merely regarded him as an ordinary boy.

Deduction—When the boy got near home, some five or six miles away, he came to a crowd round a cottage. The old woman (Margaret Crozier) who inhabited it had been found murdered. All sorts of guesses were made about who had done the deed, and suspicion seemed to centre on a small gang of three or four tramps who were going about the country robbing and threatening death to anyone who made any report of their misdeeds.

The boy heard all these things. Then he noticed some peculiar footprints in the little garden of the cottage. The nail-marks agreed with those he had seen in the boots of the man on the moor, and he naturally deduced that the man might have something to do with the murder.

Chivalry—The fact that it was a helpless old woman who had been murdered made the boy's chivalrous feeling rise against the murderer, whoever he might be.

Pluck and Self-discipline—So, although he knew that the friends of the murderer might kill him for giving information he cast his fears aside. He went at once to the constable and told him of the footmarks in the garden, and where he could find the man who had made them—if he went immediately.

Robert Hindmarsh, the boy, noticed the appearance of the tramp, without attracting much attention from the man.

Health and Strength—The man up on the moor had got so far from the scene of the murder, unseen, except by the boy, that he thought himself safe, and never thought of the boy being able to walk all the way to the scene of the murder and then to come back, as he did, with the police. So he took no precautions.

But the boy was a strong, healthy hill-boy, and did the journey rapidly and well, so that they found the man and captured him without difficulty.

The man was Willie Winter, a gipsy

16

He was tried, found guilty, and hanged at Newcastle. His body was then brought and hung on a gibbet near the scene of the murder, as was the custom in those days.

Two of the gipsies who were his accomplices were caught with some of the stolen property, and were also executed at Newcastle.

Kind-heartedness—But when the boy heard of the fate that had befallen Winter, he was overcome with misery at having caused the death of a fellow creature.

Saving Life—However, the magistrate sent for him and complimented him on the great good he had done to his fellow countrymen, probably saving some of their lives, by ridding the world of such a dangerous criminal.

Duty—He said: "You have done your duty, although it caused you personally some danger and much distress. Still, you must not mind that. It was your duty to help the police in getting justice done, and duty must always be carried out regardless of how much it costs you, even if you have to give up your life."

Example—Thus the boy did every part of the duty of a Boy Scout.

He exercised—Woodcraft; Observation, without being noticed; Deduction; Chivalry; Sense of Duty; Endurance; Kind-heartedness.

He little thought that the act which he did entirely of his own accord would years afterwards be held up as an example to you other boys in teaching you to do your duty.

In the same way, you should remember that *your* acts may be watched by others after you, and taken as an example, too.

So try to do your duty the right way on all occasions.

Camp Fire Yarn
No. 3

BECOMING A SCOUT

Tenderfoot Test · Scout Law
Scout Promise · Scout Sign and Salute
Investiture · Scout Uniform

To BE A SCOUT you should join a Scout Patrol or a Scout Troop in your neighbourhood, with the permission of your parents.

But before becoming a Scout, you must pass the **Tenderfoot Test.** This is a simple test just to show that you are worth your salt and mean to stick to it.

When you have satisfied your Scoutmaster, the man in charge of your Troop, that you can do all the things and do them properly, you will be invested as a Scout and be entitled to wear the Tenderfoot Badge.

SCOUT LAW

The Scout Law contains the rules which apply to Boy Scouts all the world over, and which you promise to obey when you are enrolled as a Scout. The Scout Law is in the front of this book (pages xi, xii and xiii). Study it carefully so that you understand the meaning of every point.

SCOUT PROMISE

At your investiture as a Scout you will make the Scout Promise in front of the rest of the Troop.

The Scout Promise you will find on page xi.

This Promise is a very difficult one to keep, but it is a most serious one and no boy is a Scout unless he does his best to live up to his Promise.

So you see, Scouting is not only fun, but it also requires a lot from you, and I know I can trust you to do everything you possibly can to keep your Scout Promise. 5

SCOUT MOTTO

The Scout Motto is:

BE PREPARED

which means you are always in a state of readiness in mind and body to do your DUTY.

Be Prepared in Mind by having disciplined yourself to be obedient to every order, and also by having thought out beforehand any accident or situation that might occur, so that you know the right thing to do at the right moment, and are willing to do it.

Be Prepared in Body by making yourself strong and active and *able* to do the right thing at the right moment. and do it.

SCOUT BADGE

The Scout Badge is the arrowhead which shows the North on a map or on a compass. It is the Badge of the Scout because it points in the right direction, and upwards. It shows the way in doing your duty and helping others. The three points of it remind you of the three points of the Scout Promise.

This arrowhead has come to be the Badge of the Scouts in almost every country in the world. In order to distinguish one nationality from the other, the country's own emblem is often placed on the front of it.

The badge of a Second Class Scout is a scroll with the Scout Motto, "Be Prepared". The scroll is turned up at the ends like a Scout's mouth, because he does his duty with a smile and willingly.

Beneath the scroll is a cord with a knot tied in it. This knot is to remind you to do a good turn daily to someone.

Together the Scout Badge and the scroll form the badge of a First Class Scout.

SCOUT SIGN AND SALUTE

The **Scout Sign** is made by raising your right hand to shoulder height, palm to the front, thumb resting on the nail of the little finger, and the other fingers upright, pointing upwards. The three fingers remind a Scout of the three parts of the Scout Promise. The Scout Sign is given at the making of the Promise, or as a greeting. When the hand held in this way is raised to the forehead, it is the **Scout Salute.**

When to Salute

All wearers of the Scout Badge ought to salute each other once a day. The first to see the other Scout is the first to salute, irrespective of rank.

Scouts will always salute as a token of respect, at the hoisting of the Flag; at the playing of the National Anthem; to the uncased

The three points of the Scout Badge and the three fingers of the Scout Sign remind a Scout of the three parts of the Scout Promise.

National Colours; to Scout Flags, when carried ceremonially; and to all funerals. On these occasions, if the Scouts are acting under orders, they obey the orders of the person in charge in regard to saluting or standing to the alert. If a Scout is not acting under orders he should salute independently. In all cases, leaders should salute.

The hand salute is only used when a Scout is not carrying his staff, and is always made with the right hand. Saluting when carrying a staff is done by bringing the left arm smartly across the body in a horizontal position, the fingers showing the Scout Sign just touching the staff.

When in uniform a Scout salutes whether he is wearing a hat or not, with one exception, namely at religious services, when all Scouts must stand at the alert, instead of saluting.

The Meaning of the Salute

A man once told me that "he was just as good as anybody else,

20

and he was blowed if ever he would raise a finger to salute his so-called 'betters'; he wasn't going to be a slave and kow-tow to them, not he!" and so on.

That is a churlish spirit, which is common among fellows who have not been brought up as Scouts.

I didn't argue with him, but I might have told him that he had the wrong idea about saluting.

A salute is a sign between men of standing. It is a privilege to be able to salute anyone.

In the old days freemen were all allowed to carry weapons, and when one met another each would hold up his right hand to show that he had no weapon in it, and that they met as friends. So also when an armed man met a defenceless person or a lady.

Slaves or serfs were not allowed to carry weapons, and so had to slink past the freemen without making any sign.

Nowadays people do not carry weapons. But those who would have been entitled to do so, such as knights, esquires, and men-at-arms, that is, those living on their own property or earning their own living, still go through the form of saluting each other by

A Scout shakes hands with another Scout with the left hand, in the Scout Handshake.

holding up their hand to their hat, or even taking it off. "Wasters" are not entitled to salute, and so should slink by, as they generally do, without taking notice of the freemen or wage-earners.

To salute merely shows that you are a right sort of fellow and mean well to the others. There is nothing slavish about it.

If a stranger makes the Scout Sign to you, you should acknowledge it at once by making the Sign back to him, and then shake hands with the LEFT HAND—the **Scout Handshake.** If he then shows his Scout Badge, or proves that he is a Scout, you must treat him as a Brother Scout, and help him.

FREEDOM AND SELF ACTUALIZATION.

... STRUCTURE POINT

INVESTITURE OF A SCOUT

Here is a suggested ceremonial for a recruit to be invested as a Scout:

The Troop is formed in horseshoe formation, with Scoutmaster and Assistant Scoutmaster in the gap. The Assistant Scoutmaster holds the hat of the recruit. When ordered to come forward by the Scoutmaster, the Patrol Leader brings the recruit to the centre. The Scoutmaster than asks: "Do you know what your honour is?"

The recruit replies: "Yes. It means that I can be trusted to be truthful and honest" (or words to that effect).

"Do you know the Scout Law?"

"Yes."

"Can I trust you, on your honour, to do your best to live up to the Scout Promise?"

Recruit then makes the Scout Sign, and so does the whole Troop while he gives the Scout Promise.

Scoutmaster: "I trust you, on your honour, to keep this Promise. You are now a Scout in the World-wide Brotherhood of Scouts".

The Scoutmaster gives him his badges and the Assistant Scoutmaster then hands him his hat. The Patrol Leader then fastens on his Patrol shoulder knot.

The Scoutmaster shakes hands with him with the left hand.

The new Scout faces about and salutes the Troop.

The Troop salutes.

The Scoutmaster gives the word, "To your Patrol, quick march".

The new Scout and his Patrol Leader march back to their Patrol.

GOING ON IN SCOUTING

When you have been invested as a Scout you can go on to the next grade, that of Second Class Scout. For this you will learn the beginnings of many useful subjects. The Badge of the Second Class Scout is the scroll alone, with the Scout Motto.

No Scout will want to remain Second Class for longer than he need and so you will become a First Class Scout as soon as you can. This will mean hard work tackling map-reading, hiking, first aid, and many other things. The First Class Badge consists of both the arrowhead and the scroll.

You can also win Proficiency Badges for your hobbies.

SCOUT UNIFORM

The Scout Uniform is very like the uniform worn by my men when I commanded the South African Constabulary. They knew what was comfortable, serviceable, and a good protection against the weather. So Scouts have much the same uniform.

With a few minor alterations the original Scout Uniform has met the ideas of Scouts around the world and has been universally

The Scout Uniform, used around the world, is very like the uniform worn by the men of the South African Constabulary.

adopted. Of course, in extreme climates it has to be modified to suit the seasons, but on the whole the different nations in the temperate climates are dressed uniformly alike.

Starting at the top, the **broad-brimmed khaki hat** is a good protection from sun and rain. It is kept on by a bootlace tied in a bow in front on the brim and going round the back of the head. This lace will come in handy in many ways when you camp. The hat has four dents in it.

Then comes the **scarf** or **neckerchief** which is folded into a triangle with the point at the back of the neck. Every Troop has its own scarf colour, and since the honour of your Troop is bound up in the scarf, you must be very careful to keep it clean and tidy. It is fastened at the throat by a knot, or "woggle", which is some form of ring made of cord, metal, or bone, or anything you like. The scarf protects your neck from sunburn and serves many purposes, such as for a bandage or as an emergency rope.

The **Scout shirt** (or jersey) is a free-and-easy thing, and nothing could be more comfortable when the sleeves are rolled up. All Scouts have them rolled up because this tends to give them greater freedom, but also as a sign that they are ready to carry out their Motto. They only roll them down when it is very cold or when their arms may become sunburnt. In cold weather the shirt can be supplemented with warmer garments over or, better, under it.

Shorts are essential to hard work, to hiking and to camping. They are less expensive and more hygienic than breeches or trousers. They give freedom and ventilation to the legs. Another advantage is that when the ground is wet, you can go about without stockings and none of your clothes gets damp.

The **stockings** are held up by garters, with green tabs showing below the turnover of the stocking top.

Personally, I consider **shoes** more suitable than high boots since they give better ventilation to the feet and therefore diminish the danger of chills and of chafes which come from damp stockings softening the feet when tightly laced boots are worn.

Wearing the Uniform

The Scout kit, through its uniformity, now constitutes a bond of brotherhood among boys across the world.

The correct wearing of the Uniform and smartness of turnout of the individual Scout makes him a credit to our Movement. It shows his pride in himself and in his Troop.

One slovenly Scout, on the other hand, inaccurately dressed may let down the whole Movement in the eyes of the public. Show me such a fellow and I can show you one who has not grasped the true Scouting spirit and who takes no pride in his membership of our great Brotherhood.

SCOUT STAFF

The Scout staff is a useful addition to the kit of the Scout. Personally, I have found it an invaluable assistant when traversing mountains or boulder-strewn country and especially in night work in forest or bush. Also, by carving upon it various signs representing his achievements, the staff gradually becomes a record as well as a treasured companion to the Scout.

The Scout staff is a strong stick about as high as your nose, marked in feet and inches for measuring.

The staff is useful for all sorts of things, such as making a stretcher, keeping back a crowd, jumping over a ditch, testing the depth of a river, keeping in touch with the rest of your Patrol in the dark. You can help another Scout over a high wall if you hold your staff horizontally between your hands and make a step for him; he can then give you a hand from above.

Several staves can be used for building a light bridge, a hut or a flag staff.

There are many other uses for the staff. In fact, you will soon find that if you don't have your staff with you, you will always be wanting it.

If you get the chance, cut your own staff. But remember to get permission first.

The Scout staff is useful for a great number of out-door activities.

Camp Fire Yarn

No. 4

SCOUT PATROLS

Patrol System · Patrol Leader
Patrol Signs · Games

EACH SCOUT TROOP consists of two or more Patrols of six to eight boys.

The main object of the Patrol System is to give real responsibility to as many boys as possible. It leads each boy to see that he has some individual responsibility for the good of his Patrol. It leads each Patrol to see that it has definite responsibility for the good of the Troop. Through the Patrol System the Scouts learn that they have considerable say in what their Troop does.

THE PATROL LEADER

Each Patrol has a boy as leader. He is called the Patrol Leader. The Scoutmaster expects a great deal from the Patrol Leader and leaves him a free hand in carrying out the work in the Patrol. The Patrol Leader selects another boy to be second in command. This boy is called a Second. The Patrol Leader is responsible for the efficiency and smartness of his Patrol. The Scouts in his Patrol obey his orders, not from fear of punishment, as is often the case in military discipline, but because they are a team playing together and backing up their leader for the honour and success of the Patrol.

And the Patrol Leader, in training and leading his Patrol, is gaining practice and experience for being a fellow who can take responsibility.

Also, besides training his Patrol, the Patrol Leader has to *lead* it, that is, he must be at least as good as any of his Scouts at the different jobs they have to do. He must never ask a fellow to do anything he would not do himself. And he must never be "down" on anyone but must get the enthusiasm and willing work of everyone by cheerily encouraging their efforts.

In every line of life young men are wanted who can be trusted to take responsibility and leadership. So the Patrol Leader who has made a success with his Patrol has every chance of making a success of his life when he goes out into the world.

Most of your work in the Patrol consists in playing Scouting games and practices by which you gain experience as Scouts.

THE COURT OF HONOUR

The Court of Honour is an important part of the Patrol System. It is a standing committee which settles the affairs of the Troop. A Court of Honour is formed of the Patrol Leaders, or, in the case of a small Troop, of the Patrol Leaders and Seconds. The Scoutmaster attends the meetings as an adviser but does not vote. Patrol Leaders in a Court of Honour have in many cases carried on the Troop in the absence of the Scoutmaster.

The Court of Honour decides programmes of work, camps, rewards and other questions affecting Troop management. The members of the Court are pledged to secrecy. Only those decisions which affect the whole Troop, that is, competitions, appointments, and so on, would be made public.

A WORD TO PATROL LEADERS

I want you Patrol Leaders to go on and train your Patrols entirely yourselves, because it is possible for you to get hold of each boy in your Patrol and make a good fellow of him. It is no use having one or two brilliant boys and the rest no good at all. You should try to make them all fairly good.

The most important step to this is your own example, because what you do yourselves, your Scouts will do also.

Show them that you can obey orders whether they are given by word of mouth or are printed or written rules, and that you carry them out whether your Scoutmaster is present or not. Show them that you can earn Proficiency Badges, and your boys will follow with very little persuasion. But remember that you must give them the *lead* and not the *push*.

PATROL NAMES AND SIGNS

Each Troop is named after the place to which it belongs. Each Patrol in the Troop is named after an animal or bird. It is a good plan to choose only animals and birds found in your district. Thus the 33rd London Troop may have five Patrols which are respectively the Wolves, the Ravens, the Curlews, the Bulls, the Owls.

Each Patrol Leader has a small flag on his staff with his Patrol animal shown on it on both sides.

Each Scout in a Patrol has his regular number. The Patrol Leader

This is the Patrol flag of the Wolf Patrol of the 1st London Troop.

is No. 1, the Second No. 2. The other Scouts have the consecutive numbers after these. Scouts usually work in pairs as comrades, Nos. 3 and 4 together, Nos. 5 and 6 together, and Nos. 7 and 8.

Here are the signs and calls of the Patrols we used at the first Scout camp at Brownsea, of course there are many more you can choose from.

CURLEW	RAVEN	WOLF	BULL
Whistle:	*Cry:*	*Howl:*	*Lowing:*
"Curley"	*"Kar-kaw"*	*"How-oooo"*	*"Um-maouw"*
Green	*Black*	*Yellow & Black*	*Red*

PATROL CALL

Each Scout in the Patrol has to be able to make the call of his Patrol animal—thus every Scout in the "Bulldogs" must be able to imitate the growl of the bulldog. This is the signal by which Scouts of a Patrol can communicate with each other when hiding or at night. No Scout is allowed to use the call of any Patrol except his own. The Patrol Leader calls his Patrol at any time by sounding his whistle and giving the Patrol call.

WOODCRAFT TRAIL SIGNS

Scout trail signs are made on the ground, close to the right-hand side of the road. They should never be made where they will damage or disfigure private property.

Road to be followed.

Letter hidden three paces from here in the direction of the arrow.

This path not to be followed.

"I have gone home."

(Signed) "Patrol Leader of the Ravens, Fifteenth London Troop."

"This is the way."

"Turn to the right."

When a Scout makes signs on the ground for others to read he also draws the head of the Patrol animal. Thus if he wants to show that a certain road should not be followed he draws a sign across it that means "Not to be followed", and adds the head of his Patrol animal to show which Patrol discovered that the road was no good, and his own number to show which Scout discovered it, thus:

At night sticks with a wisp of grass round them or stones should be laid on the road in similar forms so that they can be felt with the hand.

29

PATROL PRACTICES

Each Scout should learn the call of his Patrol animal. He should be encouraged to know all he can about its habits, etc. This can be a first step in nature lore.

Each Scout should know how to make a simple drawing of his Patrol animal. The Scouts should use this as their Patrol signature.

The special Scout signs should be used out-of-doors. They can be made in the dust, or by using sticks, and so on. A good tracking game can be arranged by using signs only.

Acting in all forms should be encouraged: mock trials and impromptu plays are excellent training and useful for evenings around the camp fire or when you have to be indoors.

GAMES

Scout Meets Scout

Single Scouts, or pairs of Scouts or complete Patrols, are taken out about two miles apart. They are then made to move towards each other, either alongside a road, or by giving each side a landmark to move towards, such as a steep hill or big tree, which is directly behind the other party and will thus ensure their coming together. The Patrol which first sees the other wins. This is signified by the Patrol Leader holding up his Patrol flag for the umpire to see, and sounding his whistle. A Patrol need not keep together, but that Patrol wins which first holds up its flag; so it is well for the Scouts to keep in touch with their Patrol Leaders by signal, voice, or message.

Scouts may employ any ruse they like, such as climbing into trees, hiding in carts, etc., but they must not dress up in disguise unless specially permitted.

This game may also be practised at night.

Debates

A good exercise for a winter's evening in the meeting room is to hold a debate on any subject of topical interest, with the Scoutmaster acting as chairman. He will see that there is a speaker prepared beforehand to introduce and support one view of the subject, and another speaker prepared to expound another view. After hearing them, he will call on the others present in turn to express their views. In the end he takes the votes for and against the motion.

At first boys will be very shy of speaking unless the subject selected by the Scoutmaster is one which really interests them and takes them out of themselves.

After a debate or two they get greater confidence, and are able to express themselves coherently. They also pick up the proper procedure for public meetings, such as seconding a motion, moving amendments, obeying the chairman's ruling, voting, according votes of thanks to the chair, etc.

Mock Trial

In place of a debate a mock trial may be of interest as a change.

For instance, the story of the Elsdon Murder given in Yarn No. 2 might form the subject of a trial.

The Scoutmaster acts as judge, and details boys to the following parts:

Prisoner	William Winter.
Witness	Boy, Robert Hindmarsh.
,, ...	Police Constable.
,, ...	Villager.
,, ...	Old woman (friend of the murdered woman).
Counsel for Prisoner.	
,, ,, Prosecution.	
Foreman and Jury (if there are enough Scouts).	

Follow as nearly as possible the procedure of a court of law. Let each make up his own evidence, speeches, or cross-examination according to his own notions and imagination, along the lines of the story, but in greater detail. Do not necessarily find the prisoner guilty unless the prosecution proves its case to the jury.

In summing up, the Scoutmaster may bring out the fact that the boy, Hindmarsh, carried out each part of the duty of a Scout, in order to bring home the lesson to the boys.

Unprepared Plays

The plot of a short, simple play is given, and each player is assigned his part, with an outline of what he has to do and say. The Scouts act it, making up the required conversation as they go along.

This develops the power of imagination and expression.

Play acting is good fun. It doesn't matter what kind of voice you have so long as you get out your words clearly and distinctly.

Scout Songs

The Scout's Chorus. This is a chant that the African Zulus used to sing to their Chief. It may be shouted on the march, or used as applause at games and meetings and camp fires. It must be sung exactly in time.

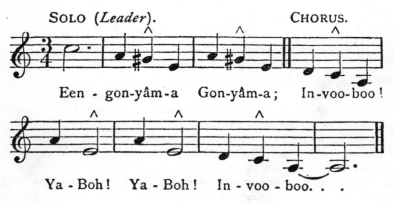

Een - gon-yâm-a   Gon-yâm-a;   In-voo-boo!

Ya - Boh!   Ya - Boh!   In - voo - boo. . .

Leader: Eengonyâma—gonyâma.

Chorus: Invooboo. Ya-Boh! Ya-Boh! Invooboo!

The meaning is—

Leader: "He is a lion!"

Chorus: "Yes! he is better than that; he is a hippopotamus!"

32

The Scout's Rally. To be shouted as a salute, or in a game, or at any other appropriate time.

SOLO (*Leader*). CHORUS.

Bè pre - pared. Zing - a - zing! Bom! Bom!

> *Leader:* Be Prepared!
> *Chorus:* Zing-a-Zing!
>   Bom! Bom!
> (Stamp or bang something at the "Bom! Bom!")

The Scout's Call. For a Scout to whistle to attract the attention of another Scout.

Scouts' Dance

Scouts form up in one line with the leader in front, each holding his staff in the right hand, and his left on the next man's shoulder.

Leader sings the Eengonyâma song. Scouts sing chorus, and advance a few steps at a time, stamping in unison on the long notes.

At the second time of singing they step backwards.

At the third, they turn to the left, still holding each other's shoulders, and move round in a large circle, repeating the chorus until they have completed the circle.

They then form into a wide circle, into the centre of which one steps forward and carries out a war dance, representing how he tracked and fought with one of his enemies. He goes through the whole fight in dumb show, until he finally kills his foe. The Scouts meantime sing the Eengonyâma chorus and dance on their own ground. As soon as he finishes the fight, the leader starts the "Be Prepared" chorus, which they repeat three times in honour of the Scout who has just danced.

Then they recommence the Eengonyama chorus, and another Scout steps into the ring, and describes in dumb show how he stalked and killed a wild buffalo. While he does the creeping up and stalking of the animal, the Scouts all crouch and sing their chorus very softly, and as he gets close to the beast, they simultaneously spring up and dance and shout the chorus loudly. When he has slain the beast, the leader again gives the "Be Prepared" chorus in his honour, which is repeated three times, the Scouts banging their staffs on the ground at the same time as they stamp

The dancing of the young men of the Kikuyu tribe in Africa provided the inspiration for the Scouts' dance.

"Bom! Bom!" At the end of the third repetition, "Bom! Bom!" is given twice.

The circle then closes together, the Scouts turn to their left again, grasping shoulders with the left hand, and move off, singing the Eengonyâma chorus, or, if it is not desired to move away, they break up after the final "Bom! Bom!"

The Eengonyâma song should be sung in a spirited way, and not droned out dismally like a dirge.

FOR WINTER IN NORTHERN COUNTRIES

Arctic Expedition

Each Patrol makes a bobsleigh with ropes and harness, for two of their number to pull (or for dogs if they have them, and can train

34

them to the work). Two Scouts go a mile or so ahead; the remainder with the sleigh follow, finding the way by means of the spoor, and by such signs as the leading Scout may draw in the snow. All other signs seen on the way are to be examined, noted, and their meaning read. The sleigh carries rations and cooking pots, and other supplies.

Build snow huts. These must be made narrow, according to the length of branches available for forming the roof, which can be made with brushwood, and covered with snow.

Snow Fort

The snow fort may be built by one Patrol according to the boys' own ideas of fortification, with loopholes for looking out. When finished it will be attacked by hostile Patrols, using snowballs as ammunition. Every Scout struck by a snow ball is counted dead. The attackers should, as a rule, number at least twice the strength of the defenders.

Siberian Man Hunt

One Scout as fugitive runs away across the snow in any direction he may please until he finds a good hiding-place, and there conceals himself. The remainder, after giving him twenty minutes' start or more, proceed to follow him by his tracks. As they approach his hiding-place, he shoots at them with snowballs, and everyone who is struck must fall out dead. The fugitive must be struck three times before he is counted dead.

In Towns

Scouts can be very useful in snowy weather by working as a Patrol under their leader in clearing away the snow from pavements, houses, etc. And in fog by acting as guides. This they may either do as a Good Turn, or accept money to be devoted to their funds.

CAMPAIGNING

Camp Fire Yarn
No. 5

LIFE IN THE OPEN

Exploration · Mountaineering · Patrolling
Night Work · Finding the Way
Finding the North · Weather Wisdom

IN SOUTH AFRICA one of the finest tribes were the Zulus. Every man was a good warrior and a good scout, because he had learned scouting as a boy.

When a boy was old enough to become a warrior, he was stripped of his clothing and painted white all over. He was given a shield with which to protect himself and an assegai or small spear for killing animals or enemies. He was then turned loose in the "bush".

If anyone saw him while he was still white he would hunt him and kill him. And that white paint took about a month to wear off —it would not wash off.

So for a month the boy had to hide away in the jungle, and live the best he could.

He had to follow up the tracks of deer and creep up near enough to spear the animal in order to get food and clothing for himself. He had to make fire to cook his food, by rubbing two sticks together. He had to be careful not to let his fire smoke too much, or it would catch the eye of scouts on the lookout to hunt him.

He had to be able to run long distances, to climb trees, and to swim rivers in order to escape from his pursuers. He had to be brave, and stand up to a lion or any other wild animal that attacked him.

He had to know which plants were good to eat and which were poisonous. He had to build himself a hut to live in, well hidden.

He had to take care that wherever he went he left no foot tracks by which he could be followed up.

For a month he had to live this life, sometimes in burning heat, sometimes in cold and rain.

When at last the white stain had worn off, he was permitted to return to his village. He was then received with great joy, and was allowed to take his place among the young warriors of the tribe. He had proved that he was able to look after himself.

From boy to man among the Zulus we have the Um-Fan (mat boy), the young warrior, and the Ring-Kop veteran.

In South America the boys of the Yaghan tribe—down in the cold, rainy regions of Patagonia—also undergo a test of pluck before they are allowed to consider themselves men. For this test the boy must drive a spear deep into his thigh and smile all the time in spite of the pain.

It is a cruel test, but it shows that those savages understood how necessary it is that boys should be trained to manliness and not be allowed to drift into being poor-spirited wasters who can only look on at men's work.

If every boy works hard at Scouting he will, at the end of it, have some claim to call himself a Scout and a man, and will find that he will have no difficulty in looking after himself.

The Cub looks up to the Boy Scout, and the Boy Scout looks up to the old scout or pioneer.

TRAINING FOR THE BACKWOODS

An old Canadian scout and trapper, over eighty years of age, Bill Hamilton, once wrote a book called *My Sixty Years in the Plains* describing the dangers of the adventurous life of the early pioneer:

"I have often been asked," Hamilton wrote, "why we exposed ourselves to such dangers. My answer has always been that there was a charm in the open-air life of a scout from which one cannot free himself after he has once come under its spell. Give me the man who has been raised among the great things of nature. He cultivates truth, independence, and self-reliance. He has generous impulses. He is true to his friends, and true to the flag of his country."

I can fully endorse what this old scout has said, and, what is more, I find that those men who come from the farthest frontiers—from what we should call a rude and savage life—are among the most generous and chivalrous of their race, especially toward women and weaker folk. They become "gentle men" by their contact with nature.

"Play Hard—Work Hard"

Theodore Roosevelt, President of the United States of America (1901–1909), also believed in outdoor life. When returning from an

38

hunting trip in East Africa he inspected some Boy Scouts in London, and expressed great admiration for them. He wrote:—

"I believe in outdoor games, and I do not mind in the least that they are rough games, or that those who take part in them are occasionally injured. I have no sympathy with the overwrought sentiment which would keep a young man in cottonwool. The out-of-doors man must always prove the better in life's contest. When you play, play hard; and when you work, work hard. But do not let your play and your sport interfere with your study."

Learn to Look after Yourself

The truth is that men brought up in a civilized country have no training whatever in looking after themselves out on the veldt or plains, or in the backwoods. The consequence is that when they go

The trained backwoodsman knows the ways of the woods. He can make himself comfortable in a thousand small ways.

into wild country they are for a long time perfectly helpless, and go through a lot of hardship and trouble which would not occur if they learned, while boys, to look after themselves in camp. They are just a lot of "tenderfoots".

They have never had to light a fire or to cook their own food—that has always been done for them. At home when they wanted water, they merely had to turn on the tap—therefore they had no idea of how to set about finding water in a desert place by looking at the grass, or bush, or by scratching at the sand till they found signs of dampness. If they lost their way, or did not know the time, they merely had to ask somebody else. They had always had houses to shelter them, and beds to lie in. They had never had to make them for themselves, nor to make or repair their own boots or clothing.

That is why a "tenderfoot" talks of "roughing it" in camp. But living in camp for a Scout who knows the game is by no means "roughing it". He knows how to make himself comfortable in a thousand small ways, he enjoys it all the more for having seen the contrast.

And even there, in the city, he can do very much more for himself than the ordinary mortal, who has never really learned to provide for his own wants. The man who has to turn his hand to many things, as the Scout does in camp, finds that when he comes into civilization, he is more easily able to obtain employment, because he is ready for whatever kind of work may turn up.

EXPLORATION

A good form of Scout work can be done by Scouts going about either as Patrols on an exploring expedition, or in pairs like knight-errants of old on a pilgrimage through the country to find people who need help, and then to help them. This can be done equally well on bicycles as on foot.

Scouts carrying out such a journey should never, if possible, sleep under a roof. On fine nights they should sleep in the open wherever they may be. In bad weather, they would get permission to occupy a hay loft or barn.

You should on all occasions take a map with you, and find your way by it without having to ask the way of passers-by.

Map Sketching

Also make a sketch-map. This does not need to be elaborate, as long as someone else can find his way by it. Be certain to include the north line and a rough scale.

Explorers, of course, keep a log or journal, giving a short account of each day's journey, with simple drawings or photographs of interesting things they see.

The Object of Your Expedition

As a rule you should have some object in your expedition: that is to say, if you are a Patrol of town boys, you would go off with the idea of scouting some special spot, say a mountain, or a famous lake, or possibly some old castle or battlefield, or a seaside beach. Or you may be on your way to join one of the larger camps.

If, on the other hand, you are a Patrol from the country, you can make your way up to a big town, with the idea of seeing its buildings, its zoological gardens, museums, etc.

You would, of course, have to do your daily good turn whenever opportunity presented itself, but besides that, you should do good turns to farmers and others who may allow you the use of their barns and land, as a return for their kindness.

MOUNTAINEERING

Mountaineering is grand sport in many parts of the world. Finding your way and making yourself comfortable in the mountains bring into practice all your Scoutcraft.

On steep hill sides the Scout staff will often come in handy for balancing yourself.

In mountain climbing you are continually changing your direction, because, moving up and down in the deep gullies of the mountainside, you lose sight of the landmarks which usually guide you. You have to watch your direction by the sun and by your compass, and keep on estimating in what direction your proper line of travel lies.

Then again you are very liable to be caught in fogs and mists, which upset the calculations even of men who know every inch of the country.

Lost in the Mountains

I had such an experience in Scotland one year, when, in company with a Highlander who knew the ground, I got lost in the mist. Supposing that he knew the way, I committed myself entirely to his guidance. But after going some distance I felt bound to remark to him that I noticed the wind had suddenly changed. It had been blowing from our left when we started, and was now blowing hard on our right cheek. However, he seemed in no way disturbed and led on. Presently I remarked that the wind was blowing behind us, so that either the wind, or the mountain, or we ourselves were turning round. Eventually it proved, as I expected, that it was not the wind that had turned, or the mountain. It was ourselves who had wandered round in a complete circle. We were back almost at the point we started from. Scouts working on a mountain ought to practise the art of roping themselves together, as mountaineers do.

PATROLLING

Scouts go about Scouting as a Patrol or in pairs, or sometimes singly.

When patrolling, the Scouts of a Patrol seldom move close together. They spread out to see more country. Also, in this way, they will not all get caught if cut off or ambushed by the "enemy".

A Patrol of six Scouts best moves in the shape of a kite with the Patrol Leader in the centre. No. 2 Scout is in front, Nos. 5 and 4 to the right and left, No. 3 to the rear, and No. 6 with the leader (No. 1) in the centre.

If there are eight in the Patrol, the Patrol Leader takes the Tenderfoot with him, No. 2 takes No. 6, and No. 3 takes No. 7.

Patrols going over open country where they are likely to be seen by enemies or animals should get across it as quickly as possible, by moving at Scout's Pace, walking and running alternately for short spells of fifty paces from one point of cover to another. As soon as they are hidden in cover they can rest and look round before making the next move.

If you are the leading Scout and get out of sight ahead of your Patrol, you can bend branches of bushes or of reeds and grass every few yards, making the heads point *forward* to show your path. In this way the Patrol or anyone coming after you can easily follow and can judge from the freshness of the grass pretty well how long ago you passed. Besides, you can always find your way back again. Or you can make marks in the sand, or lay stones, or show which way you have gone by the signs which I have given you in Yarn No. 4.

NIGHT WORK

Scouts must be able to find their way equally well by night or by day. But unless they practise it frequently, they are very apt to lose themselves by night. Distances seem greater and landmarks are hard to see. Also you are apt to make more noise than by day, by accidentally treading on dry sticks or kicking stones.

If you are watching for an enemy at night, you have to trust much more to your ears than to your eyes. Your nose will also help you, for a Scout is well-practised at smelling out things. A man who has not damaged his sense of smell by smoking can often smell an enemy a good distance away. I have done it many times myself.

When patrolling at night, Scouts keep closer together than by day, and in very dark places, such as woods, they keep in touch with each other in single file by each catching hold of the end of the next Scout's staff.

When working singly in the dark, the Scout staff is most useful for feeling the way and pushing aside branches.

Scouts working apart from each other at night keep up communication by occasionally giving the call of their Patrol animal.

All Scouts should know how to guide themselves by the stars.

FINDING THE WAY

Among the Red Indian scouts, the man who was good at finding his way in a strange country was termed a "pathfinder". It was a great honour to be called by that name.

Many a "tenderfoot" has become lost in the veldt or forest, and has never been seen again, because he knew no scouting, nor had what is called "eye for the country".

In one case a man got off a coach, which was driving through Matabeleland, while the mules were being changed, and walked off a few yards into the bush. When the coach was ready to start the drivers called for him in every direction, then searched for him. They followed the man's tracks as far as they could, in the very difficult soil of that country, but could not find him. At last, the coach, unable to wait any longer, continued its journey, after some one else had taken over the search. Several weeks afterwards, the

The coach through Matabeleland was pulled by eight mules.

man was discovered, dead, nearly fifteen miles from where he had left the coach.

Don't Get Lost

It often happens that when you are tramping alone through the bush, you become careless in noticing in what direction you are moving. You frequently change direction to get round a fallen tree, or over a rock or other obstacle and, having passed it, do not take up exactly the correct direction again. A man's inclination somehow is to keep edging to his right, and the consequence is that when you think you are going straight, you are really not doing so at all. Unless you watch the sun, or your compass, or your landmarks, you are very apt to find yourself going round in a big circle.

In such a case a "tenderfoot", when he suddenly finds he has lost his bearings, at once loses his head and gets excited. He probably begins to run, when the right thing to do is to force yourself to keep cool and give yourself something useful to do—that is, to track your own footprints back again; or, if you fail in this, to collect firewood for making signal fires to direct those who will be looking for you.

The main point is not to get lost in the first instance.

Notice the Directions

When you start out for a walk or on patrol, note the direction by the compass. Also notice which direction the wind is blowing;

this is a great help, especially if you have no compass, or if the sun is not shining.

Every old scout notices which way the wind is blowing when he turns out in the morning.

To find the way the wind is blowing when there is only very light air, throw up little bits of dry grass. Or hold up a handful of light dust and let it fall. Or wet your thumb and let the wind blow on it; the cold side of it will then tell you from which direction the wind comes.

Using Landmarks

Then you should notice all important landmarks for finding your way.

In the country the landmarks may be hills or prominent towers, steeples, curious trees, rocks, gates, mounds, bridges—any points, in fact, by which you could find your way back again, or by which you could instruct someone else to follow the same route. If you remember your landmarks going out you can always find your way back by them; but you should take care occasionally to look back at them after passing them, so that you can recognize them for your return journey.

The same holds good when you arrive in a strange town by train. The moment you step out from the station notice where the sun is, or which way the smoke is blowing. Also notice your landmarks—which in this case would be prominent buildings, churches, factory chimneys, names of streets and shops—so that when you have gone down several streets you can turn round and find your way back to the station without difficulty. It is wonderfully easy when you have practised it a little, yet many people get lost when they have turned a few corners in a town they do not know.

Concentrate on Your Job

When you are acting as scout or guide for a party, move ahead of it and fix your whole attention and all your thoughts on what you are doing. You have to go by the very smallest signs, and if you talk and think of other things you are very apt to miss them. Old scouts generally are very silent people, from this habit of fixing their attention on the work in hand.

Very often a "tenderfoot" out for the first time will think that the leading scout looks lonely and will go up to walk or ride alongside of him and begin a conversation—until the scout shows by his manner or otherwise that he does not want the "tenderfoot" there.

On small steamers you may see a notice, "Don't speak to the man at the wheel". The same thing applies to a scout who is guiding a party. When acting as scout you must keep all your thoughts on the one subject, like Kim did when Lurgan tried to mesmerize him.

USING A COMPASS

I am certain that you know that the needle of a compass has the habit of swinging round until it points in one definite direction.

If you followed the direction indicated by one end of the needle you would come out at a spot north of Canada, about 1400 miles from the North Pole. The reason for this is that at this spot there

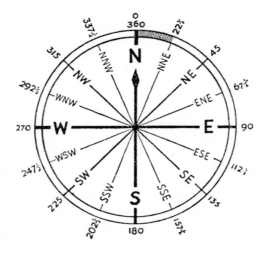

is a powerful magnetic force. It is this force which attracts the north point of the needle and make it point to "Magnetic North".

North is only one of the compass points. Every sailor knows the other points of the compass by heart, and so should a Scout. I have talked about north, but that is only because we usually think of north as a starting point. That is just for convenience—we could just as well use south.

Explorers seldom refer to compass points. They use compass degrees instead because they are more exact.

When you look at the compass chart you will notice that it is marked not only with the points, but also with figures running clockwise from 0 at the north point round to north again which also has the figure 360. So any point can be given either as a compass name or as a degree number. Thus, east is 90 degrees, south is 180, west is 270, and so on. Instead of saying S.E. we can say 135 degrees.

How a Compass Helped My Career

Knowing the right way to use a compass helped to give me a good start in my army career.

It was this way.

With a number of other young officers I was being tested in surveying. We had to take a reading with our compass to a certain

Compass work means extreme care to take an accurate reading.

spot, and from there to another point, and from there to a third point. If one did it correctly, this last reading should land us exactly at the spot whence we started.

But it means extreme care to take an accurate reading. If you misread your compass by not much more than a hair's breadth you would fail. Only one of our party had been exact enough to succeed, and who do you think that was?

Little me!

As a result of this and a few good marks in other subjects, I got promoted with extra pay, with which I was able to buy the best horse I ever had.

FINDING THE NORTH WITHOUT A COMPASS

Besides the "Magnetic North" which you find with your compass, there is the other north of the North Pole at the top of the earth. This is the real north and for that reason is named "True North".

North by the Sun

If you have no compass to show you "Magnetic North", the sun will tell you by day where "True North" is, and from that you can figure out the other directions.

At six o'clock in the morning Greenwich Mean Time the sun is east. At nine it is south-east. At noon it is south. At three o'clock in the afternoon it is south-west, and at six o'clock it is west. In

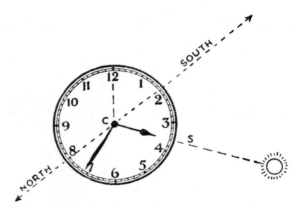

When the sun is out, a watch will help you find your directions.

winter it will have set before six o'clock, but will not have reached west when it is set. This applies roughly in the Northern Hemisphere. (In the Southern Hemisphere, at six o'clock the sun is east, at nine north-east, at noon north, at three north-west, at six west.)

The Phoenicians who sailed round Africa in ancient times noticed that when they started the sun rose on their left-hand side—they were going south. Then they reported that they came to a strange country where the sun rose in the wrong quarter, namely on their right hand. The truth was that they had gone round the Cape of Good Hope, and were headed north again, up the east side of Africa.

To find the south at any time of day by the sun, hold your watch flat, face upwards, so that the sun shines on it. Turn it round till the hour hand points at the sun: allow for Summer Time if it is in operation. Without moving the watch, lay a pencil or stick across the face of the watch so that it rests on the centre of the dial and points out half-way between the figure XII and the hour hand. The direction in which it points is south. This applies only in the Northern

Hemisphere. (In the Southern Hemisphere turn the XII, instead of the hand, to the sun, and south will then lie between the two as before.)

North by the Stars

Various groups of stars have been given names because they seemed to make some kind of picture outline of men and animals.

The Plough or the Big Dipper is an easy one to find. It is shaped something like a plough or dipper. It is the most useful star group for a Scout to know, because in the northern part of the world it shows him where north is. The Plough is also called the Great Bear. The stars in the curve make its tail. It is the only bear I know that wears a long tail.

Pole Star—The two stars in the Plough called the Pointers tell you where the North or Pole Star is. It is the last star in the tail of the Little Bear. All stars and constellations move round the sky during the night, but the Pole Star remains fixed in the north.

Two stars of the Plough or Big Dipper point toward the Pole Star.

Orion—Another group of stars, or constellation, represents a man wearing a sword and belt, and is named Orion. It is easily recognized by three stars in a line, the "belt", and three smaller stars in another line, close by, the "sword". Two stars to right and left below the sword are Orion's feet, two more above the belt are his shoulders, and a group of three small stars between them make his head.

The Zulus call Orion's belt and sword the "Ingolubu", or three pigs pursued by three dogs. The Masai tribe in East Africa say that the three stars in Orion's belt are three bachelors being followed by

A line through Orion will eventually reach the Pole or North Star.

three old maids. You see, scouts all know Orion, though under different names.

The great point about Orion is that by him you can always tell which way the North or Pole Star lies, and you can see Orion whether you are in the south or the north part of the world.

If you draw a line, by holding up your staff against the sky, from the centre star of Orion's belt through the centre of his head, and

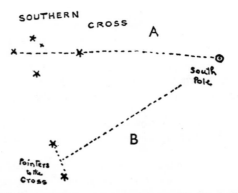

In the Southern Hemisphere, the Southern Cross tells the directions

carry that line on through two big stars till it comes to a third, that third star is the North or Pole Star.

Southern Cross—On the south side of the world, in South Africa, South America, New Zealand and Australia, the Plough is not visible. Here the Southern Cross points toward south (see diagram). If you carry your eye along the same direction, A, as the long stem of the Cross for a distance of about three times its length, the point you hit will be about due south. Or if you imagine a line between the two Pointers and another imaginary line, B, standing upright on this first line and continued until it cuts the line A in continuation of the stem of the Cross, the point where A and B cut each other will be the south.

WEATHER WISDOM

Every Scout ought to be able to read signs of the weather, especially when going camping, and to read a barometer.

He should remember the following points:

Red at night, shepherd's delight (i.e. fine day coming).

Red in morning, shepherd's warning (i.e. rain).

Yellow sunset means wind.

Pale yellow sunset means rain.

Dew and fog in early morning means fine weather.

Low dawn means fine weather.

High dawn means wind (high dawn is when the sun rises over a bank of clouds, high above the horizon).

Soft clouds, fine weather.

Hard-edged clouds, wind.

Rolled or jagged clouds, strong wind.

> "*When the wind's before the rain,*
> *Soon you may make sail again;*
> *When the rain's before the wind,*
> *Then your sheets and halyards mind.*"

PATROL PRACTICES IN FINDING THE WAY

Use compass directions whenever possible, such as "N.W. corner of room", "E. side of camp site", etc.

Practise moving in the direction of a compass point. Take a direction, say N.E. Pick out some landmark—tree, mound, rock—in line with the direction given; this mark should not be too far away. Walk to that point, and repeat the operation by picking out another mark on which to move.

Then continue further practice using degrees instead of points.

Practise finding compass directions with watch and by the stars.

Send out Patrols with compass directions to take them by separate routes to meeting place.

When possible, point out constellations in night sky. Learn to recognize the Great Bear and the Pole Star and Orion.

Night movements can be practised in daylight by covering the eyes with a bandage made of several thicknesses of black crêpe or similar material. The staff should be used.

Use local map for map reading and finding way by the map.

GAMES IN PATHFINDING

Follow the Map

A Patrol is taken in patrol formation into a strange town or into an intricate piece of strange country, with a map. Here sealed instructions are opened, telling where the Patrol is, and where it is to go to. Each Scout now in turn leads the Patrol, say, for seven minutes if cycling, fifteen minutes if walking. Each Scout is to find the way entirely by the map, and points are given for ability in reading.

On Trek

Make a "wilderness" trek, each Scout carrying his kit and food. Walk in single file, with a Scout 200 yards out in front to indicate the road to follow by Scout signs. Make a bridge over a stream or a raft over a lake; cross boggy ground on faggots.

To teach your Scouts individually, ideas of direction and distance, send each out in a different direction on some such order as this: "Go two miles to the North-north-east. Write a report to show exactly where you are, with a sketch map to explain it. Bring in your report as quickly as possible". Then test by ordnance maps or otherwise to see how far he was out of the distance and direction ordered.

Send out Scouts in pairs, to compete each pair against the other. Each pair to be sent by a different route to gain the same spot, finding the way by map, and to reach the goal without being seen by

Learn to pack your camp gear properly. In Africa and North America, they often use a tump-line on the head to help support the load.

the others on the way. This develops map-reading, eye for country, concealment, look-out, etc.

For judging time: send out Scouts in different directions, each with a slip of paper that tells him for how long he is to be away— say seven minutes for one, ten for another, and so on. Note down exact time of starting, and take it again on the return of the Scouts. They must be put on their honour not to consult watches or clocks.

Find the North

Scouts are posted thirty yards apart, and each lays his staff on the ground pointing to what he considers the exact north (or south), without using any instrument. He steps back three paces away from his staff. The umpire compares each stick with the compass. The one that is nearest, wins. This is a useful game to play at night, or on sunless days as well as sunny days.

Night Patrolling

Scouts can practise hearing and seeing at night by acting as "sentries", who stand or walk about, while other Scouts try to stalk up to them. If a sentry hears a sound he calls or whistles. The stalking Scouts must at once halt and lie still. The umpire comes to the sentry and asks which direction the sound came from. If he is right, the sentry wins. If the stalker can creep up within fifteen yards of the sentry without being seen, he deposits some article, such as a

53

The Red Indians used to transport their teepees and equipment on a carrier made by lashing sticks together. It was called a "travois".

handkerchief, on the ground at that point, and creeps away again. Then he makes a noise to cause the sentry to sound an alarm, and when the umpire comes up, he explains what he has done. This game can also be practised by day, with the sentries blindfolded.

Compass Points

Eight staffs are arranged in star fashion on the ground, all radiating from the centre. One staff should point due north.

One Scout takes up his position at the outer end of each staff, and represents one of the eight principal points of the compass.

The Scoutmaster now calls out any two points, such as S.E. and N., and the two Scouts concerned must immediately change places. To change, Scouts must not cross the staffs, but must go outside the circle of players. Anyone moving out of place without his point being named, or moving to a wrong place or even hesitating, should lose a mark. When three marks have been lost the Scout should fall out.

As the game goes on blank spaces will occur. These will make it slightly harder for the remaining boys.

To make the game more difficult sixteen points may be used instead of eight.

When played indoors the lines of the compass may be drawn in chalk on the floor.

Alarm: Catch the Thief

A red rag is hung up in the camp or troop room in the morning. The umpire goes round to each Scout in turn, while they are at work or play, and whispers to him, "There is a thief in the camp". But to one he whispers, "There is a thief in the camp, and you are he— Marble Arch!" or some other well-known spot about a mile away.

That Scout then knows that he must steal the rag at any time within the next three hours, and bolt with it to the Marble Arch. Nobody else knows who is to be the thief, where he will run to, and when he will steal it. Directly anyone notices that the red rag is stolen, he gives the alarm, and all stop what they may be doing at the time, and dart off in pursuit of the thief. The Scout who gets the rag or a bit of it wins. If none succeeds in doing this, the thief wins. He must carry the rag tied round his neck, and not in his pocket, or hidden away.

Surveying the Country

As soon as a camp has been pitched, the first thing to be done is to find out about the country around the camp site, and this makes an excellent subject for a Patrol competition.

Each Patrol Leader is given a sheet of paper upon which to make a sketch map of the country for perhaps two miles around. He then sends out his Scouts in all directions to survey and bring back a report of every important feature—roads, railways, streams, etc.—choosing the best Scouts for the more difficult directions. Each Patrol Leader makes up his map entirely from the reports of his own Scouts.

The Patrol whose leader brings to the Scouter the best map in the shortest time, wins.

Note—Many of these games and practices can be carried out in town just as well as in the country.

Camp Fire Yarn
No. 6

SEA SCOUTING

**Lifeboatmen · Swimming
Boat Cruising · Sea Games**

THERE ARE PERHAPS no greater heroes and no truer Scouts than the sailors who man the lifeboats around the coasts of the oceans of the world. During dangerous storms they must BE PREPARED to turn out at any minute, and risk their lives in order to save others. Because they do it often and so quietly we have come to look upon it almost as an everyday affair, but it is none the less splendid of them and worthy of our admiration.

I am glad that so many Boy Scouts are taking up Sea Scouting, and by learning boat management and seamanship are also learning to take their place in the service of their country as seamen in the navy, or in the merchant service, or as lifeboatmen along the coasts.

A ship can be either a heaven or a hell—it depends entirely on the fellows in her. If they are surly, inclined to grouse, and untidy, they will be an unhappy ship's company. If they are, like Scouts, cheerily determined to make the best of things, to give and take, and to keep their place tidy and clean, they will be a happy family and enjoy their life at sea.

SWIMMING

Every boy should learn to swim. I've known lots of fellows pick it up the first time they try, others take longer. I did myself—I couldn't at first get the hang of it. In my heart of hearts I think I really feared the water a bit, but one day, getting out of my depth, I found myself swimming quite easily. I had made too much of an effort and a stiff struggle of it before—but I found the way was to take it slowly and calmly. I got to like the water, and swimming became easy.

All you have to do is at first to try to swim like a dog, as if crawling along in the water. Don't try all at once to swim with the breast stroke. When paddling along like a dog, get a friend to support you at first with his hand under your tummy.

There is jolly good fun in bathing—but ever so much more if the bathing includes a swim. What a fool the fellow looks who has to paddle about in shallow water and can't join his pals in their trips to sea or down the river.

But there's something more than fun in it.

If you go boating or sailing it is not fair on the other chaps to do so if you can't swim. If the boat capsizes and all are swimmers, it is

TOMMY THE TENDERFOOT No. 1   *TOMMY AT THE LAKE*

Tommy sees all of them happy but him,
They are plunging and diving—but Tommy can't swim.

rather a lark. But if there is a non-swimmer there, the others have to risk their lives to keep him afloat.

Then, too, there may come the awful time when you see someone drowning. If you are a swimmer, in you go, get hold of him the right way, and bring him ashore. And you have saved a fellow creature's life! But if you can't swim? Then you have a horrible time. You know you ought to do something better than merely call for help, while your fellow creature is fighting and struggling for his life and gradually becoming weaker before your eyes. I won't describe it—it is a horrible nightmare, and will be all the rest of your life when you think that it was partly your fault that the poor fellow was drowned. Why your fault? Because if you had been a true Scout you would have learnt swimming and would have been able to save him.

57

MANAGING A BOAT

Also, if you live near water you should be able to manage a boat. You should know how to bring it properly alongside a ship or pier, either by rowing it or steering it in a wide circle so that it comes up alongside with its head pointing the same way as the bow of the ship or towards the current. You should be able to row one oar in time with the rest of a boat's crew, or to use a pair of oars, or to scull a boat by "screwing" a single oar over the stern. In rowing, the object of feathering or turning the blade of the oar flat when it is out of the water is to save it from catching the wind and thereby checking the pace of the boat.

You should know how to throw a coil of rope so as to fling it on to another boat or wharf, or how to catch and make fast a rope thrown to you. Also how to throw a lifebuoy to a drowning man.

You should be able to make a raft out of any materials that you can get hold of, such as planks, logs, barrels, sacks of straw, and so on. Often on a hike you may want to cross a river with your food and baggage where no boats are available.

BOAT CRUISING

Instead of hiking or cycling, it is an excellent practice for a Patrol to take a boat and explore a river or make a trip through the country, camping out in the same way as in a tramping camp. But no one should be allowed in the boat who is not a good swimmer, able to swim at least fifty yards with clothes on (shirt, shorts, and socks as a minimum), because accidents may happen, and if all are swimmers it does not matter.

One of my most enjoyable Sea Scout experiences was a river cruise I made with two of my brothers. We took a canvas folding boat up the Thames as far as we could get her to float. We got right up in the Chiltern Hills where no boat had ever been seen before. We carried our cooking kit, tent and bedding with us and camped out at night.

When we reached the source of the river we carried the boat over the watershed and launched her again on the stream which ran down to the westward and which in a few miles became the Avon.

Through Bath and through Bristol we journeyed, rowing, sailing, poling, or towing, as circumstances required, until we reached the mighty waters of the Severn.

Across this we sailed with the centre board down, till we successfully reached Chepstow on the other side. Here we made our way up the rapids of the Wye through its beautiful scenery, to our home near Llandogo.

From London to Wales, almost all the way by water, with loads of adventure and lots of fun!

Learn to row a boat properly, and to "scull" with one oar.

But it was no more than any of you could do if you liked to try. So, come along, Scouts—make yourselves efficient, and if you enjoy your Sea Scouting as much as I enjoyed mine you will have a wonderful time.

SEA GAMES

Smugglers (For night or day)

One party of smugglers from the sea endeavour to land and conceal their goods (a brick or stone per man) in a base called the "Smugglers' Cave", and get away in their boat again. Another party of revenue men is distributed to watch a long stretch of the coast with single Scouts.

As soon as one revenue man sees the smugglers land he gives the alarm, and collects the rest to attack, but the attack cannot be

59

successful unless there are at least as many revenue men on the spot as smugglers. The revenue men must remain bivouacked at their station until the alarm is given by the look-out men.

Whale Hunt

The whale is made of a big log of wood with a roughly-shaped head and tail. Two boats will usually carry out the whale hunt, each boat manned by one Patrol—the Patrol Leader acting as captain, the Second as bowman or harpooner, the remainder of the Patrol as oarsmen. Each boat belongs to a different harbour, the two harbours being about a mile apart. The umpire takes the whale and lets it loose about half-way between the two harbours, and on a given signal, the two boats race out to see who can get to the whale first.

The harpooner who first arrives within range of the whale drives

his harpoon into it, and the boat promptly turns round and tows the whale to its harbour.

The second boat pursues, and when it overtakes the other, also harpoons the whale, turns around, and endeavours to tow the whale back to its harbour.

In this way the two boats have a tug-of-war, and eventually the better boat tows the whale, and possibly, the opposing boat into its harbour.

Camp Fire Yarn
No. 7

SIGNALS AND COMMANDS

Hidden Dispatches · Signal Fires
Sound Signals · Words of Command
Whistle and Flag Signals

SCOUTS HAVE TO BE CLEVER at passing news secretly from one place to another, or in signalling to each other.

Before the siege of Mafeking, which I told you about in my first yarn, I received a secret message from some unknown friend in the Transvaal, giving me news of the enemy's plans, the number of his men, horses, and guns. This news came in a very small letter rolled up in a little ball the size of a pill, then put inside a tiny hole in a rough walking stick, and plugged in there with wax. The stick was given to an African, who merely had orders to come into Mafeking and give me the stick as a present. Naturally, when he brought me the stick and said it was from a white man, I guessed there must be something special about it, and soon found the hidden letter.

I received a secret letter from another friend once. He had written it in the Hindustani language, but in English lettering. Anybody else studying it would have been quite puzzled about the language in which it was written, but to me it was clear as daylight.

When we sent letters out from Mafeking during the siege, we gave them to the Africans, who were able to creep out between the Boer outposts. Once through the line of sentries, the Boers mistook them for their own, and took no further notice of them. They carried the messages in this way: the letters were written on thin paper, and half a dozen or more were crumpled up tightly into a little ball, then rolled up into a piece of lead paper, such as tea is packed in. The scout would carry a number of these little balls in his hand, or hanging round his neck loosely on strings. If he saw he was in danger of being captured by an enemy, he would notice landmarks round about him and drop all the balls on the ground, where they looked like small stones. Then he would walk boldly on until accosted by the enemy, who, if he searched him, would find nothing.

The messenger would wait around for perhaps a day or two, until the coast was clear, then come back to the spot where the landmarks

The aborigines of Australia often used signal fires to send messages.

told him the letters were lying. "Landmarks", you may remember, mean any objects—trees, mounds, rocks, or other details—which act as sign-posts for a Scout who notices and remembers them.

SIGNALLING

Signalling is well worth knowing. It is good fun to be able to signal to your pal across the street without other people understanding what you are talking about. But I found it really valuable for communicating with a friend out in the wild—once when we were on separate mountains, and another time when we were on opposite sides of a big river, and one of us had important news to communicate.

Signal Fires

Scouts of many countries use fires for signalling purposes—smoke fires by day and flame fires by night.

Smoke Signals—Three big puffs in slow succession mean "Go on". A succession of small puffs means "Rally, come here". A continual column of smoke means "Halt". Alternate small puffs and big ones mean "Danger".

To make a smoke fire, light your fire in the ordinary way with plenty of thin dry sticks and twigs, and as soon as it is burning well, put on green leaves and grass, or damped hay, to make it smoke.

Special drums are used in Africa to signal from village to village.

Cover the fire with a damp blanket. Take off the blanket to let up a puff of smoke, then put it over the fire again. The size of the puff depends on how long you lift the blanket. For a short puff, hold it up while you count two, then replace the blanket while you count eight. For a long puff hold up the blanket for about six seconds.

Flare Signals—Long or short flares at night mean the same as the above smoke signals by day.

You light a flare fire with dry sticks and brushwood, so as to make as bright a flame as possible.

Two Scouts hold up a blanket in front of the fire, that is, between it and those to whom you are signalling, so that your friends do not see the flame till you want them to. Then you drop the blanket

Here is another kind of signal "drum" used in Africa.

while you count two for a short flash, or six for a long one, hiding the fire while you count four between each flash.

Sound Signals

In the American Civil War, Captain Clowry, a scout officer, wanted to give warning to a large force of his own army that the enemy was going to attack unexpectedly during the night. But he could not get to his friends because there was a flooded river between them which he could not cross, and a rain storm was raging.

What would you have done if you had been Captain Clowry?

A good idea struck him. He got hold of an old railway engine that was standing near him. He lit the fire and got up steam in her, and then started to blow the whistle with short and long blasts in the Morse alphabet. Soon his friends heard and understood, and answered back with a bugle. He then spelt out a message of warning to them, which they read and acted upon. And so their force of twenty-thousand men was saved from surprise.

Certain tribes in Africa signal news to each other by means of beats on a drum. Others use wooden war gongs.

Morse and Semaphore Signalling

Every Scout ought to learn the **Morse** code for signalling. It can be used to send messages by "dots" and "dashes" for some distance by flags; or by sounds, such as bugle; or by flashes (heliograph or electric light).

Semaphore signalling, which is done by waving your arms at different angles to each other, is even easier to learn. Here you form the different letters by putting your arms at different angles. Be sure to make these angles correctly. The diagram on page 66 shows the signs as they appear to a "reader". It may look complicated in the picture, but you will find it is very simple.

The sender must always face the station he is sending to. He gets the attention of the receiving station by the *calling up signal* VE—VE—VE or AAAA. When the receiving station is ready, it gives the *carry on signal* K. If it is not ready, it sends Q, meaning *wait*.

When the receiving station has read a word correctly, it sends E or T (for Morse), or C or A (for Semaphore). If any word is not answered, the sending station knows that the receiving station has not read it and so repeats it until it is answered.

If you make a mistake, send the *erase signal* of 8 Es, and then repeat the word.

If you are going to send numbers, use the regular Morse numerals, but in Semaphore spell the numbers out in letters. They will be checked by being repeated back by the receiving station.

A ·—	J ·———	S ···	2 ··———
B —···	K —·—	T —	3 ···——
C —·—·	L ·—··	U ··—	4 ····—
D —··	M ——	V ···—	5 ·····
E ·	N —·	W ·——	6 —····
F ··—·	O ———	X —··—	7 ——···
G ——·	P ·——·	Y —·——	8 ———··
H ····	Q ——·—	Z ——··	9 ————·
I ··	R ·—·	1 ·————	0 —————

The MORSE code letters and numerals are made up of dots and dashes.

The end of a word is indicated by a short pause in light and sound signalling, or, with flags, by bringing them down to the front.

You finish a message by sending the *end of message signal* AR.

The receiving station answers with the *message received signal* R if the message has been received correctly.

Once you know the Morse or Semaphore alphabet, all you need is practice. A Scout is not asked to send long sentences, or to send over long distances, or at a high speed. All that is expected of you is that you should know your alphabet and read and send simple

A		**H**		**O**		**V**	
B		**I**		**P**		**W**	
C		**J**		**Q**		**X**	
D		**K**		**R**		**Y**	
E		**L**		**S**		**Z**	
F		**M**		**T**		**NUMERALS TO FOLLOW**	
G		**N**		**U**		**LETTERS TO FOLLOW** (J)	

SEMAPHORE letters are made by holding two flags at different angles.

sentences or words really well. Do your best, so that when it comes to sending across a big field, or from hill to hill, your message will be easy to read.

If you want to write a dispatch that will puzzle most people to read, use the Morse or Semaphore letters in place of the ordinary alphabet. It will be quite readable to any of your friends who understand signalling.

COMMANDS AND SIGNALS

A Patrol Leader often has a whistle, and a lanyard or cord for keeping it The following commands and signals should be at your fingertips, so that you can use them in your Patrol.

Words of Command
"Fall in" (in line).
"Alert" (stand up smartly).
"At ease" (stand at ease).

"Sit easy" or "Sit at ease" (sit or lie down without leaving the ranks).

"Dismiss" (break off).

"Right turn" (or "left turn"); (each Scout turns accordingly).

"Patrol right turn" (or "left turn"); (each Patrol with its Scouts in line wheels to that hand).

"Quick march" (walk smartly, stepping off on the left foot).

"Halt" (stop, standing still at the "Alert")

"Double" or "At the double" (run at smart pace, arms hanging loose).

"Scout Pace" (walk so many paces and run so many paces alternately—about 50 of each).

Signal	Meaning and Use
VE, VE, VE, or AAAA	Calling up signal.
K	Carry on (answer to VE if ready to receive message).
Q	Wait (answer to VE if not ready to receive message).
T or E (Morse) C or A (Semaphore)	General answer (used to answer all signals unless otherwise stated).
8 dots (Semaphore 8 Es)	Erase (to erase anything sent incorrectly).
AR	End of message signal.
R	Message received correctly (answer to AR).

Whistle Signals

When a Scoutmaster wants to call the Troop together he whistles "The Scout Call", or uses a special Troop call.

Patrol Leaders thereupon call together their Patrols by giving their Patrol call. Then they take their Patrol "at the double" to the Scoutmaster.

Here are some whistle signals for Scout wide games.

1. One long blast means "Silence", "Alert"; "Look out for my next signal".

2. A succession of long, slow blasts means "Go out", "Get farther away", or "Advance", "Extend," "Scatter".

3. A succession of short, sharp blasts means "Rally", "Close in", "Come together", "Fall in".

4. A succession of short and long blasts alternately means "Alarm", "Look out", "Be ready", "Man your alarm posts".

5. Three short blasts followed by one long one from the Scoutmaster calls up the Patrol Leaders—i.e., "Leaders come here".

Any signal must be instantly obeyed at the double as fast as you can run—no matter what other job you may be doing at the time.

Hand Signals

Hand Signals—which can also be made by Patrol Leaders with their Patrol flags when necessary.

Hand waved several times across the face from side to side, or flag waved horizontally from side to side opposite the face means "No", "Never mind", "As you were".

Hand or flag held high, and waved very slowly from side to side, at full extent of arm means "Extend", "Go farther out", "Scatter".

Hand or flag held high, and waved quickly from side to side at full extent of arm means "Close in", "Rally", "Come here".

Hand or flag pointing in any direction, means "Go in that direction".

Clenched hand or flag jumped rapidly up and down several times means "Run".

Hand or flag held straight up over head, means "Stop", "Halt".

When a leader is shouting an order or message to a Scout who is some way off, the Scout, if he hears what is being said, should hold up his hand level with his head all the time. If he cannot hear, he should stand still, making no sign. The leader will then repeat louder, or beckon to the Scout to come in nearer.

Make up your own signals for other commands to your Patrol.

PATROL PRACTICES IN SIGNALLING

Practise the laying, lighting and use of signal fires of smoke or flame.

_____

Practise whistle and drill signals.

_____

Have a competition in the Patrol in concealing dispatches on the person: give each Scout a small piece of paper and allow him to hide it on himself. Pair Scouts off and let each search the other. The one whose paper takes longest to find is the winner.

Each Patrol invents its own secret code. The other Patrols try to decipher it.

Patrols compete in finding the most ingenious way of sending a Morse message without use of special apparatus.

All signalling practices should be as real as possible. From the beginning separate letters can be sent and read across as wide a space as may be available, preferably out-of-doors.

Here is an English sentence you can use for practice in signalling: "The quick brown fox jumps over the lazy dog." It contains all the letters of the alphabet.

GAME IN MESSAGE CARRYING

Dispatch Running

A Scout is chosen to carry a dispatch to a "besieged" place—which may be a real village, farm or house, or someone stationed at an appointed spot. The dispatch-runner must wear a coloured rag, at least two feet long, pinned to his shoulder, and with this in its proper place he must reach his goal.

The enemy besieging the place must prevent him reaching it, but cannot, of course, go within the lines of the supposed defenders, that is, within 300 yards of the besieged place—boundaries for this should be decided upon beforehand. Anyone found within that limit by the umpire will be ruled out as shot by the defenders.

To catch the dispatch-runner the enemy must take the rag from his shoulder. They know he starts from a certain direction at a certain time—the spot should be a mile or so from the besieged town—and they may take any steps to capture him they like, except that they may not actually witness his departure from the starting-place.

The game may be played in a town with two houses chosen as starting-place and besieged town respectively, and the dispatch-runner can adopt any disguise (except that of a woman), as long as he wears the rag pinned to his shoulder.

The people of old had their own signals. Here's one that has meant
"Attention" through all ages.

Camp Fire Yarn
No. 8

PIONEERING

**Knot Tying · Hut-Building
Felling Trees · Bridging
Self-Measurement · Judging Heights
and Distances**

PIONEERS ARE MEN who go ahead to open a way in the jungle or elsewhere for those coming after them.

When I was on service on the West Coast of Africa, I had command of a large force of local scouts, and, like all scouts, we tried to make ourselves useful in every way to our main army, which was coming along behind us. We not only looked out for the enemy and watched his moves, but we also did what we could to improve the road for our own army, since it was merely a narrow track through thick jungle and swamps. So we became pioneers as well as scouts. In the course of our march we built nearly two hundred bridges over streams, by tying poles together.

But when I first set the scouts to do this important work I found that, out of the thousand men, a great many did not know how to use an axe to cut down trees, and, except one company of about sixty men, none knew how to make knots—not even bad knots.

SAVING LIFE WITH KNOTS

Just before I arrived in Canada a number of years ago, an awful tragedy had happened at the Niagara Falls.

It was mid-winter. Three people, a man and his wife and a boy of seventeen, were walking across a bridge which the ice had formed over the rushing river under the falls, when it suddenly began to

71

crack and to break up. The man and his wife found themselves on one floe of ice floating away from the main part, and the boy was on another.

All around them the water was covered with similar floating blocks of ice, grinding and bumping against each other. The three people were at the mercy of the current, which here moved slowly, but gradually and surely carried them downstream towards the awful rapids a mile away.

People on the banks saw their dangerous position, and thousands collected, but not one seemed able to do anything to help them. Swimming was impossible. So was a boat rescue.

For an hour the poor wretches floated along. Then the river carried them under two bridges, which span the river just before the rapids.

On the bridges, 160 feet above the water, men had lowered ropes so that they hung down in the path of the drifting people.

As they passed by, the boy managed to grasp a rope, and willing hands proceeded to haul him up. But when they had him up about half-way, the poor fellow could hold on no longer. He fell down in the icy stream, and was never seen again.

The man on the other floe also grasped a rope which he tried to fasten around his wife, so that she, at any rate, might be saved. But the current was now rushing them along. His hands were numb. He failed to fasten the rope. It slipped from his hands.

And a few seconds later both he and his wife ended their tortures by being sucked under the water in the heavy swirling rapids.

What Would You Have Done?

It is easy to be wise after an event, but this disaster is worth thinking out. What would you have done had you been there?

One of our Canadian Scoutmasters told me that he was travelling in a train shortly after this accident, when some of his fellow-travellers were talking it over. They did not know that he was connected with the Scouts in any way, and one of them said:

"Well, I believe that if any Boy Scouts had been there they would have found some plan for saving those poor people."

People often think: "What is the good of learning such a simple thing as tying knots?" Well, here was a case in which that knowledge might have saved three lives.

When the ropes were lowered from the bridge they should have had a loop or two tied in them for the victims to put around themselves, or to put their arms or legs through. As it was, the ropes had no loops, and the people, not knowing how to tie bowlines or any other type of loop, were unable to save themselves.

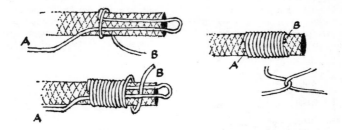

To prevent the end of a rope from becoming frayed, you should whip it. Place a piece of twine in a loop along the rope. Then twist the longer part (B) round and round up to within a quarter of an inch of the end. Pull each turn tightly and pack each neatly to the next. Now slip end B through the loop, and pull firmly on A—don't snatch it, or it may break. This pulls end B down under the whipping (about half-way down will do). Finally cut off the spare ends neatly.

USEFUL KNOTS

Every Scout ought to be able to tie knots.

To tie a knot seems a simple thing, and yet there are right ways and wrong ways of doing it, and Scouts ought to know the right way. A life may depend on a knot being properly tied.

The right kind of knot to tie is one which you can be certain will hold under any amount of strain, and which you can undo easily if you wish to.

A bad knot is one which slips when a hard pull comes on it, or which gets jammed so tight that you cannot untie it.

The best way to learn is to get a fellow who knows to show you. You need to practise a lot, or you will soon forget the knots. Use pieces of rope or cord and not messy bits of string or bootlaces!

On pages 74 and 75 are useful knots which every Scout ought to know, and ought to use whenever he is tying string or rope.

To prevent the end of a rope from becoming frayed and unlaid you should whip it. This is done by wrapping thin string round it several times and finishing it off so that the ends do not show. There are several methods of doing this; the picture on this page shows an easy and efficient way.

1. THE REEF KNOT, *for tying two ropes together under strain, as in tying up a parcel. Being a flat knot, it is much used in ambulance work. The best simple knot, as it will not slip and is easy to untie.*

2. SHEET BEND, *or common bend, for joining ropes of equal or unequal thickness together. Make loop with one rope and pass other end through and around whole loop and bend it under its own standing part.*

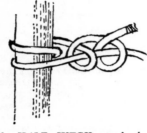

3. HALF HITCH, *made by passing rope-end round standing part and behind itself. If free end is turned back and forms a loop, the hitch can be easily loosened. A round turn and two half hitches are used for tying a rope to a spar.*

4. THE SHEEP SHANK, *for shortening ropes. Gather up the amount to be shortened as in illustration. Then make a half-hitch round each of the bends.*

5. THE BOWLINE, *a loop that will not slip, to tie round a person being lowered from a building, etc. Form a loop, then in the standing part form a second and smaller loop. Through this pass the end of the large loop and behind the standing part and down through the small loop.*

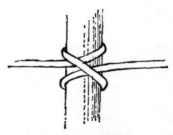

6. CLOVE HITCH, *for fastening a rope to a spar. Either end will stand a strain without slipping, either lengthways or downwards.*

74

We had no rope with us in West Africa, so we used strong creeping plants, and thin withes or long whippy sticks, which we made still more pliant or bendable by holding one end under foot and twisting the other round and round with our hands. Willow and hazel make good withes. You cannot tie all knots with them, as with rope, but you can generally make a timber hitch.

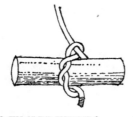

7. *TIMBER HITCH for securing the end of a rope to a spar or log.*

8. *FISHERMAN'S KNOT for tying together two wet or slippery lines.*

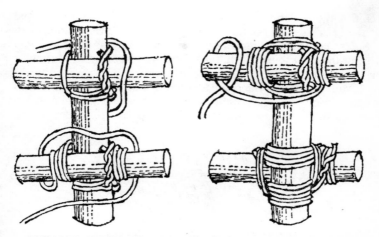

SQUARE LASHING. Begin with clove hitch under horizontal spar; follow round as shown; pull tight at each stage; pack turns together neatly without crossing. After several complete turns, frapping turns (at right angles to main lashing) are made; these must be very tight. Finish off with clove hitch round handiest spar, keeping clove hitch at right angles to last turn. Go slowly, and keep all tight and firm.

75

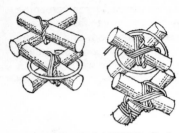

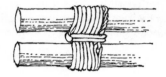

DIAGONAL LASHING. Begin with timber hitch round both spars. Take turns round each fork. Frap. End with clove hitch.

SHEAR LASHING. Clove hitch round one spar. Then turns round both spars. Frap. End with clove hitch round one spar.

12 HUT BUILDING

To live comfortably in camp a Scout must know how to make a bivouac shelter for the night, or a hut if he is going to be in camp for a long time.

What sort of shelter you put up depends on the country and weather.

Notice the direction from which the wind generally blows, and put the back of your shelter that way, with your fire in front of it. If you are going into camp where there are plenty of trees, and you have got the right to use them, then there are several types of shelters you may make.

A bivouac shelter is the simplest form of hut. Two upright stakes are driven firmly into the ground, with a ridge-pole placed in position along the tops. Against this a number of poles are made to lean

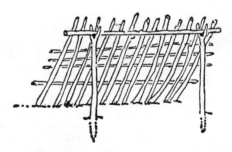

A bivouac shelter is a simple hut, which you can make quickly.

from the windward side, with crossbars to support the branches, reeds, sods or twigs, or whatever is to form your roofing material.

For a single man this shelter can be made quite small, about 3 ft. high in front, 3 ft. wide and 6 ft. long. You build your fire about 4 ft. in front of the shelter, and lie in it alongside your fire.

If the "shack" is for more than one man, you build it 5 ft. or 6 ft. high in front, and 6 to 7 ft. deep, so that several fellows can lie alongside each other, feet to the fire.

Thatching Your Hut

When you start to thatch your framework, begin at the bottom and lay your roofing material in layers, one above the other in the way that slates are put on a roof. In this way you make it watertight.

For thatching you can use thick evergreen branches, or grass, reeds, sods, bark or slabs of wood (called "shingles"), or small twigs of heather closely woven in.

It is generally advisable to lay a few branches and stout poles over the thatch when finished in order to keep it on if a gale springs up.

Other Huts

If you want to build a complete hut, you can make a lean-to from each side on the same ridge-pole. But the single lean-to, with its fire in front of it, is quite good enough for most people.

Another way to build a shelter hut is to lean a ridge-pole or back-bone from the ground into the fork of a small tree about 5 ft. above the ground, the butt of the pole being about 7 ft. to windward of the tree. Then put up a side pole leaning against this, and roof over in the same way as for a lean-to.

A pole resting in a tree crotch can be the foundation of your hut.

Where you have no poles available you can do as the South African natives do—pile up a lot of brushwood, heather, etc., into a small wall made in a semicircle to keep out the cold wind—and make your fire in the open part.

Zulus make their huts by planting a circle of long sticks upright in the ground. They then bend the tops towards the centre and tie them together. Next they weave whippy sticks horizontally in and out among the uprights until they have made a kind of circular birdcage. This they cover with a straw mat, or thatch it, or weave straw in among the sticks. Sometimes a small hole is left at the top, to act as a chimney.

The Zulu but is started by placing a circle of long sticks upright in the ground. The tips are tied together, and a framework is made.

The Red Indians make their "teepee" by tying several long poles together in the form of a pyramid, and covering them with canvas or skins sewn together.

This type of shelter is called a "wab" by the natives of Somaliland.

78

If your tent or hut is too hot in the sun, put blankets or more straw over the top. The thicker the roof, the cooler the tent is in summer. If the hut is too cold, make the bottom of the walls thicker, or build a small wall of sods about a foot high round the base of the wall outside.

Never forget to dig a drain all round your hut, so that if heavy rain comes in the night your floor will not get flooded from outside.

YOUR AXE

A backwoodsman has to be pretty useful with his axe. To become a good axeman a fellow must know, first, how the thing ought to be done, and secondly, he must have lots of practice in doing it before he can be considered any good.

Only bad workmen complain of the tools—so before starting to work, be sure that your tool is a good one.

Sharpening the Axe

Then see that your axe is sharp—really sharp, not merely with a good edge on it. A slightly blunt axe is no more good for cutting down a tree than a very blunt knife is for cutting a pencil. Learn how to sharpen your axe on a grindstone, while you are in civilization,

TOMMY THE TENDERFOOT No. 2   *TOMMY FELLS A TREE*
Poor Tommy's forgotten to sharpen his axe,
So the tree only suffers a series of whacks.

79

where grindstones can be found and where there are men to show you.

In India, when we went "pig sticking" (that is, hunting wild boar with spears), we found how very necessary it was to keep our spears as sharp as razors. Every time we killed a boar we sharpened up our spear-heads again, ready for the next fight. We could not carry grindstones about with us, but we carried a small, fine file, with which we were able to touch up the edge.

Many an old backwoodsman carries such a file with him to keep his axe keen. There is a saying with these men that "You may lend your last dollar to a friend, but never lend him your axe—unless you know that he is a good axeman and will not blunt it".

Protect Your Axe

Only a fool will go banging about with an axe—hacking at trees, chopping at roots and branches on the ground, in this way destroying valuable trees and at the same time blunting the axe at every stroke on earth and stones. And when his arms tire, he will throw the axe down, leaving it lying around on the ground, where it may catch and cut the toe of someone moving about after dark.

When you want to leave your axe, strike straight down with it into a tree stump, and leave it sticking there till required again, or make a special "mask" for the blade of a piece of wood, or put it in its leather case.

Using the Axe

In using the axe, the "tenderfoot" generally tries to cover his bad aim by the extra strength of his blows. If an old hand is looking on, he is smiling to himself and thinking of the backache he got himself the first time that he did it.

Don't try to put force into the blow, merely be careful about aiming it so that it falls exactly where you want it. The swing and weight of the axe will do the rest. Make the blows at a slant, not straight down.

A good axeman uses his axe equally well left-handed or right. It is all a matter of practice.

Tree Felling

When you want to fell a tree for a useful purpose, get permission first. Before starting to fell your tree, first clear away all branches which might interfere with the swing of your axe and therefore spoil your aim. Also clear away any brambles or undergrowth that might trip you at the critical moment. Make sure that onlookers are well away from you.

The way to fell a tree is first to cut a big chunk out on the side to which you want the tree to fall, and then to cut into the opposite side to fell it. Plan your work so that the tree will fall clear of other trees and not get hung up in their branches.

Begin your first notch, or "kerf", as it is called, by chopping two marks, the upper one at a distance above the other equal to the thickness of the tree. Then cut alternately, first a horizontal cut at the lower mark, then a sideways, downward cut at the upper one, and jerk out the chunk between the two. Go on doing this till you get to the centre of the tree.

Use two kerfs for felling a tree, with the lower kerf on the side the tree is leaning. The tree will then fall in that direction.

Now go to the opposite side of the tree and cut another kerf here, only about three inches above the level of the lower mark of the first kerf.

Cut out chunks when you are at it—not a lot of little chips, which are signs to anyone coming there later that a "tenderfoot" has been at work. It is all a matter of aiming your stroke well.

Then, when your tree falls, look out for the butt. This often jumps back from the stump. Never stand directly behind it—many a tenderfoot has been killed that way. When the stem cracks and the tree begins to topple over, move forward in the direction of the fall, and at the same time outwards, away from the butt.

Trimming and Logging

When the tree is down, it must be trimmed, that is, the boughs and branches must be cut off, leaving a clean trunk. This is done by working from the butt end of the trunk towards the top. Cut off each bough from below, as close to the trunk as possible.

The trunk is then cut into lengths. This is called "logging". Cut from one side towards the middle, making the kerf half as wide as the tree is thick. Then turn the tree over and make a similar kerf from the other side, until the logs come apart.

2. BRIDGE BUILDING

As I told you before, my scouts in Ashanti, when also acting as pioneers, had to build nearly two hundred bridges. And they had to make them out of any kind of material that they could find on the spot.

There are many ways of making bridges.

Pioneer bridges are generally made by lashing poles together.

In the Himalaya mountains, they make bridges out of three ropes stretched across the river and connected together every few yards by V-shaped sticks, so that one rope forms the footpath and the other two make the handrail on either side. They are a jumpy kind of bridge to walk across. But they take you over and they are easily made.

The simplest way for bridging a narrow, deep stream is to fell a

In the Himalaya mountains, they make bridges of three ropes.

tree, or two trees side by side, on the bank, so that they fall across the stream. With an adze you then flatten the top side. Put up a handrail, and there you have a very good bridge.

Rafts, too, can be used to cross a stream. Build your raft along-side the bank—in the water, if the river is shallow; on the bank if it is deep. When the raft is finished, hold on to the down-stream end, push the other out from the bank, and let the stream carry it down into position.

To make a Ladder with a Pole—Tie sticks firmly across the pole

82

at intervals to form steps. A pole can be made by tying several
Scouts' staffs together.

SELF MEASURES

Every pioneer should know his exact personal measurement in the
following details, of which I give the average man's measure:

Nail joint of forefinger, or breadth of thumb . .	1 inch
Span of thumb and forefinger	8 inches
Span of thumb and little finger	9 inches
Wrist to elbow (this also gives you the length of your foot)	10 inches
Elbow to tip of forefinger (called "cubit") . . .	17 inches
Middle of kneecap to ground	18 inches

Extended arms, from finger-tip to finger-tip, nearly equals your
height.

Pulse beats about 75 times a minute. Each beat is a little quicker
than a second.

Step: a step is about 30 inches; about 120 steps equal 100 yards.
Fast walking steps are shorter than slow ones.

When walking fast you walk a mile in 16 minutes, or nearly four
miles an hour.

Some of the "bridges" of Kashmir, in India, consist of a single rope.

D

JUDGING DISTANCES

Every Scout should be able to judge distance from an inch up to a mile and more.

If you remember your self measures accurately, they are a great help to you in measuring things. Also it is useful to cut notches in your staff, showing such measurements as one inch, six inches, one foot and one yard. These you can measure off with a tape measure before you use your staff.

Judging the distance of a journey is generally done by seeing how long you have been travelling, and at what rate. Suppose you walk at the rate of four miles an hour. If you have been walking for an hour and a half you know that you have done about six miles.

Distance can also be judged by sound. If you see a gun fired in the distance and you count the number of seconds between the flash and the sound of the explosion reaching you, you will be able to tell how far off you are from the gun, Sound travels at the rate of 365 yards in a second—as many yards as there are days in the year.

Test the following from your own observations.

At 50 yards, the mouth and eyes of a person can be clearly seen. At 100 yards, eyes appear as dots. At 200 yards, buttons and details of

TOMMY THE TENDERFOOT No. 3   TOMMY BUILDS A BRIDGE
Your knots give the strength to a bridge, as you know.
But Tommy's weak lashings just ruined the show.

uniform can still be seen. At 300 yards, the face can be seen. At 400 yards, the movement of the legs can be seen. At 500 yards the colour of the uniform can be seen.

For distances over these, think out for yourself which point is half-way to the object. Estimate how far this may be from you, and then double it to obtain the distance. Another way is to estimate the farthest distance that the object can be away, and the very nearest it could be, and strike a mean between the two.

Objects appear *nearer* than they really are when the light is bright and shining on the object; when looking across water or snow; when looking uphill or down. Objects appear *farther off* when in the shade; when across a valley; when the background is of the same colour; when the observer is lying down or kneeling; when there is a heat haze over the ground.

Distances Across a River

The way to estimate the distance across a river is to notice an object X, such as a tree or rock, on the bank opposite to where you stand at A (see diagram). Start off at right angles to A X, and walk,

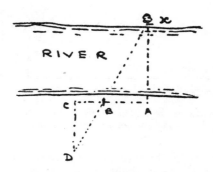

By laying out the triangles as shown in the diagram, you can determine the width of a river with fair accuracy.

say, ninety yards along your bank. On arriving at sixty yards, plant a stick or stone, B. On arriving at C, thirty yards beyond B and ninety from the start at A, turn at right angles and walk inland, counting your steps until you bring the stick and the distant tree in line. The number of steps you have taken from the bank, C D, will then give you the half distance across A X.

85

ESTIMATING HEIGHTS

A Scout must also be able to estimate heights, from a few inches up to three thousand feet or more. He ought to be able to judge the height of a fence, the depth of a ditch, or the height of an embankment, of a house, tree, tower, hill, or mountain. It is easy to do when you have practised it a few times, but it is very difficult to teach it by book.

To find the height of an object, such as a tree or house, walk a distance of eleven feet or yards or any unit you like and set up a staff with another Scout to hold it. Now walk one more unit of your chosen measurement, making twelve in all. Get your eye down to ground level at this spot and look up at the tree. The second Scout then slides his hand up or down the staff until your eye, his hand, and the top of the tree are all in line. Measure the distance in inches along the staff from the ground to the Scout's hand; call these inches

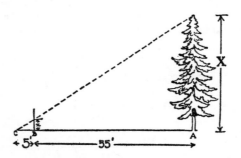

You can determine the height of a tree with the aid of a Scout staff which you have marked in inches.

feet, and that is the height of the object in feet. You can use any unit of measurement you find suitable as long as you make it eleven to one, and you call inches on the staff, feet.

WEIGHTS AND NUMBERS

You should also know how to estimate weights—a letter of an ounce, or a fish or a potato of one pound, or a sack of bran, and also the probable weight of a man from his appearance. These, again, are only learnt by practice.

Learn also to judge numbers—to tell at a glance approximately how many people are in a crowd, or on a bus, or in a big crowd; how many sheep in a flock; how many marbles on a tray, and so on. You can practise for yourself at all times in the street or field.

13. PATROL PRACTICES IN PIONEERING

Practise knot tying against time, by having races between the Scouts in pairs. The losers pair off again for further races, until the slowest knot tier is found. In this way (which can be used for practice in other Scoutcrafts also), the worst performers get the most practice —and the competition is just as great to avoid being the worst as it would be in striving to be the best, and win a prize.

Knot tying races in the dark are fun. The Patrol Leader turns

A parbuckle is an effective way for moving a heavy log—or some other kind of heavy object.

out the lights for a few seconds after naming the knot to be tied. Instead of turning off the lights, the competitors may be blindfolded.

Make models of bridges with Scout staffs, tying them together with cord or rope.

GAME

Scout Pace

The umpire stations three individuals or groups, each group differently clothed as far as possible, and carrying different articles (such as stick, bundle, paper, etc.), at distances from 300 to 1,200 yards from starting-point. If there are other people about, these groups might be told to kneel on one knee, or take up some such position to distinguish them from passers-by. The umpire makes out a circular course of three points for the competitors to run, say, about ¼ mile, with a few jumps if possible.

The competitors start and run to No. 1 point. Here the umpire tells them the compass-direction of the group they have to report on. Each competitor on seeing this group writes a report showing—

1. How many in the group.
2. How clothed or how distinguishable.
3. Position as regards any landmark near them.
4. Estimation of distance from his own position.

He then runs to the next point and repeats the same on another group, and so on; and finally he runs with his report to the winning post.

You can make a simple raft from "sausages"—waterproof covers filled with straw or dry leaves. Lash them to a frame of Scout staves.

Marks—Full marks, 5 for each correct and complete description of a group—that is, an aggregate of 15 marks for the course. One mark deducted for every ten seconds later than the first boy handing in his report at the winning post. Marks or half-marks deducted for mistakes or omissions in reports.

A Patrol hut may be made by placing slender trees together, and by covering the framework with sods.

Camp Fire Yarn

No. 9

CAMPING

Comfort in Camp · Ground
Camp Equipment · Camp Pitching
Fire Building · Keeping Camp Clean

SOME PEOPLE TALK OF "ROUGHING IT" in camp. Well a "tenderfoot" may find it rough and uncomfortable. But there is no "roughing it" for a backwoodsman; he knows how to look after himself and make himself comfortable. If he has no tent, he doesn't sit down to shiver and grouse, but sets to work to rig up a shelter or hut for himself. He chooses a good spot for it, where he is not likely to be flooded out if a storm of rain were to come on. Then he lights a camp fire, and makes himself a soft mattress of ferns or straw.

A Scout is full of resource. He can find a way out of any difficulty or discomfort.

GROUND

When you go camping, you must first decide where you will have your camp, and then what kind of camp it shall be.

The nearer it is to your homes, the less will be the expense of travelling.

To my mind, the best place for a camp is close by a wood where you have permission to cut firewood and to build huts. So if you know of an owner in your neighbourhood who may let you use a corner of his wood, there is your chance. Inside a wood the ground may be damp and the trees will continue dripping in wet weather. Be on the look-out for this. If you build good rain-proof huts, you need no tents.

The seaside also gives some good camp grounds if you find a place where boats are available and bathing possible. Sometimes you can get the use of a boathouse to live in. Don't forget that you will want good water and some firewood.

Or you can go to mountains, moor, or river, and get permission to pitch your camp.

In choosing the camp site, always think what it would be if the weather became very rainy and windy. Choose the driest and most sheltered spot, not too far away from your water supply. Remember that a good water supply is of first importance. And make sure that your drinking water is pure.

HIKE CAMPS

Instead of a fixed or "standing camp", many Scouts prefer a "hike camp".

Of course, it is much better fun to go over new country. But to make a hike camp enjoyable you want good weather.

In arranging your hike, your first point will be to select the line of country you want to visit, and mark out from the map where you will halt each night. You will find that about five miles a day is as much as you will want to do.

You might want to make a "trek-cart" for carrying your tents, blankets, groundsheets, and so on.

At the end of each day's march you would get permission from a farmer to pitch your camp in his field, or get the use of his barn to sleep in—especially if the weather be wet.

TENTS

Before you know which type of tent you will want, you must decide whether it will be wanted for a standing or moving camp.

For a standing camp, from which you don't mean to move, I prefer the kind used by explorers called a "ridge tent" or "wall tent". They are unequalled for comfort and for making the camp look neat. If they have fly-sheets, they will be quite waterproof, even if you touch the inside of the tent, and the fly-sheet will keep the tent cool in hot sunshine and warm in frosty weather.

Smaller Scout tents also do very well for camp if you can have two or more for each Patrol. You can make your own tent during the winter months—and this, perhaps, is the best way of all, as it comes cheapest in the end. And if, while you are about it, you make one or

The "ridge tent" or "wall tent" is one of the favourite tent models used by explorers in many parts of the world.

two extra ones, you may be able to sell them at a good profit.

Where the expense of tents prohibits buying them, remember that used tents may often be hired for a week or more at small cost.

CAMP EQUIPMENT

Your next point is to look to the equipment—that is to say, what you will need in the way of cooking gear, buckets, tools, and so on. Here is a rough list of things that are useful in a standing camp, but they will not all be necessary in a bivouac or hike camp.

For Tent—Bucket, lantern and candles, matches, mallet, basin, spade, axe, hank of cord, Patrol flag, and strap for hanging things on the tent pole.

For Kitchen—Saucepan or stewpot, fry-pan, kettle, grid-iron, matches, bucket, butcher's knife, ladle, cleaning rags, bags for potatoes, etc.

For Each Scout—Waterproof groundsheet, two blankets or sleeping bag, cord or strap for tying them up, straw mattress (to be made in camp—twine and straw required), ration bags. It is important that enough sleeping bags or blankets be provided to enable each Scout to make up a separate bed.

Personal Equipment—Each Scout will need:

Complete Scout Uniform, including headgear
Pyjamas or change for night
Spare shirt and shorts
Change of underwear   Mending materials
Sweater   Plates, cup or mug

92

Rain coat	Knife, fork and spoon
Spare shoes and socks	Matches
Bathing trunks	Tea towel
Towel	Haversack or pack
Handkerchiefs	

Soap, comb, brush, toothbrush, in toilet bag.

An old camper always has with him in camp three or four little linen bags for carrying his provisions. Of course, he makes these for himself before going out into camp.

The ration bag need not be bigger than 6 inches deep by 3 inches wide, and should have a tape run through the hem of the neck with which to draw it tight.

While you are about it, it is also useful to make yourself some bigger bags to keep odds and ends in, in camp—such as string, spare buttons, needle case, scissors, and so on.

I have linen bags, too, for putting my boots into when packing up. It prevents them from dirtying the clothes among which they are packed.

FOOD

If fresh meat is used, be sure that it is *fresh*, and remember that eggs, rice, and porridge keep better. Fruit is easy to stew and good to eat. Chocolate is very useful in camp and on the march.

A good kind of bread for camp is what the Boers and most South African hunters used, and that is "rusks". Rusks are easily made. You buy a stale loaf at the baker's at half-price, cut it up into thick slices or square junks, and then bake these in an oven or toast them before a hot fire till they are quite hard. They do very well instead of bread. Soft bread easily gets damp and sour and stale in camp.

You can smile at the rain if you have pitched your tent properly.

MAKING CAMP

In Scout camps the tents are not pitched in lines and streets as in military camps, but are dotted about in Patrol units, fifty or a hundred yards apart or more, in a big circle round the Scoutmaster's tent, which, with the flag and camp fire, is generally in the centre.

Pitching Tents

When you have chosen the spot for your camp, pitch your tent with the door away from the wind.

If heavy rain comes on, dig a small trench about three inches deep all round the tent to prevent it from getting flooded. This trench should lead the water away downhill. Dig a small hole the size of a teacup alongside the foot of the pole into which to shift it if rain comes on. This enables you to slacken all ropes at once to allow for their shrinking when they get wet.

Water Supply

If there is a spring or stream, the best part of it must be kept strictly clear and clean for drinking water. Farther downstream, a place may be appointed for bathing, washing clothes, and so on.

The greatest care is always taken by Scouts to keep their drinking water supply very clean, otherwise they may get sickness among them.

TOMMY THE TENDERFOOT No. 4   *TOMMY GOES CAMPING*

Arriving in camp brimming over with hopes
He finds out that tents are supported by ropes

All water has a large number of germs in it, too small to be seen without the help of a microscope. Some of them are dangerous, some are not. You can't tell whether the dangerous ones are there, so if you are in doubt about the water, it is safest to kill all the germs by boiling the water. Then let it cool again before drinking it. In boiling the water, don't let it merely come to the boil and then take it off, but let it boil fully for a quarter of an hour, as germs are very tough customers, and take a lot of boiling before they get killed.

Kitchens

The cooking fire is made to leeward, or down-wind of the camp, so that the smoke and sparks from the fire don't blow into the tents. Cooking fires are described on pages 102 and 103.

Scouts always take special care to keep the kitchen particularly clean, as, if scraps are left lying about, flies collect and are very likely to poison the food, and this may bring sickness to the Scouts.

Note to Parents

Camping is the great point in Scouting which appeals to the boy, and the opportunity for teaching him self-reliance and resourcefulness, besides giving him health.

Some parents who have never had experience of camp life themselves, look upon camping with misgivings as possibly likely to be too rough and risky for their boys. But when they see their lads return full of health and happiness outwardly, and morally improved in the points of practical manliness and comradeship, they cannot fail to appreciate the good which comes from such an outing.

I sincerely hope, therefore, that your boys will be encouraged to go to camp whenever they can.

So keep the camp kitchen and the ground around it very clean at all times.

To do this you will want a wet and a dry pit. These are holes about eighteen inches square and at least two feet deep. The top of the wet one is covered with a layer of straw or grass, and all greasy water is poured through this into the pit. The covering collects the grease in the water and prevents it from clogging up the ground. The straw or grass should be burnt every day and renewed.

Into the dry pit is put everything else that will not burn. Tin cans should be burnt first and then hammered out flat before being put in the dry pit. Burn everything you can or your pit will very soon be full. The rubbish should be covered with a layer of earth every evening.

Latrines

Another very important point for the health of the Scouts is to dig a trench to serve as a latrine. On reaching the camping ground the latrine is the very first thing to attend to—and all Scouts should bear this in mind.

Before pitching tents or lighting the fire the latrine is dug and screens erected around it. The trench should be two feet deep, three feet long, and one foot wide, so that the user can squat astride of it, one foot on each side. A thick sprinkling of earth should be thrown in after use, and the whole trench carefully filled in with earth after a few days' use.

There should also be a wet latrine made by digging a hole and half-filling it with stones for drainage.

Even in a one-night camp, Scouts should dig a latrine trench. And when rearing away from camp a Scout will always dig a small pit a few inches deep, which he will fill in again after use. Neglect of this not only makes a place unhealthy, but also makes farmers and landowners disinclined to give the use of their ground for Scouts to camp on. So don't forget it, Scouts!

Camp Routine

Here are alternative programmes:

A		B	
7.00 a.m.	Cooks roused.	7.00 a.m.	Cooks roused.
7.30 a.m.	Campers roused, wash, etc.	7.30 a.m.	Campers roused, wash, etc.
8.15 a.m.	Breakfast.	8.15 a.m.	Breakfast.
8.45–10.00 a.m.	Washing-up, cleaning tents and ground, airing blankets, etc.	8.45–10.00 a.m.	Washing-up, cleaning tents and ground, airing blankets, etc.
10.00 a.m.	Inspection. Flag break; prayers.	10.00 a.m.	Inspection. Flag break; prayers.
10.15–1.00 p.m.	Scouting activities.	10.15–1.00 p.m.	Scouting activities.
1.00 p.m.	Dinner.	1.00 p.m.	Light lunch.
1.30–2.30 p.m.	Rest hour.	2.00–5.30 p.m.	Wide games, and Scout activity.
2.30–5.00 p.m.	Wide games, and Scout activity.	5.30 p.m.	Tea, and biscuits.
5.00 p.m.	Tea.	5.45–6.45 p.m.	Camp games.
6.00–7.30 p.m.	Camp games or free.	7.00 p.m.	Dinner, followed by free time.
8.30 p.m.	Camp fire: one hour is long enough; a long yarn will provide variation from songs and choruses.	8.30 p.m.	Camp fire: one hour is long enough; a long yarn will provide variation from songs and choruses.
10.00 p.m.	Lights out.	10·00 p.m.	Lights out.

N.B.—There should be silence in camp after "Lights Out," and in no case should there be any noise after 10.30.

A night game should be included in the programme on one evening, and rising time next day adjusted accordingly.

BATHING AND SWIMMING

When in camp, bathing will be one of your joys and one of your duties—a joy because it is such fun, a duty because no Scout can consider himself a full-blown Scout until he is able to swim and to save life in the water. But there are dangers about bathing for which every sensible Scout will be prepared.

A bulletin board may be put up for "Standing Orders" and "Camp Routine". Notice the Patrol dining shelter in the background.

First, there is the danger of cramp. If you bathe within an hour and a half after taking a meal, that is, before your food is digested, you are very likely to get cramp. Cramp doubles you up in extreme pain so that you cannot move your arms or legs—and down you go. You may drown—and it will be your own fault.

There must always be a bathing picket posted, while bathing is going on, of two good swimmers, who will not bathe themselves but will be ready, undressed, prepared to jump in at any moment and help a bather if he is in difficulties. The guards should not bathe until the others have left the water, and a life line must be available.

Many lives are lost every summer through foolishness on the part of boys bathing, because they don't think of these things. Bathing must only be permitted in safe places and under strict supervision.

TRESPASSING

Be careful to get permission from the owners of land before you go on to it. You have no right to go anywhere off the roads without leave, but most owners will give you this if you go and tell them who you are and what you want to do.

When going over their land remember above all things:

1. Leave all gates as you found them.
2. Disturb animals and game as little as you possibly can.
3. Do no damage to fences, crops, or trees.

Any firewood that you require you must ask for before taking it. And be careful not to take out of hedges dead wood which is being used to fill up a gap.

LOAFERS IN CAMP

A camp is a roomy place. But there is no room in it for one chap, and that is the fellow who does not want to take his share in the many little odd jobs that have to be done. There is no room for the shirker or the grouser—well, there is no room for them in the Boy Scouts at all, but least of all in camp.

Every fellow must help, and help cheerily in making it comfortable for all. In this way comradeship grows.

TOMMY THE TENDERFOOT No. 5   *TOMMY SLEEPS OUT*

Plenty of blankets below—he'd been told.
But Tommy knew better—and so he got cold.

COMFORT IN CAMP

Camp Beds

There are many ways of making a comfortable bed in camp, but always have a waterproof groundsheet over the ground between your body and the earth. Cut grass or straw or bracken is good to lay down thickly where you are going to lie.

I think you never find out how full of corners you are till you have to sleep on a hard bit of ground where you cannot get straw or grass.

Of course, every Scout knows that the worst corner in him is his hip-bone, and if you have to sleep on hard ground the secret of comfort is to scoop out a little hole, about the size of a tea-cup, where your hip-bone will rest. It makes all the difference to your sleeping.

Your night's rest is an important thing; a fellow who does not get a good sleep at night soon knocks up, and cannot get through a day's work like the one who sleeps in comfort. So my best advice is: make a good thick straw mattress for yourself.

Making a Mattress

To make a mattress, set up a camp loom (as described at the end of this yarn) and weave it out of bracken, ferns, heather, straw, or grass, six feet long, and two feet nine inches across. With this same loom you can make straw mats, with which to form tents, or shelters, or walls (page 109).

Another good way of giving yourself a comfortable bed is to make a big bag of canvas or stout linen, 6 ft. long and 3 ft. wide. This

This type of sleeping bag makes it possible to camp without a tent.

will do to roll up your kit in for travelling. When you are in camp you can stuff it with straw, or leaves, or bracken, etc., and use it as a nice soft mattress.

A pillow is also a useful thing for comfort in camp. For this you only need a strong pillow-case about two feet long by one foot wide. This you can also make for yourself. It will serve as your clothes-bag by day and your pillow by night with your clothes, neatly rolled and packed in it, serving as the stuffing.

I have often used my boots as a pillow, rolled up in a coat so that they don't slip apart.

How to Squat

It is something to know how to sit down in a wet camp. You "squat" instead of sitting. Indians squat on their heels, but this is a tiring way if you have not done it as a child. It comes easy if you put a sloping stone or chock of wood under your heels.

The old camper has his own way of squatting, to keep off the ground.

South African Boers and other camp men squat on one heel. It is a little tiring at first.

FIRE BUILDING

North American Indians were always clever with their fires. Four kinds of fires were used. The Council Fire inside the teepee was a formal kind of thing. The Friendly Fire—somewhat larger than the Council Fire—was to warm everybody in the village. The Signal Fire, was built for sending up smoke signals. The Cooking Fire was a very small fire of glowing red-hot embers.

Scouts use the same kinds of fires.

Clearing the Ground

Before lighting your fire, remember always to do as every backwoodsman does, and that is to remove all grass, dry leaves, bracken, heather, from round the spot, to prevent the fire from spreading to the surrounding grass or bush. Many bad bush fires have been caused by young "tenderfoots" fooling about with blazes which they imagined to be camp fires. Where there is danger of a grass fire, have branches or old sacks ready with which you can beat it out.

Scouts should always be on the look-out to beat out a bush fire that had been accidently started at any time, as a Good Turn to the owner of the land or to people who may have herds and crops in danger.

Laying the Fire

It is no use to learn how to light a fire by hearsay. The only way is to pay attention to the instructions given you, and then practise laying and lighting a fire yourself.

In the book called *Two Little Savages*, instructions for laying a fire are given in the following rhyme:—

"First a curl of birch bark as dry as it can be,
Then some twigs of soft wood dead from off a tree,
Last of all some pine knots to make a kettle foam,
And there's a fire to make you think you're sitting right at home."

Remember the usual fault of a beginner is to try to make too big a fire. You will never see a backwoodsman do that—he uses the smallest possible amount of wood for his fire.

First collect your firewood. Green, fresh-cut wood is no good, nor is dead wood that has lain long on the ground. Get permission to break dead branches off trees for it.

With a fire built this way, one match may be all you will need.

To make your fire, you put a few sticks flat on the ground, especially if the ground be damp. On this flooring lay your "punk"—that is, shavings, splinters, or any other material that will easily catch fire from your match.

TOMMY THE TENDERFOOT No. 6   *TOMMY BUILDS A FIRE*

On lighting of fires he sets everyone right.
But his own little bonfire refuses to ignite.

101

On this you pile, in pyramid fashion, thin twigs, splinters, and slithers of dry wood, leaning on the "punk" and against each other. These are called kindling.

A good kind of kindling can easily be made by slitting a stick into several slices or shavings, as shown. This is called a firestick. If stood up, with the shavings downwards towards the ground, it quickly catches light and flares up.

A few stouter sticks are added over the kindling to make the fire.

Lighting the Fire

Set light to all this, putting your match under the bottom of the "punk".

"Firesticks" whittled from dry wood make a good fire lighters.

When the wood has really got on fire, add more and larger sticks, and finally logs.

A "tenderfoot" after lighting his fire will blow out his match and throw it on the ground. A backwoodsman will break the match in half before throwing it away. Why? Because if the match is not really out and is still smouldering it will tell him so—by burning his hand.

Several Kinds of Fires

A great thing for a cooking fire is to get a good pile of red-hot wood embers, and if you use three large logs, they should be placed on the

The "star fire" consists of logs placed like the spokes of a wheel.

ground, star-shaped, like the spokes of a wheel, with their ends centred in the fire. A fire made in this way need never go out, for as the logs burn away you keep pushing them towards the centre of the fire, always making fresh red-hot embers there. This makes a fire which gives very little flame or smoke.

If you want to keep a fire *flaming* during the night for light or to warm you, use the star fire with one long log reaching to your hand, so that you can push it in from time to time to the centre without the trouble of getting up to stoke the fire.

To keep your fire *smouldering* overnight, cover it over with a heap of ashes. It will then be ready for early use in the morning, when you can easily blow it into a glow.

Here is a way they use in North America for making a fire for heating your tent.

Drive two stout stakes into the ground about four feet apart, both leaning a bit backwards. Cut down a young tree with a trunk some six inches thick; chop it into four-foot lengths. Lay three or more logs, one on top of another, leaning against the upright stakes. This "reflector" forms the back of your fireplace. Two short logs are then laid as fire-dogs, with a log across them as front bar of the fire. Inside this "grate" you build a pyramid-shaped fire, which then gives out great heat. The "grate" must, of course, be built so that it faces the wind.

Putting Out the Fire

A Scout is very careful about fires. When he uses one he sees that it is well out before he leaves the place. The fire should be doused

The "reflector fire" is used in North America for heating your tent, especially when you go camping in the winter time.

with water and earth, and stamped down well, so that there is not a spark left that might later start a fire. Finally the original turf—which was put on one side before you made the fire—is put back so that hardly a trace is left.

Tongs are useful about a camp fire. They can be made from a rod of beech or other tough wood, about four feet long and one inch thick. Shave it away in the middle to about half its proper thickness; put this part into the hot embers of the fire for a few moments, and bend the stick over till the two ends come together. Then flatten away

Notch the middle of the stick before bending it into fire tongs.

the inside edges of the ends so that they have a better grip—and there are your tongs.

Making Fire without Matches

What would you do if you needed a fire and had no matches?

A Zulu boy's way of getting over the difficulty is to find a piece of hard stick and drill a hole with it in a piece of soft wood. By twirling it rapidly between his hands he manages to make embers which then

The Australian boys light a fire by twirling a stick in softer wood.

set light to dry grass or the lining of the bark of trees, and from this he makes his fire.

It is a long way from South Africa to Australia—across thousands of miles of ocean. Yet, when you get to Australia, you find that the aborigines there had many of the same customs and many of the same dodges that were practised by the people of South Africa.

The Red Indians of North America also have their method of fire-lighting, which is very much used by the Boy Scouts there.

In this case, the boy takes the spindle of hard wood and holding it upright with one hand, the palm of which is protected by a wood or stone hand piece, he twists it rapidly round by means of a bow whose string is twisted round the spindle.

The point of the spindle then works its way into a board of soft wood, which the boy holds in place with his foot.

A little slit at the side of the board leads to the hole made by the spindle, and the hot ember which comes away from the wood falls into this small opening and sets fire to the tinder which the boy has placed under it.

So a fellow who has once learnt this way of making fire, and knows which kind of wood to use (for not all kinds are suitable), can go out into the backwoods, without having to carry a match-box with him and can keep himself warm or cook his grub at any time he would wish by lighting his fire in *the backwoods way*.

The people of Borneo make fire by sawing a log with a whippy cane.

DRYING CLOTHES

You sometimes get wet in camp, and you will see "tenderfoots" remaining in their wet clothes until they get dry again. No old Scout would do so, as that is the way to catch cold.

When you are wet, take the first opportunity of getting your wet clothes off and drying them, even though you may not have other clothes to put on, as happened to me many a time. I have sat naked under a waggon while my one suit of clothes was drying over a fire

The way to dry clothes is to make a fire of hot embers, and then build a small beehive-shaped cage of sticks over it. Hang your clothes all over this cage, and they will very quickly dry.

In hot weather it is dangerous to sit in your clothes when they have become wet from your perspiration. On the West Coast of Africa I always carried a spare shirt hanging down my back, with the sleeves tied round my neck. As soon as I halted I would take off the wet shirt I was wearing, and put on the dry, which had been hanging out in

The Red Indian and Scout method of fire-lighting uses bow and drill.

the sun on my back. By this means I never got sick when almost everyone else did.

TIDINESS

The camp ground should at all times be kept clean and tidy, not only (as I have pointed out) to keep flies away, but also because Scouts are always tidy, whether in camp or not, as a matter of habit. If you are not tidy at home, you won't be tidy in camp; and if you're not tidy in camp, you will be only a "tenderfoot" and no Scout.

A broom is useful for keeping the camp clean, and can easily be made with a few sprigs of birch bound tightly round a stake.

A Scout is tidy also in his tent, bunk, or room, because he may be suddenly called upon to go off on an alarm, or something unexpected. If he does not know exactly where to lay his hand on his things, he will be a long time in turning out, especially if called up in the middle of the night.

So on going to bed, even when at home, practise the habit of folding up your clothes and putting them where you can find them at once in the dark and get into them quickly.

CAMP FIRES

Songs, recitations and small plays can be performed round the camp fire, and every Scout should be made to contribute something to the programme, whether he thinks he is a performer or not.

A different Patrol may be responsible for each night of the week

106

to provide for the performance. The Patrol can then prepare before-hand for the Camp Fire.

Camp Fire is one of the happiest hours of camp. Songs, recitations and small plays follow each other on the programme.

CLEANING CAMP GROUND

Never forget that the state of an old camp ground, after the camp has finished, tells exactly whether the Patrol or Troop which has used it was a smart one or not. No Scouts who are any good ever leave a camp ground dirty. They sweep up and bury or burn every scrap of rubbish. Farmers then don't have the trouble of having to clean their ground after you leave, and they are, therefore, all the more willing to let you use it again.

It is a big disgrace for any Troop or Patrol or lone camper to leave the camp ground dirty and untidy.

Remember the only two things you leave behind you on breaking up camp:

1. **Nothing.**
2. **Your thanks to the owner of the ground.**

PAYMENT

Another point to remember is that when you use a farmer's ground you ought to repay him for the use of it. If you do not do this with money you can do it in other ways. You can—and ought to—do jobs that are useful for him. You can mend his fences or gates, or dig up weeds, and so on.

You should always be doing good turns both to the farmer and to the people living near your camp, so that they will be glad to have you there.

PATROL PRACTICES IN CAMPING

The best practice in camping is camping whenever possible— single nights, weekends, and longer camps.

In going to camp with the Troop it is essential to have a few "Standing Orders", which can be added to from time to time, if necessary. The Patrol Leaders are held fully responsible that their Scouts carry them out exactly.

Such orders will contain the camp routine and might point out that each Patrol will camp separately from the others, and that there will be a comparison between the respective cleanliness and good order of tents and surrounding ground.

Each Patrol usually has its tents grouped together, well away from the other Patrols, but within call of the Scoutmaster's tent which generally is in the centre.

Bathing in camp is under strict supervision to prevent non-swimmers getting into dangerous water.

The following rules would be strictly followed:

(1) No Scout shall be allowed to bathe except under the personal supervision of the Scouter in charge of the party or some responsible adult appointed by him for the purpose. The safety of the place must have been previously ascertained and all reasonable precautions must be taken, including the provision of a life line.

(2) A picket of two good swimmers, preferably trained swimmers and life savers, must be on duty, undressed, in a boat or on shore as the circumstances may demand, ready to help any boy in distress. The picket itself may not bathe until the others have left the water.

In the Boy Scouts of America, a so-called "buddy-system" is used. In this system, the Scouts are divided into pairs, or buddies. The two boys of the buddy team are of about equal swimming ability. When in the water, each buddy is responsible for the safety of the other, under the general supervision of the Scouter in charge of the whole party.

Making a Camp Loom—Plant a row (No. 1 row) of five stakes firmly in the ground, 7 or 8 inches apart. Opposite to them, at a distance of 6 to 7 ft., drive in a row (No. 2 row) of two stakes and a crossbar (or of five stakes). Fasten a cord or twine to the head of each stake in No. 1 row and stretch it to the corresponding stake in No. 2 row and make it fast there. Then carry the continuation of the cord back over No. 1 row for some 5 ft. extra, and fasten it to a loose crossbar or "beam". Fasten other cords from the other stakes in No. 1 row to the stakes of No. 2 row, and then to the beam, tying them here the same distance apart that the stakes are apart.

The beam is now moved up and down at slow intervals by one Scout, while another Scout lays bundles of fern or straw in layers

On a camp loom it is easy to weave a comfortable mattress out of bracken, ferns, heather, straw or grass.

alternately under and over the stretched strings. The bundles are thus bound in by the rising or lowering of the cords attached to the beam.

If you move the beam first slightly to the right and then to the left so that the strings fall first on one side and then on the other side of the stretched strings it will twist the cords and make the binding much more secure.

Camp Fire Yarn
No. 10

CAMP COOKING

Cooking · Hay-Box Cooking
Bread Making · Cleanliness

EVERY SCOUT MUST, OF COURSE, know how to cook his own meat and vegetables, and to make bread for himself, without regular cooking utensils.

COOKING MEAT

Meat may be cooked by sticking it on sharp sticks and hanging it close to the fire, so that it gets broiled. Or use the lid of an old cake tin as a kind of frying-pan. Put grease in it to prevent the meat from sticking.

Or make "Kabobs:" cut your meat up into a slice about half or three-quarters of an inch thick. Cut this up into small pieces about one to one and a half inches across. String a lot of these chunks on to a stick or iron rod, and plant it in front of the fire, or suspend it over the hot embers for a few minutes till the meat is roasted.

Meat can also be wrapped in a few sheets of wet paper, or in a coating of clay, and put in the red-hot embers of the fire, where it will cook by itself.

Hunter's Stew—Cut lean meat or game into small chunks about an inch or one and a half inches square. Mix some flour, salt, and pepper together, and rub your meat well in it. Brown it in a little fat in the pot, shuffling the pot so as to sear, but not burn the surfaces

110

of the meat. Add clean water, and hang pot high over the fire. It is
important that the water should not boil hard, but merely simmer.
Later add cut-up vegetables, such as potatoes, carrots and onions.
The water should just cover the food—no more. Cook until tender.

Cooking Birds and Fish

Birds and fish can be cooked in the same manner. A bird is most
easily plucked immediately after being killed. But there is no need
to pluck it before cooking it in clay, as the feathers will stick to the
clay when it hardens in the heat, and when you break it open the
bird will come out cooked, without its feathers, like the kernel out
of a nutshell.

Another way is to clean out the inside of a bird, get a stone about

*A fire place may be made of two lines of sods, bricks, thick logs, or
stones. Place or hang your pots over it.*

the size of its inside, and heat it till nearly red hot. Place it inside the
bird, and put the bird on a gridiron, or on a wooden spit over the
fire.

FIRE PLACES

Usually a Scout has his own pot of "billy" or camp kettle. In that
you can boil water or cook your vegetables or stew your meat.

To cook in your pot, you can either stand it on the ends of the logs
of a star fire (where it may fall over unless care is taken), or, better,
stand it on the ground among the hot embers of the fire. Or rig up
a tripod of three green poles over the fire, tying them together at the
top, and hanging the pot by a wire or chain from the poles.

Even better, make a fire of two lines of sods, bricks, thick logs, or stones. The lines should be flat at the top and about six feet long, four inches apart at one end and eight inches at the other—the big end toward the wind.

Then you should make your own pot hooks and hangers for holding your cooking pots over the fire.

COOKING HINTS

When boiling a pot of water on the fire, do not jamb the lid on too firmly. When the steam forms inside the pot, it must have some means of escape. To find out when the water is beginning to boil, you need not take off the lid and look, but just hold the end of a stick or knife to the pot, and if the water is boiling you will feel the pot trembling.

Oatmeal Porridge—Pour into a pot one cup of water for each person. Add a pinch of salt for each cup. When the water boils, sprinkle oatmeal in it while stirring with a stick or large spoon. The amount of oatmeal depends upon whether you want the porridge thick or thin. Simmer the porridge until it is done, stirring all the time.

Don't do as I did once when I was a "tenderfoot". It was my turn to cook, so I thought I would vary the dinner by giving them soup, I had some pea-flour, and I mixed it with water and boiled it up, and served it as pea-soup. But I did not put in any stock or meat juice of any kind, I didn't know that it was necessary or would be noticeable. But they noticed it directly, called my beautiful soup a "wet pea-pudding", and told me I might eat it myself—not only told me I *might*, but they jolly well *made* me eat it. I never made the mistake again.

Hay-Box Cooking

Hay-box cooking is the best way of getting your cooking done in camp, as you only have to start it and the hay-box does the rest. You can then go out and play your camp games with the other fellows, and come back to find that your dinner has cooked itself—that is, if you started it right. If you didn't—well, you won't find yourself very popular with the Patrol!

This is how you start it: get a box. Line it with several thicknesses of newspaper at sides and bottom, then fill it with hay or more newspapers; pack this all tight with a space in the middle for your cooking pot. Plenty of hay below as well as round the pot. Make a cushion packed with hay for the top, or a thick pad of folded newspapers.

Get your stewpot full of food, and as soon as it is well on the boil, pop it into the hay-box. Pack the hay or paper tight round it and over it, put on the covering pad, and jam down the lid with a weight on it.

Meat will take four or five hours to cook in this way. Oatmeal you should boil for five minutes, and leave in hay-box all night. It will be ready for your early breakfast.

Bread Making

"The three Bs of life in camp are the ability to cook bannocks, beans, and bacon."

To make bread, or bannocks, or "dampers", the usual way is to mix flour with a pinch or two of salt and of baking powder, then make a pile of it and scoop out the centre until it forms a cup for the water, which is then poured in. Mix everything well together until it forms a lump of dough. With a little fresh flour sprinkled over the hands to prevent the dough sticking to them, pat it and make it into the shape of a large bun or several smaller buns.

Then put it on a gridiron over hot embers. Or sweep part of the fire to one side, and put the dough on the hot ground left there and pile hot ashes round it and let it bake.

Only small loaves can be made in this way.

Bread can be made without any oven at all. Twist the dough around a stick and bake it over glowing embers.

Twist

Still another way is to cut a stout stick, sharpen its thin end, peel it, and heat it in the fire. Make a long strip of dough, about two inches wide and half an inch thick and wind it spirally down the stick. Plant the stick close to the fire and let the dough toast, just giving the stick a turn now and then.

Baking Oven

If real bread is required, a kind of oven should be made, either by using an old earthenware pot or a tin box, and putting it into the fire and piling embers all over it. Or make a clay oven, light a fire inside it, and then, when it is well heated, rake out the fire, and put the dough inside, and shut up the entrance tightly till the bread is baked.

CLEANLINESS

Scouts take special care to keep the kitchen particularly clean. They are careful to clean their cooking pots, plates, forks, knives, very thoroughly. They know that if dirt and scraps of food are left about, flies will collect.

Flies are dangerous, because they carry disease germs on their feet, and if they settle on your food they often leave the poison there for you to eat—and then you wonder why you get ill.

For this reason you should be careful to keep your camp kitchen very clean, so that flies won't come there. All slops and scraps should be burned or thrown into a properly dug hole, where they can be buried, and not scattered all over the place.

Patrol Leaders are responsible for seeing that this is always done. Remember, "A Scout is clean".

PATROL PRACTICES IN COOKING

Scouts should be able to cook before they go to camp. Teach them the most important things, such as cooking potatoes and porridge, meat and vegetables. These can be practised during the winter.

Practise mixing dough and baking twists and dampers.

Make a hay-box and use it.

Make your own linen ration bags.

Patrols should compete in preparing menus, working out quantities, etc.

Bring raw rations on a hike, make a fire and cook your own meal.

Experiment with different types of fire places until you arrive at the one you think most suitable for your Patrol Cooking. Then try making a number of kitchen gadgets.

TRACKING

Camp Fire Yarn
No. 11

OBSERVATION OF "SIGN"

Noticing "Sign" · Details of People
"Sign" Round a Dead Body
Details in the Country
Use of Eyes, Ears, and Nose by Scouts
Night Scouting

"SIGN" IS THE WORD used by Scouts to mean any little details, such as footprints, broken twigs, trampled grass, scraps of food, a drop of blood, a hair, and so on—anything that may help as clues in getting the information they are in search of.

Mrs. Walter Smithson, when travelling in Kashmir, was following up, with some Indian trackers, the "pugs" of a panther which had killed and carried off a young buck. He had crossed a wide bare slab of rock which, of course, gave no mark of his soft feet. The tracker went at once to the far side of the rock where it came to a sharp edge. He wetted his finger, and just passed it along the edge till he found a few buck's hairs sticking to it. This showed him where the panther had passed down off the rock, dragging the buck with him. Those few hairs were what Scouts call "sign".

Mrs. Smithson's tracker also found bears by noticing small "sign". On one occasion he noticed a fresh scratch in the bark of a tree evidently made by a bear's claw, and on the other he found a single black hair sticking to the bark of a tree, which told him that a bear had rubbed against it.

NOTICING "SIGN"

One of the most important things that a Scout has to learn, whether he is a war scout or a hunter or peace scout, is *to let nothing escape*

116

his attention. He must notice small points and signs, and then make out the meaning of them. It takes a good deal of practice before a "tenderfoot" gets into the habit of really noting everything and letting nothing escape his eye. It can be learnt just as well in a town as in the country.

And in the same way you should notice any strange sound or any peculiar smell and think for yourself what it may mean. Unless you learn to notice "sign" you will have very little of "this and that" to put together, and so you will be no use as a Scout.

Remember, a Scout always considers it a great disgrace if an outsider discovers a thing before he has seen it for himself, whether that thing is far away in the distance or close by under his feet.

If you go out with a really trained Scout you will see that his eyes are constantly moving, looking out in every direction near and far, noticing everything that is going on.

Once I was walking with one in Hyde Park in London. He presently remarked, "That horse is going a little lame". There was no horse near us, but I found he was looking at one far away across the Serpentine Lake. The next moment he picked up a peculiar button lying by the path. His eyes, you see, were looking both far away and near.

"Have You Seen a Man?"

In the streets of a strange town a Scout will notice his way by the principal buildings and side-streets, and by what shops he passes and what is in their windows; also what vehicles pass him.

Most especially he will notice people—what their faces are like, their dress, their boots, their way of walking—so that if, for instance, he should be asked by a policeman, "Have you seen a man with dark overhanging eyebrows, dressed in a blue suit, going down this street?" he should be able to give some such answer as "Yes—he was walking a little lame with the right foot, wore foreign-looking

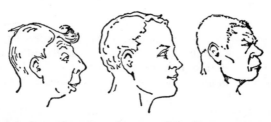

Notice the faces of people so that you will be able to recognize them.

117

boots, was carrying a parcel in his hand. He turned down Gold Street, the second turning on the left from here, about three minutes ago."

Information of that kind has often been of the greatest value in tracing out a criminal.

You remember in the story of *Kim* how Kim was taught observation by means of a game in which he had to describe from memory a trayful of small objects shown to him for a minute and then covered over.

We use this "Kim's Game", because it is excellent practice for Scouts.

There was a revolutionary society in Italy called the Camorra, that used to train its boys to be quick at noticing and remembering things. When walking through the street of the city, the Camorrist would suddenly stop and ask his boy: "How was the woman dressed who sat at the door of the fourth house on the right in the last street?" or, "What were the two men talking about at the corner

It is easy enough to disguise yourself with simple means, if you know how. How many things did this man change to alter his appearance? Notice that the thing that makes the main difference is his changed posture.

three streets back?" or, "Where was the cab ordered to drive to, and what was its number?" or, "What is the height of that house and what is the width of its upper-floor window?" and so on. Or the boy was given a minute to look in a shop window, and then describe all that was in it.

A Scout must also have his eyes on the ground, especially along the edge of the pavement against the houses or the gutter. I have

118

often found valuable trinkets that have been dropped, and which have been walked over by numbers of people, and kicked to one side without being noticed.

Every town Scout should know, as a matter of course, where the nearest chemist's shop is (in case of accidents), and the nearest police "fixed point", police station, doctor, hospital, fire alarm, telephone, ambulance station, etc.

DETAILS OF PEOPLE

When you are travelling by train or bus, always notice every little thing about your fellow-travellers. Notice their faces, dress, way of talking, and so on, so that you could describe them each pretty accurately afterwards. And try to make out from their appearance and behaviour their probable business, whether they are happy, or ill, or in need of help.

But in doing this you must not let them see you are watching them, else it puts them on their guard. Remember the shepherd-boy I told you about in Yarn No. 2, who noticed the gipsy's boots, but did not look at him, and so did not make the gipsy suspicious of him.

Can you tell their characters by the way they wear their hats?

Close observation of people and ability to read their character and their thoughts are of immense value in trade and commerce, especially for a shop-assistant or salesman in persuading people to buy goods, or in detecting would-be swindlers.

It is said that you can tell a man's character from the way he wears his hat. If it is slightly on one side, the wearer is supposed to be good-natured; if it is worn very much on one side, he is a swaggerer; if on the back of his head, he is bad at paying his debts; if worn straight on the top, he is probably honest but very dull.

The way a man (or a woman) walks is often a good guide to his

119

character—witness the fussy, swaggering little man paddling along with short steps with much arm action; the nervous man's hurried, jerky stride; the slow slouch of the loafer; the smooth, quick, and silent step of the Scout, and so on.

PRACTICE OBSERVATION

With a little practice in observation, you can tell pretty accurately a man's character from his dress.

The shoes are very generally the best test of all the details of clothing.

Sometime ago, I was with a lady in the country, and a young lady was walking just in front of us.

"I wonder who she is?" said my friend.

"Well," I said, "maybe you will know if you know whose maid she is."

TOMMY THE TENDERFOOT No. 7   TOMMY THE PATHFINDER
"Which way to turn me I cannot divine.
Of friend or of foeman I can't see a sign."

The girl was very well dressed, but when I saw her shoes I guessed that the dress had belonged to some one else, had been given to her and refitted by herself—but that as regards shoes she felt more comfortable in her own. She went up to the house at which we were staying—to the servants' entrance—and we found that she was one of the maids.

120

I once was able to be of service to a lady who was in poor circumstances. I had guessed it from noticing, while walking behind her, that though she was well dressed the soles of her shoes were in the last stage of disrepair. I don't suppose she ever knew how I guessed that she needed help.

But it is surprising how much of the sole of the shoe you can see when walking behind a person—and it is equally surprising how much meaning you can read from that shoe. It is said that to wear out soles and heels equally is to give evidence of business capacity and honesty; to wear your heels down on the outside means that you are a man of imagination and love of adventure; but heels worn down on the inside signify weakness and indecision of character, and this last sign is more infallible in the case of man than in that of woman.

It is an amusing practice, when you are in a railway carriage or omnibus with other people, to look only at their feet and guess, without looking any higher, what sort of people they are, old or young well-to-do or poor, fat or thin, and so on, and then look up and see how near you have been to the truth.

I was speaking with a detective not long ago about a gentleman we had both been talking to, and we were trying to make out his character.

I remarked, "Well, at any rate, he is a fisherman."

My companion could not see why—but then he was not a fisherman himself.

I had noticed a lot of little tufts of cloth sticking up on the left cuff of his coat. A good many fishermen, when they take their flies off the line, stick them into their cap to dry; others stick them into their sleeve. When dry they pull them out, which often tears a thread or two of the cloth.

Remember how Sherlock Holmes met a stranger and noticed that he was looking fairly well-to-do, in new clothes with a mourning band on his sleeve, with a soldierly bearing, and a sailor's way of walking, sunburnt, with tattoo marks on his hand. What should you have supposed that man to be? Well, Sherlock Holmes guessed, correctly, that he had lately retired from the Royal Marines as a Sergeant, his wife had died, and he had some small children at home.

SIGN ROUND A DEAD BODY

It may happen to some of you that one day you will be the first to find the body of a dead man. In such a case the smallest signs that are to be seen on and near the body must be examined and noted down, before the body is moved or the ground disturbed and trampled down. Besides noticing the exact position of the body (which should, if possible, be photographed exactly as found) the ground all round should be very carefully examined—without treading on it yourself more than is absolutely necessary, for fear of spoiling existing tracks. If you can also draw a little map of how the body lay and where the signs round it were, it might be of value.

I know of two cases where bodies have been found which were at first supposed to be of people who had hanged themselves. But close examination of the ground round them—in one case some torn twigs and trampled grass, and in the other a crumpled carpet —showed that murder had been committed, and that the bodies had been hanged after death to make it appear as though the people had committed suicide.

Finger-Prints

Finger-prints are some of the first things the police look for on all likely articles. If they do not correspond to those of the murdered man they may be those of his murderer, who could then be identified by comparing the impression with his fingers.

There was the case of a learned old gentleman who was found dead in his bedroom with a wound in his forehead and another in his left temple.

Very often after a murder, the murderer, with his hands bloody from the deed and running away, may catch hold of the door, or a jug of water to wash his hands.

In the present case a newspaper lying on the table had the marks of three blood-stained fingers on it.

The son of the dead man was suspected and was arrested by the police.

But careful examination of the room and the prints of the finger-marks showed that the old gentleman had become ill in the night. He had got out of bed to get some medicine, but near the table a new spasm seized him and he fell, striking his head violently against the corner of the table, and made the wound on his temple, which just fitted the corner. In trying to get up he had caught hold of the table and had made the bloody finger-marks on the newspaper lying on it. Then he had fallen again, cutting his head a second time on the foot of the bed.

The finger-prints were compared with the dead man's fingers and were found to be exactly the same. Well, you don't find two men in 64,000,000,000,000 with the same pattern on the skin of their fingers. So it was evident there had been no murder, and the dead man's son was released as innocent.

Other Marks

In a Russian city a banker was found murdered. Near the body was discovered a cigar-holder with an amber mouthpiece. This mouthpiece was of a peculiar shape and could only be held in the mouth in one position, and it had two teeth marks in it. The marks showed that the two teeth were of different lengths.

The teeth of the murdered man were quite regular, so the cigar-holder was evidently not his. But his nephew had teeth which corresponded to the marks on the mouthpiece. He was arrested, and then further proof came up and showed that he was the murderer.

There is a similar story in *Sherlock Holmes' Memoirs* called "The Resident Patient". Here a man was found hanging and was considered to be a suicide till Sherlock Holmes came in and showed by various signs—such as cigar ends bitten by different teeth, footprints —that three men had been in the room with the man for some time previous to his death and had hanged him.

DETAILS IN THE COUNTRY

If you are in the country you should notice landmarks, that is, objects which will help you to find your way or prevent you getting lost, such as distant hills, church towers, and nearer objects such as peculiar buildings, trees, gates, rocks, etc.

A great deal of dust does not always mean many people. Here is a ruse that was used to draw the attention of the enemy: branches of trees were towed along a dusty road, to imitate moving cavalry.

And remember, in noticing such landmarks, that you may want to use your knowledge of them some day for telling someone else how to find his way, so you must notice them pretty closely to be able to describe them unmistakably and in their proper order. You must notice and *remember* every by-road and foot-path.

Then you must also notice smaller signs, such as birds getting up and flying hurriedly, which means somebody or some animal is there. Rising dust shows animals, men, or vehicles moving.

Of course, when in the country you should notice just as much as in town, all passers-by very carefully—how they are dressed, what their faces are like, their way of walking—and examine their footmarks and jot down sketches of them in your notebook, so that you would know the footmarks again if you found them somewhere else, as the shepherd boy did in the story at the beginning of this book.

Also notice tracks of animals, birds, wheels, etc., for from these you can read valuable information.

Track reading is of such importance that I shall give you a yarn on that subject by itself.

USING YOUR EYES

Let nothing be too small for your notice. A button, a match, the ash from a cigar, a feather, or a leaf, might be of great importance.

A Scout must not only look to his front, but also to either side and behind him; he must have "eyes at the back of his head", as the saying is.

Often, by suddenly looking back, you will see an enemy's scout or a thief showing himself in a way that he would not have done had he thought you would look round.

There is an interesting story by Fenimore Cooper called *The Pathfinder*, in which the action of a Red Indian scout is well described. He had "eyes at the back of his head", and, after passing some bushes, caught sight of a withered leaf or two among the fresh ones. This made him suspect that somebody had put the leaves there to make a better hiding-place, and so he discovered some hidden fugitives.

NIGHT SCOUTING

A Scout has to be able to notice small details by night as well as by day.

At night he has to do it chiefly by listening, occasionally by feeling or smelling.

In the stillness of the night, sounds carry farther than by day. If you put your ear to the ground or place it against a stick, or especially against a drum, which is touching the ground, you will hear the shake of horses' hoofs or the thud of a man's footfall a long way off.

Another way is to open a knife with a blade at each end; stick one blade into the ground, hold the other carefully between your teeth and you will hear all the better.

The human voice, even though talking low, carries to a great distance, and is not likely to be mistaken for any other sound.

I have often passed through outposts at night after having found where the pickets were posted by hearing the low talking of the men or the snoring of those asleep.

PATROL PRACTICES IN OBSERVATION

IN TOWN: teach your boys first, in walking down a street, to notice the different kinds of shops they pass and to remember them in their proper order. Then to notice and remember the names on the shops. Then to notice and remember the contents of a shop window after two minutes' gaze. Finally to notice the contents of several shop windows in succession with half a minute at each.

Make the boys notice prominent buildings as landmarks, the number of turnings off the street they are using, names of other streets, details of cars passing by, and especially, details of people as to dress, features and way of walking. Take them out the first time to show them how to do it. After that send them out and question them on their return.

Make the Scouts learn for themselves to notice and remember the whereabouts of all fire alarms, police points, hospitals, etc.

IN THE COUNTRY: take the Patrol out for a walk and teach the boys to notice distant prominent features as landmarks, such as hills, church steeples, and the like, and as nearer landmarks such things as peculiar buildings, trees, rocks, gates, etc. Also have them notice by-roads or paths, different kinds of trees, birds, animals, tracks, and also people and vehicles.

Send the boys out on a walk. On their return examine them

125

one by one, or have them all in and let them write their answers
to, say, six questions which you give them with reference to certain
points which they should have noticed. It adds to the value of the
practice if you make certain small marks on the ground beforehand,
or leave buttons or matches, etc., for the boys to notice or to pick
up and bring in, as a means of making them examine the ground
close to them, as well as distant objects.

At Troop meeting, arrange for an "incident" to take place without
warning, such as this: A man rushes in, "knocks down" the Scoutmaster, and escapes. Then each Patrol writes a report of what
happened, a description of the man, etc.

GAMES IN OBSERVATION

Thimble Finding (Indoors)

Send the Patrol out of the room.

Take a thimble, ring, coin, bit of paper, or any small article,
and place it where it is perfectly visible, but in a spot where it is
not likely to be noticed. Let the Patrol come in and look for it.
When one of the Scouts sees it, he should go and quietly sit down
without indicating to the others where it is.

After a fair time he should be told to point it out to those who
have not succeeded in finding it.

Far and Near (For town or country)

Umpire goes along a given road or line of country with a Patrol
in patrol formation. He carries a scoring card with the name of
each Scout on it.

Each Scout looks out for the details required, and, directly he
notices one, he runs to the umpire and informs him or hands in the
article, if it is an article he finds. The umpire enters a mark accordingly against his name. The Scout who gains most marks in the walk
wins.

Details like the following should be chosen, to develop the Scout's
observation and to encourage him to look far and near, up and
down. The details should be varied every time the game is played,
and about eight or ten should be given at a time.

Every match found	1 point
Every button found	1 ,,
Bird's tracks	2 points
Grey horse seen	2 ,,

Pigeon flying	2 points
Sparrow sitting	1 point
Ash-tree	2 points
Broken window	1 point

(And so on).

Shop Window (Outdoors in town)

Umpire takes a Patrol down a street past six shops and gives them half a minute at each shop. Then, after moving them to some distance off, he gives each boy a pencil and card, and tells him to write from memory what he noticed in, say, the third and fifth shops. The Scout who sets down most articles correctly wins. It is useful practice to match one boy against another in heats—the losers competing again, till you arrive at the worst. This gives the worst Scouts the most practice.

Room Observation (Indoors)

Send each Scout in turn into a room for half a minute. When he comes out, take down a list of furniture and articles which he has noticed. The boy who notices most wins.

The simplest way of scoring is to make a list of the articles in the room on your scoring paper, with a column against them for marks for each Scout. The marks can then easily be totalled up.

Smugglers Over the Border

The "border" is a certain line of country about four hundred yards long, preferably a road or wide path or bit of sand, on which foot-tracks can easily be seen. One Patrol watches the border with sentries posted along this road; with a reserve posted farther inland, about half-way between the "border" and the "town". The "town" would be a base marked by a tree, building, or flags, about half a mile distant from the border. A hostile Patrol of smugglers assembles about half a mile on the other side of the border. They will all cross the border, in any formation they please, either singly or together or scattered, and make for the town, either walking or running, or at Scout Pace. Only one among them is supposed to be smuggling, and he wears tracking irons. The sentries walk up and down their beat (they may not run till after the "alarm"), waiting for the tracks of the smuggler. Directly a sentry sees the track, he gives the alarm signal to the reserve and starts himself to follow up the track as fast as he can. The reserve thereupon co-operates with him and they all try to catch the smuggler before he can reach

"Old Spotty-Face" is a good game for practising observation. It also helps to sharpen the eye sight.

the town. Once within the boundary of the town he is safe and wins the game.

Old Spotty-Face

Prepare squares of cardboard divided into about a dozen or more small squares. Each Scout should take one, and should have a pencil and go off a few hundred yards.

The leader then takes a large sheet of cardboard, with the same number of squares ruled on it of about three inch sides. The leader has a number of black paper discs, half an inch in diameter, and pins ready, and sticks about half a dozen on to his card, dotted about where he likes. He holds up his card so that it can be seen by the Scouts. They then gradually approach, and as they get within sight they mark their cards with the same pattern of spots. The one who does so at the farthest distance from the leader wins.

Give five points for every spot correctly shown, deduct one point for every two inches nearer than the furthest man.

Scout's Nose (Indoors)

Prepare a number of paper bags, all alike, and put in each a different-smelling article, such as chopped onion in one, coffee in another, rose leaves, leather, aniseed, toilet soap, orange peel, etc. Put these packets in a row a couple of feet apart, and let each competitor walk down the line and have five seconds' sniff at each. At the end he has one minute in which to write down or to state to the umpire the names of the different objects smelled, from memory, in their correct order.

Fugitives

Each Scout in the Patrol has a round disc of white cardboard with a number printed plainly upon it, pinned on to the back of his shirt.

One member of the Patrol is then chosen as the "fugitive", while the rest act as hunters.

The "fugitive", who wears tracking-irons, or leaves some kind of trail behind him, is given, say, ten minutes' start. The rest of the Patrol then start out and endeavour to track him down.

As soon as a "hunter" can get near enough to the "fugitive", without being seen, to take down his number, the latter is caught. But if the "fugitive" can, by any means, turn the tables and get any of his pursuers' numbers, the latter are out of action.

As soon as a number is taken down, the Scout who takes it must call it out, to let his captive know he is out of action.

This game necessitates some careful stalking. A sharp Scout in the Patrol should be chosen for the "fugitive", as he has not only to elude perhaps six or seven pursuers, but he must also endeavour to "capture" them, unless he wishes to get killed himself.

Camp Fire Yarn
No. 12

SPOORING

Men's Tracks · Animals' Tracks
The Age of Tracks · Hints on "Spooring"

GENERAL DODGE, OF THE AMERICAN ARMY, described how he once had to pursue a party of Red Indians who had murdered some people.

The murderers had nearly a week's start, and had gone away on horseback. Except for one, they were all riding unshod horses.

General Dodge got a splendid tracking-scout named Espinosa to help him. After tracking the Indians for many miles, Espinosa suddenly got off his horse and pulled four horseshose out of a hidden crevice in the rocks. The rider of the shod horse had evidently pulled them off so that they should not leave a track.

For six days Dodge and his men pursued the band, and for a great part of the time there was no sign visible to an ordinary eye. After going for 150 miles they eventually overtook and captured the whole party. It was entirely due to Espinosa's good tracking.

TRACKING BY NIGHT

On another occasion some American troops were following up a number of Red Indians, who had been raiding and murdering whites. They had some other Red Indian scouts to assist them in tracking.

In order to make a successful attack, the troops marched by night, and the trackers found the way in the darkness by feeling the tracks of the enemy with their fingers. They led on at a fairly good pace for many miles; but suddenly they halted and reported that the track they had been following had been crossed by a fresh track. When the commanding officer came up, he found the Indians still holding the track with their hands, so that there should be no mistake.

A light was brought and it was found that the new track was that of a bear which had walked across the trail of the enemy! The march continued without further incident, and the enemy was surprised and caught in the early hours of the morning.

The American Scout, Frederick Burnham, who was with Wilson's men in South Africa when they were massacred on the Shangani River in Matabeleland, was sent away with a dispatch shortly before they were surrounded. He travelled during the night to escape the observation of the enemy. He found his way by feeling for the tracks left in the mud by the column when it marched up there in the morning

I myself led a column through an intricate part of the Matopo Hills in Rhodesia by night to attack the enemy's stronghold which I had reconnoitred the previous day. I found the way by feeling my own tracks, sometimes with my hands and sometimes through the soles of my shoes, which had worn very thin. I never had any difficulty in finding the line.

Frederick Burnham, American scout, became famous in Matabeleland.

THE IMPORTANCE OF TRACKING

Tracking, or following up tracks, is called by different names in different countries. Thus, in South Africa, you would talk only of "spooring", that is, following up the "spoor"; in India, it would be following the "pugs", or "pugging"; in North America, it is also called "trailing".

It is one of the principal ways by which Scouts gain information and hunters find their game. But to become a good tracker you must begin young and practise it at all times when you are out walking, whether in town or country.

If at first you constantly remind yourself to do it, you will soon find that you do it as a habit without having to remind yourself. It is a very useful habit, and makes the dullest walk interesting.

Hunters when they are looking about in a country to find game first look for any tracks, old or new, to see if there are any animals in the country. Then they study the newer marks to find out where the animals are hiding themselves. Then, after they have found a fresh track, they follow it up till they find the animal and kill it. Afterwards they often have to retrace their own tracks to find their way back to camp. War scouts do much the same as regards their enemies.

MEN'S TRACKS

First of all you must be able to distinguish one man's footmark from that of another, by its size, shape, and nails, etc. And, similarly, the prints of horses and other animals.

From a man's track, that is, from the size of his foot and the length of his stride, you can tell, to a certain extent, his height.

In taking notes of a track you should pick out a well-marked print, very carefully measure its length, length of heel, width of sole, width at instep, width of heel, number of rows of nails, and number of nails in each row, heel and toe-plates or nails, shape of nail-heads, nails missing, etc.

It is best to make a diagram of the foot-print thus.

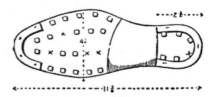

Notice the length of the shoe, the width of the sole, the length of the heel, as well as details. X indicates missing nails.

You should also measure very carefully the length of the man's step from the heel of one foot to the heel of the other.

132

A man was once found drowned in a river. It was supposed that he must have fallen in accidentally, and that the cuts on his head were caused by stones, etc., in the river. But someone took a drawing of his boots, and after searching the river-bank came on his tracks, and followed them up to a spot where there had evidently been a struggle: the ground was much trampled and bushes broken down to the water's edge, and there were tracks of two other men's feet. Though these men were never found, it showed the case to be one of probable murder, which would not otherwise have been suspected.

Differences Between Bare-Foot Tracks

It is very puzzling for a beginner to tell the difference between a lot of footmarks of bare feet—they all look so much alike—but this is the way that the Indian police trackers do it.

When measuring the footprint of the man you are after draw a line from the tip of the big toe to the tip of the little toe, and then notice where the other toes come with regard to this line, and put it down in your note-book. Then when you come to a number of tracks you have only to try this same line on one or two of them till you find the one you want. All people vary a little in the position of their toes.

Try it with the other Scouts in your Patrol, each of you making a footprint with his bare foot, and then noting how it is different from the others when the toe line is drawn.

THE PACE OF TRACKS

A Scout must learn to recognize at a glance at what pace the maker of the tracks was going.

To distinguish between bare-foot tracks, draw a line from tip of big toe to tip of little toe, then notice how the other toes lie.

A man walking puts the whole flat of his foot on the ground, each foot a little under a yard from the other. In running, the toes are more deeply dug into the ground, and a little dirt is kicked up, and the feet are more than a yard apart. Sometimes men walk backwards in order to deceive anyone who may be tracking, but a good Scout can generally tell this at once by the stride being shorter, the toes more turned in, and the heel marks deeper.

HORSES' TRACKS

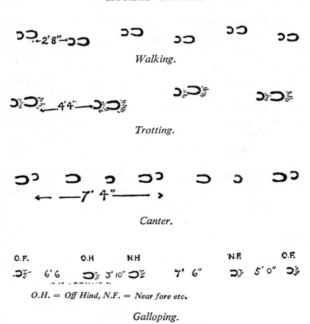

Walking.

Trotting.

Canter.

O.H. = Off Hind, N.F. = Near fore etc.

Galloping.

When you find the tracks of horses, try to discover at what speed the animals were travelling. This is indicated by the distances between the imprints of the fore feet and the hind feet. In the sketches above, the long feet are the hind feet.

With animals, if they are moving fast, their toes are more deeply dug into the ground, and they kick up the dirt, and their paces are longer than when going slowly.

You ought to be able to tell the pace at which a horse has been going directly you see the tracks.

At a walk the horse makes two pairs of hoof prints—the near

134

(left) hind foot close in front of near fore foot mark, and the off (right) fore foot similarly just behind the print of the off hind foot. At a trot the track is similar, but the stride is longer.

The hind feet are generally longer and narrower in shape than the fore feet.

It was a trick with highwaymen of old, and with horse stealers, to put their horses' shoes on the wrong way round in order to deceive trackers who might try to follow them up. But a good tracker would not be taken in. Similarly, thieves often walk backwards for the same reason, but a clever tracker will very soon recognize the deception.

Wheel tracks should also be studied till you can tell the difference between the tracks of motor-cars or bicycles, *and the direction they were going*.

THE AGE OF TRACKS

In addition to learning to recognize the pace of tracks, you must get to know how old they are. This is a most important point, and requires a very great amount of practice and experience before you can judge it really well.

So much depends on the state of the ground and weather, and its effects on the "spoor". If you follow one track, say, on a dry, windy day, over varying ground, you will find that when it is on light, sandy soil, it will look old in a very short time, because any damp earth

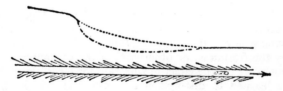

The direction of a bicycle's travel is shown by the way dirt is thrown backward. Also by the loops made in the track where the rider made a turn or wobble: the thinner end of the loop points in the direction he went.

that it may kick up from under the surface will dry very rapidly to the same colour as the surface dust, and the sharp edges of the foot-marks will soon be rounded off by the breeze playing over the dry dust in which they are formed. When it gets into damp ground, the same track will look much fresher, because the sun will have only partially dried up the upturned soil, and the wind will not, therefore,

135

have bevelled off the sharp edges of the impression. If it gets into damp clay, under shade of trees, etc., where the sun does not get at it, the same track, which may have looked a day old in the sand, will here look quite fresh.

Of course, a great clue to the age of tracks will often be found in spots of rain having fallen on them since they were made (if you know at what time the rain fell), dust or grass seeds blown into them (if you noticed at what time the wind was blowing), or the crossing of

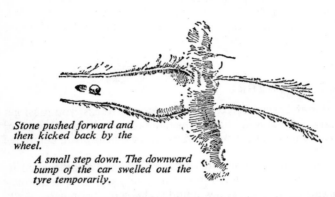

Stone pushed forward and then kicked back by the wheel.

A small step down. The downward bump of the car swelled out the tyre temporarily.

In following the track of a bicycle (or motor-car), study especially spots where the road is uneven. Here there will be many "sign".

other tracks over the original ones, or, where the grass has been trodden down, the extent to which it has since dried or withered. In following a horse, the length of time since it passed can also be judged by the freshness, or otherwise, of the droppings, due allowance being made for the effect of sun, rain, or birds, upon them.

Having learned to distinguish the pace and age of spoor, you must next learn to follow it over all kinds of ground. This is an accomplishment that you can practise all your life, and will still find yourself continually improving.

Then there is a great deal to learn from the ashes of fires—whether they are still warm or cold, scraps showing what kind of food the people were eating, whether plentiful or scarce.

You must not only keep a sharp lookout for Scout "signs" made by your own Scouts, but also for those made by "hostile" Scouts.

The following are some of the signs made by tramps on walls or fences near houses where they have been begging, which they chalk up to warn others of their class:

⊙ Very bad: they give you in charge here.

⋏ No good.

△ Too many tramps have been here already.

▢ Bad people.

Tracking for Stolen Goods

There are very good trackers in the Sudan and Egypt, and I saw some of their work there.

The Colonel of the Egyptian Cavalry had had some things stolen out of his house, so a tracker was sent for from the neighbouring Jaalin tribe.

Some time, you may come upon these tracks. They are, left to right, deer, sheep, wolf and fox.

He soon found the footprints of the thief and followed them a long way out on to the desert, and found the spot where he had buried the stolen goods. His tracks then came back to the barracks.

So the whole of the regiment was paraded without shoes on, for the tracker to examine. And at the end, when he had seen every man walk, he said, "No, the thief is not there." Just then the Colonel's servant came up to him with a message, and the tracker who was standing by, said to the Colonel, "That is the man who buried the stolen goods."

The servant, surprised at being found out, then confessed that it was he who had stolen his master's property, thinking that he would be the last man to be suspected.

HINTS ON SPOORING

When getting on to very fresh spoor of man or beast, the old Scout will generally avoid following it closely, because the hunted animal will frequently look back to see if it is being followed. The tracker therefore makes a circle, and comes back on to where he would expect

137

Old hand comes on a buck spoor.

to find the spoor again. If he finds it, he makes another circle farther
ahead till he finds no spoor. Then he knows he is ahead of his game,
so he gradually circles nearer till he finds it, taking care, of course,
not to get to windward of the animal when within scenting distance.

Some trackers of Scinde followed up a stolen camel from Karachi
to Sehwan, 150 miles over sand and bare rock. The thieves, to escape
detection, drove the camel up and down a crowded street, in order
to get the trail mixed up with others—but the trackers foresaw this
and made a "cast" round the town, and hit on the outgoing spoor
on the far side, which they successfully followed up.

Look Ahead Over Hard Ground

In tracking where the spoor is difficult to see, such as on hard
ground, or in grass, note the direction of the last footprint that you
can see, and look on in the same direction, but well ahead of you,
say 20 or 30 yards. In grass you will then generally see the blades
bent or trodden, and on hard ground, possibly stones displaced or
scratched, and so on—small signs which, seen in a line one behind
the other, give a kind of track that otherwise would not be noticed.

I once tracked a bicycle on a hard macadam road where it really
made no impression at all, but by looking along the surface of the
road for a long distance ahead of me, under the rising sun as it happened, the line it had taken was quite visible through the almost
invisible coating of dew upon the ground. Standing on the track
and looking upon it close to my feet I could not see the slightest sign
of it.

The great thing is to look for a difficult track against the sun, so that the slightest dent in the ground throws a shadow.

"Casting" for a Lost Track

If you lose sight of the track you must make a "cast" to find it again. To do this put your handkerchief, staff, or other mark at the last footmark that you noticed, then work round it in a wide circle, say, 30, 50, or 100 yards away from it as a centre—choosing the most favourable ground, soft ground if possible, to find signs of the outward track. If you are with a Patrol it is generally best for the Patrol to halt while one or perhaps two men make the cast. If everybody starts trying to find the spoor they very soon defeat their object by treading it out or confusing it with their own footmarks—too many cooks easily spoil the broth in such a case.

In making a cast, use your common sense as to which direction the enemy has probably taken, and try it there.

I remember an instance of tracking a boar which illustrates what I mean. The boar had been running through some muddy inundated fields, and was easy enough to follow until he turned off over some very hard and stony ground, where after a little while not a sign of his spoor was to be seen. A cast had accordingly to be made. The last footmark was marked, and the tracker moved round a wide circle, examining the ground most carefully, but not a sign was found. Then the tracker took a look round the country, and, putting himself in place of the pig, said "Now in which direction would I have gone?" Some distance to the front of him, as the original track led, stood a long hedge of prickly cactus; in it were two gaps. The tracker went to one of these as being the line the boar would probably take, Here the ground was still very hard, and no footmark was visible, but on a leaf of the cactus in the gap was a pellet of wet mud; and this gave the desired clue. There was no mud on this hard ground, but the pig had evidently brought some on his feet from the wet ground he had been travelling through. This one little sign enabled the tracker to work on in the right direction to another and another, until eventually he got on to the spoor again in favourable ground, and was able to follow up the boar to his resting-place.

Fitting Your Stride to the Track

I have watched a tracker in the Sudan following tracks where for a time they were quite invisible to the ordinary eye in this way. While the track was clear he made his own stride exactly to fit that of the track, so that he walked step for step with it, and he tapped

These are the tracks of two birds. One lives generally on the ground, the other in bushes and trees. Which track belongs to which bird?

the ground with his staff as he walked along—ticking off each foot-print, as it were. When the footprints disappeared on hard ground, or had been buried by drifting sand, he still walked on at the same pace, tap-tapping the ground with his staff at the spot where there ought to have been a footprint. Occasionally he saw a slight depression or mark, which showed that there had been a footprint there, and thus he knew he was still on the right line.

PATROL PRACTICES IN SPOORING

Prepare a tracking ground by picking a piece of soft ground, about ten to fifteen yards square, and making it quite smooth with a roller by sweeping it over. Part of the ground should be wet as if by rain, the other part dry. Make one boy walk across it, then run, then bicycle. Explain the difference in the tracks, so that the Scouts of the Patrol can tell at once from any tracks they may see afterwards whether a person was walking or running.

Send out a boy to make tracks and let the Patrol track him and notice when any other tracks override his, showing what people or animals have passed since. The boy may wear tracking irons strapped to the soles of his boots. Or he may have a few nails hammered into the sole or into the butt of his staff in a pattern that will make an unmistakable track.

Study the age of tracks by making fresh tracks a day later along-side the old. Notice the difference in appearance, so that the Scouts can learn to judge the age of tracks.

Make each Scout make a track of his shoe in soft ground and draw a diagram of it on paper.

140

Send Patrols along different roads, and let them return with reports on tracks seen—whether of people, or vehicles or animals.

Make plaster casts of tracks. Build a wall round the track, of mud. Pour water into a mug or cup, slowly add plaster of Paris, stir all the time, until it is like very thick cream—just pourable. Then pour into track. When almost dry, scratch on date, where found, etc. When absolutely dry, dig out carefully and wash.

GAMES IN SPOORING

Track Memory

Make a Patrol sit with their feet up, so that other Scouts can study them. Give the Scouts, say, three minutes to study the shoes. Then leaving the Scouts in a room or out of sight, let one of the Patrol make some footmarks in a good bit of ground. Call up the Scouts one by one and let each see the track and say who made it.

Track Drawing

Take out a Patrol; set it on to a foot track. See which Scout can make the most accurate drawing of one of the footprints of the track. The Scouts should be allowed to follow up the track till they get to a bit of ground where a good impression of it can be found.

Spot the Thief

Get a stranger to make a track unseen by the Scouts. The Scouts study his track so as to know it again.

Then put the stranger among eight or ten others and let them all make their tracks for the boys to see, going by in rotation. Each Scout then in turn whispers to the umpire which man made the original track—describing him by his number in filing past. The Scout who answers correctly wins. If more than one answers correctly, the one who then draws the best diagram of the footprint from memory wins.

Follow the Trail

Send out a "hare", either walking or cycling, with a pocketful of chicken feed, nutshells, confetti paper, etc., dropping a little here and there to give a trail for the Patrol to follow.

Or use Scout signs, scratched in the ground or formed from twigs, hiding a letter at some point.

Camp Fire Yarn
No. 13

READING "SIGN", OR DEDUCTION

Putting This and That Together
Instances of Deduction
Sherlock Holmes

WHEN A SCOUT HAS LEARNED to notice "sign", he must then learn to "put this and that together", and so read a meaning from what he has seen. This is called "deduction".

Here is an example which shows how the young Scout can read the meaning from "sign", when he has been trained to it.

Old Blenkinsop rushed out of his little store near the African Kaffir village.

"Hi! Stop thief!" he shouted. "He's stolen my sugar. Stop him!"

Stop whom? There was nobody in sight running away.

"Who stole it?" asked the policeman.

"I don't know, but a whole bag of sugar is missing. It was there only a few minutes ago."

A police tracker was called in—and it looked a pretty impossible job for him to single out the tracks of the thief from among dozens of other naked footprints about the store. However, he presently started off hopefully at a jog-trot, away out into the bush. In some places he went over hard stony ground but he never checked his pace, although no footmarks could be seen.

At length the tracker suddenly stopped and cast around, having evidently lost the trail. Then a grin came on his face as he pointed with his thumb over his shoulder up the tree near which he was standing. There, concealed among the branches they saw a man with the missing bag of sugar.

How had the tracker spotted him? His sharp eyes had seen some grains of sugar sparkling in the dust. The bag leaked, leaving a very slight trail of these grains. He followed that trail and when it came to an end in the bush the tracker noticed a string of ants going up a tree. They were after the sugar, and so was he, and between them they brought about the capture of the thief.

I expect that Old Blenkinsop patted the tracker on the back for his cleverness in using his eyes to see the grains of sugar and the ants, and in using his wits to see why the ants were climbing the tree.

The Lost Soldier

A cavalry soldier was lost in India, and some of his comrades were hunting all over to find him. They came across an Indian boy and asked him if he had seen the lost man. He immediately said: "Do you mean a very tall soldier, riding a roan horse that was slightly lame?"

They said, "Yes, that was the man. Where did you see him?"

The boy replied, "I have not seen him, but I know where he has gone."

Thereupon they arrested him, thinking that probably the man had been murdered and made away with, and that the boy had heard about it.

But eventually he explained that he had seen tracks of the man.

A lame horse made these tracks. The question is: which leg is he lame in?
The long feet are the hind feet.

He pointed out the tracks to them, and finally brought them to a place where the signs showed that the man had made a halt. Here the horse had rubbed itself against a tree, and had left some of its hairs sticking to the bark, which showed that it was a roan (speckled) horse. Its hoof marks showed that it was lame, that is, one foot was not so deeply imprinted on the ground and did not take so long a pace as the other feet. That the rider was a soldier was shown by the track of his boot, which was an army boot.

Then they asked the boy, "How could you tell that he was a tall

143

man?" and the boy pointed to where the soldier had broken a branch from the tree, which would have been out of reach of a man of ordinary height.

Deduction is exactly like reading a book.

A boy who has never been taught to read, and who sees you reading from a book, would ask, "How do you do it?" You would point out to him that a number of small signs on a page are letters. These letters when grouped form words. And words form sentences, and sentences give information.

Similarly, a trained Scout will see little signs and tracks. He puts them together in his mind and quickly reads a meaning from them which an untrained man would never arrive at.

From frequent practice he gets to read the meaning at a glance, just as you do a book, without the delay of spelling out each word, letter by letter.

INSTANCES OF DEDUCTION

I was one day, during the Matabele War in Africa, out scouting with an African over a wide grassy plain near the Matopo Hills.

Suddenly we crossed a track freshly made in grass, where the blades of grass were still green and damp, though pressed down—all were bending one way, which showed the direction in which the people had been travelling. Following up the track for a bit it got on to a patch of sand, and we then saw that it was the spoor of several women (small feet with straight edge, and short steps) and boys (small feet, curved edge, and longer steps) walking, not running, towards the hills, about five miles away, where we believed the enemy was hiding.

Then we saw a leaf lying about ten yards off the track. There were no trees for miles, but we knew that trees having this kind of leaf grew at a village fifteen miles away, in the direction from which the footmarks were coming. It seemed likely therefore that the women had come from that village, bringing the leaf with them, and had gone to the hills.

On picking up the leaf we found it was damp, and smelled of native beer. The short steps showed that the women were carrying loads. So we guessed that according to the custom they had been carrying pots of native beer on their heads, with the mouths of the pots stopped up with bunches of leaves. One of these leaves had fallen out; and since we found it ten yards off the track, it showed that at the time it fell a wind was blowing. There was no wind now, that is,

144

at seven o'clock, but there had been some about five o'clock.

So we guessed from all these little signs that a party of women and boys had brought beer during the night from the village fifteen miles away, and had taken it to the enemy in the hills, arriving there soon after six o'clock.

A single leaf that had blown off a pot carried by an African woman made it possible to secure information about the enemy.

The men would probably start to drink the beer at once (as it goes sour in a few hours), and would, by the time we could get there, be getting sleepy and keeping a bad look-out, so we should have a favourable chance of looking at their position.

We accordingly followed the women's tracks, found the enemy, made our observations, and got away with our information without any difficulty.

And it was chiefly done on the evidence of that one leaf.

So you see the importance of noticing even a little thing like that.

Dust Helping in Deduction

By noticing very small signs detectives have discovered crimes.

In one case a crime had been committed, and a stranger's coat was found which gave no clue to the owner.

The coat was put into a stout bag, and beaten with a stick. The dust was collected from the bag, and examined under a powerful magnifying glass, and was found to consist of fine sawdust, which showed that the owner of the coat was probably a carpenter, or sawyer, or joiner. The dust was then put under a more powerful magnifying glass—called a microscope—and it was then seen that it also contained some tiny grains of gelatine and powdered glue. These things are not used by carpenters or sawyers, so the coat was shown to belong to a joiner, and the police got on the track of the criminal.

Dust out of pockets, or in the recesses of a pocket-knife, and so on, tells a great deal, if closely examined.

SHERLOCK HOLMES

Dr. Bell of Edinburgh is said to be the original from whom Sir Arthur Conan Doyle drew his idea of Sherlock Holmes.

The doctor was once teaching a class of medical students at a hospital how to treat people. A patient was brought in, so that the doctor might show how an injured man should be cared for. The patient in this case came limping in, and the doctor turned to one of the students and asked him:

"What is the matter with this man?"

The student replied, "I don't know, sir. I haven't asked him."

The doctor said: "Well, there is no need to ask him, you should see for yourself—he has injured his right knee—he is limping on that leg. He injured it by burning it in the fire—you see how his trouser is burnt away at the knee. This is Monday morning. Yesterday was fine, Saturday was wet and muddy. The man's trousers are muddy all over. He had a fall in the mud on Saturday night."

Then he turned to the man and said: "You drew your wages on Saturday and got drunk, and in trying to get your clothes dry by the fire when you got home, you fell on the fire and burnt your knee—isn't that so?"

"Yes, sir," replied the man.

I saw a case in the paper once where a judge at the county court used his powers of "noticing little things", and "putting this and that together". He was trying a man as a debtor.

The man pleaded that he was out of work, and could get no employment.

The judge said: "Then what are you doing with that pencil behind your ear if you are not in business?"

The man had to admit that he had been helping his wife in

her business, which, it turned out, was a very profitable one. The judge thereupon ordered him to pay his debt.

TRUE SCOUTING STORIES

Captain Stigand a cavalry officer, writing of his experiences gave the following instances of scouts reading important meanings from small signs.

When he was going round outside his camp one morning, he noticed fresh spoor of a horse which had been walking. He knew that all his horses went at a jog-trot only, so it must have been a stranger's horse. He realized that a mounted enemy scout had been quietly looking at his camp in the night.

Coming to a village in Central Africa from which the inhabitants had fled; Stigand could not tell what tribe it belonged to till he found a crocodile's foot in one of the huts. This showed that the village belonged to the Awisa tribe, as they eat crocodiles, and the neighbouring tribes do not.

A man was seen riding a camel over half a mile away. An African who was watching him said, "It is a man of slave blood."

"How can you tell at this distance?"

"Because he is swinging his leg. A true Arab rides with his legs close to the camel's side."

The tracks right outside your door may have a story to tell if you can read them. These tracks are from a simple story of a dog chasing a cat, and its owner's anger.

Finding Lost Property

An officer lost his field-glasses during some manoeuvres on the desert five miles from Cairo, and he sent for Egyptian trackers to look for them.

The horse was brought out and led about, so that the trackers could study its footprints. These they carried in their minds, and went out to where the manoeuvres had been. There, among the hundreds of hoof marks of the cavalry and artillery, the trackers soon found those of the officer's horse, and followed them up where-ever he had ridden, till they found the field-glasses lying where they had dropped out of their case on the desert.

The footmarks of different camels look very much alike. But Egyptian trackers are trained to follow them and track down stolen camels.

The "Lost" Camel

Egyptian trackers are particularly good at spooring camels. To anyone not accustomed to them, the footmarks of one camel look very like those of any other camel. But to a trained eye they are all as different as people's faces, and experienced trackers remember them very much as you would remember the faces of people you had seen.

Some years ago a camel was stolen near Cairo. The police tracker was sent for and shown its spoor. He followed it for a long way until it got into some streets, where it was entirely lost among other footmarks.

A year later the same police tracker suddenly came on the fresh track of this camel—he had remembered its appearance all that time.

148

It had evidently been driven with another camel whose track he also recognized. He knew they were made by a camel which belonged to a well-known camel thief. So, without trying to follow the tracks through the city, the tracker went with a policeman straight to the man's stable, and there found the long-missing camel.

South American Trackers

The "Gauchos", or cowboys, of South America are fine scouts. The cattle lands are now for the most part enclosed, but formerly the gauchos had to track stolen and lost beasts for miles and were therefore good trackers. One of these men was once sent to track a stolen horse, but failed to find it. Ten months later, in a different part of the country, he suddenly noticed the fresh spoor of this horse on the ground. He at once followed it up and recovered the horse.

EXAMPLE OF PRACTICE IN DEDUCTION

A simple deduction from signs noticed in my walk one morning on a stormy mountain path in Kashmir.

Signs Observed—Tree-stump, about three feet high, by the path. A stone about the size of a cocoanut lying near it, to which were sticking some bits of bruised walnut rind, dried up. Some walnut rind also lying on the stump. Farther along the path, thirty yards to the south of the stump, were lying bits of walnut shell of four walnuts. Close by was a high sloping rock, alongside the path. The only walnut tree in sight was 150 yards north of the stump.

At the foot of the stump was a cake of hardened mud which showed the impression of a grass shoe.

What would you make out from those signs?

My solution of it was this.

A man had gone southward on a long journey along the path two days ago carrying a load and had rested at the rock while he ate walnuts.

My deductions were these.

It was a man carrying a load, because carriers when they want to rest do not sit down, but rest their load against a sloping rock and lean back. Had he had no load, he would probably have sat down on the stump, but he preferred to go thirty yards farther to where the rock was. Women do not carry loads there, so it was a man. He broke the shells of his walnuts on the tree stump with the stone, having brought them from the tree 150 yards north—so he was travelling south. He was on a long journey, as he was wearing shoes, and not going barefooted, as he would be if only strolling near his home. Three days ago there was rain, the cake of mud had been picked up while the ground was still wet—but it had not been since rained upon, and was now dry. The walnut rind was also dry, and confirmed the time that had elapsed.

There is no important story attached to this, but it is just an example of everyday practice which should be carried out by Scouts.

PATROL PRACTICES IN DEDUCTION

Read aloud a story in which a good amount of observation of details occurs, with consequent deductions, such as in either the *Memoirs* or the *Adventures of Sherlock Holmes*. Then question the boys as to which details suggested certain solutions, to see that they really have grasped the method.

Make tracks on soft ground of different incidents—such as a cyclist meeting a boy on foot, getting off his bicycle to talk to his friend, then setting out again. Let the boys study the tracks and deduce their meaning.

Place on a tray a collection of articles which might come from a man's pockets. Ask the Scouts to deduce what kind of man he was, his interests, etc.

GAMES IN DEDUCTION

Strangers

Get some people who are strangers to the boys to come along as passers-by in the street or road, and let the boys separately notice all about them. After an interval ask each boy for a full description of the passers-by as to appearance, peculiar recognizable points, and what he guesses their business to be.

Or let each boy have two minutes' conversation with some stranger, and try to find out what he can about him in that time by questioning and observation.

"Crime" Deduction—Detective

Set a room or prepare a piece of ground with small signs, tracks, etc. Read aloud the story of a crime up to the point when the signs are made and let each boy in turn examine the scene for a given time, and then privately give his solution of it.

The very simplest schemes should be given at first. They can gradually be elaborated.

For instance, have a number of footmarks and used matches by a tree, showing where a man had difficulty in lighting his pipe, etc.

For a more finished theme take a mystery like that in *Memoirs of Sherlock Holmes* called "The Resident Patient". Set a room to represent the patient's room where he was found hanging, with footprints of muddy boots on the carpet, cigar ends bitten or cut in the fireplace, cigar ashes, screw-driver and screws, etc. Put down a strip of newspapers for "stepping stones" on which competitors shall walk (so as not to confuse existing tracks). Let each Scout (or Patrol) come in separately and give him three minutes in which to investigate. Then give him half an hour to make up his solution, written or verbal.

"Track the Assassin"

The assassin escapes after having "stabbed his victim", carrying in his hand the "dripping dagger". The remainder, a minute later, start out to track him by the "drops of blood" (represented by confetti) which fall at every third step. His confederate (the umpire) tells him beforehand where to make for. If he gets there without being touched by his pursuers, over eight minutes ahead of them, he wins.

WOODCRAFT

Camp Fire Yarn
No. 14

STALKING

How to Hide Yourself
How to Learn Stalking
Games in Stalking

WHEN YOU WANT TO OBSERVE wild animals, you have to stalk them, that is, creep up to them without them seeing or smelling you.

A hunter keeps himself entirely hidden when he is stalking wild animals. So does the war scout when watching or looking for the enemy. A policeman does not catch pickpockets by standing about in uniform watching for them. He dresses like one of the crowd, and as often as not gazes into a shop window and sees all that goes on behind him reflected as if in a looking-glass.

If a guilty person finds himself watched, it puts him on his guard, while an innocent person becomes annoyed. So, when you are observing a person, don't do so by openly staring at him, but notice the details you want to at one glance or two. If you want to study him more, walk behind him. You can learn just as much from a back view—in fact more than you can from a front view—and, unless the person is a Scout and looks round frequently, he does not know that you are observing him.

War scouts and hunters stalking game always carry out two important things when they don't want to be seen.

One is—they take care that the ground, or trees, or buildings, behind them are of the same colour as their clothes.

And the other is—if an enemy or a deer is looking for them they remain perfectly still without moving while he is there.

In that way a Scout, even though he is out in the open, will often escape being noticed.

152

Choosing the Background

In choosing your background, consider the colour of your clothes. If you are dressed in khaki, don't go and stand in front of a white-washed wall, or in front of a dark-shaded bush, but go where there is khaki-coloured sand or grass or rocks behind you—and remain perfectly still. It will be very difficult for an enemy to distinguish you, even at a short distance.

If you are in dark clothes, get among dark bushes, or in the shadow of trees or rocks, but be careful that the ground beyond you is also dark—if there is light-coloured ground beyond the trees under which you are standing, for instance, you will stand out clearly defined against it.

In making use of hills as look-out places, be very careful not to show yourself on the top or sky-line. That is the fault which a tenderfoot generally makes.

TOMMY THE TENDERFOOT No. 8   TOMMY'S STALKING
"Keep up your end when you're stalking your foes."
(It might read in two ways as Tommy now knows.)

Slow Motion

It is quite a lesson to watch a Zulu scout making use of a hilltop or rising ground as a look-out place. He will crawl up on all fours, lying flat in the grass. On reaching the top he will very slowly raise his head, inch by inch, till he can see the view. If he sees the enemy on beyond, he will have a good look, and, if he thinks they are watching him, will keep his head perfectly steady for a long time, hoping that he will be mistaken for a stump or a stone. If he is not detected, he will very gradually lower his head, inch by inch, into the grass again, and crawl quietly away. Any quick or sudden move-ment of the head on the sky-line would be very liable to attract attention, even at a considerable distance.

At night, keep as much as possible in low ground, ditches, etc., so that you are down in the dark, while an enemy who comes near will be visible to you outlined on higher ground against the stars.

By squatting low in the shadow of the bush at night, and keeping quite still, I have let an enemy's scout come and stand within three feet of me, so that when he turned his back towards me I was able to stand up where I was, and fling my arms round him.

Silent Walking

A point also to remember in keeping hidden while moving, especially at night, is to walk quietly. The thump of an ordinary man's heel on the ground can be heard a good distance off. A Scout or hunter always walks lightly, on the balls of his feet, not on his heels. This you should practise whenever you are walking, by day or by night, indoors as well as out, so that it becomes a habit with you to walk as lightly and silently as possible. You will find that as you grow into it your power of walking long distances will grow—you will not tire so soon as you would if clumping along in the heavy-footed manner of most people.

Keep Down-Wind

Remember always that to stalk a wild animal, or a good scout, you must keep downwind of him, even if the wind is so slight as to be merely a faint air.

Before starting to stalk your enemy, then, you should be sure which way the wind is blowing, and work up against it. To find this out, wet your thumb all round with your tongue, and then hold it up and see which side feels coldest. Or you can throw some light dust, or dry grass or leaves in the air, and see which way they drift.

Using Disguise

The Red Indian scouts, when they wanted to reconnoitre an enemy's camp, used to tie a wolf's skin on their backs and walk on all fours, and prowl round the camps at night, imitating the howl of a wolf. Also, when peeping over a ridge or any place where their head might be seen against the sky-line, they put on a cap made of wolf's-head skin with ears on it so that they might be mistaken for a wolf, if seen.

In Australia, the aborigines stalk emus—great birds something like an ostrich—by putting an emu's skin over themselves, and walking with body bent and one hand held up to represent the bird's head and neck.

Scouts, when looking out among grass, often tie a string or band

An aborigine of Australia stalking emus, with an emu skin over him. He carries a boomerang in his hand and a spear between his toes.

round their head, and stick grass in it, some upright, some drooping over their face, so that their head is invisible. When hiding behind a big stone or mound, they don't look over the top, but round the side of it.

PATROL PRACTICES IN STALKING

Demonstrate the value of adapting colour of clothes to background by sending out one boy about 500 yards to stand against different backgrounds in turn, till he gets one similar to his own clothes. The rest of the Patrol will watch and notice how invisible the boy becomes when he gets a suitable background. A boy in a grey suit, for example, standing in front of dark bushes is quite visible, but he becomes less so if he stands in front of a grey rock or house. A boy in a dark suit is very visible in a green field, but not when he stands in an open doorway against dark interior shadow.

Demonstrate the effect of movement. Place Scouts in fair concealment (shrubs, etc.), and show how difficult it is to spot them until they move.

Practise quick rushes from cover to cover; crawling along ditches and behind ridges, and from bush to bush.

Try stalking in the dusk. Some of the games given could be played in twilight or in darkness. Do not begin with absolutely black night.

GAMES IN STALKING

Scout Hunting

One Scout is given time to go out and hide himself, the remainder then start to find him. He wins if he is not found, or if he can get back to the starting-point within a given time without being touched.

Message Running

A Scout is told to bring a note to a certain spot or house from a distance within a given time. Other "hostile" Scouts are told to prevent any message getting to this place, and to hide themselves at different points to stop the dispatch carrier getting in with it.

To count as a capture, two Scouts must touch the message runner before he reaches the spot for delivering the message.

Deer Stalking

Patrol Leader acts as a deer—not hiding, but standing, moving a little now and then if he likes.

Scouts go out to find him and each in his own way tries to get up to him unseen.

The moment the Patrol Leader sees a Scout he directs him to stand up as having failed. After a certain time the Patrol Leader calls "time". All stand up at the spot which they have reached, and the nearest wins.

The same game may be played to test the Scouts in stepping lightly—the umpire being blindfolded. The practice should preferably be carried out where there are dry twigs and gravel lying about. The Scout may start to stalk the blind enemy at 100 yards' distance, and he must do it fairly fast—say in one minute and a half—to touch the blind man before he hears him.

Flag Raiding

Two or more Patrols on each side.

Each side forms an outpost within a given tract of country to protect three flags (or at night three lanterns two feet above ground), planted not less than 200 yards (100 yards at night) from it. Those protecting an outpost will be posted in concealment either all together or spread out in pairs. They will then send out Scouts to discover the enemy's position. When they have found out where the outpost is, they try to creep round it out of sight, till they can get to the flags and bring them away to their own line. One Scout may not take away more than one flag.

This is the general position of a Patrol on such an outpost:—

$+$ $+$ $+$

$+$ $+$ $+$

Pair of Scouts.   *Pair of Scouts.*   *Pair of Scouts.*

$+$

Patrol Leader.

P P P

Flags

Any Scout coming within fifty yards of a stronger party will be put out of action if seen by the enemy. If he can creep by without being seen it is all right.

Scouts posted to watch at outposts cannot move from their ground, but their strength counts as double, and they may send single messengers to their neighbours or to their own scouting party.

An umpire should be with each outpost and with each scouting Patrol.

At a given hour, operations cease, and all assemble at the given spot to hand in their reports. The following points might be awarded:

For each flag or lamp captured and brought in . .   5 points

For each report or sketch of the position of the
enemy's outposts . . . . up to   5 points

For each report of movement of enemy's scouting
Patrols . . . .   2 points

The side which makes the biggest total wins.

NOTE: For games such as the above—usually called *Wide Games*, because they are played in open country—some method of "killing" or "capturing" is often needed. A strand of wool—a different colour for each side—or a piece of 1 in. gauze bandage can be worn round the arm, visible between elbow and shoulder. When broken, the victim goes to an umpire to get a new "life" in order to continue in the fun. It is important that the smallest Scout should have as good a chance as the heftiest.

Ambushing

The Troop splits up into two parties, one of which goes out in advance and hides in bushes, etc., by the roadside. The other party follows, and calls out those Scouts whom they can see *without leaving the road*. They continue as long as desired; one party alternately hiding and seeking.

At first, time should be given for the hiders to arrange them-

157

Try these stalking methods. Cling as close to the ground as possible.

selves; later they should be able to do so quickly. Opportunity can always be taken when someone drops out for the rest of the party to get under cover as quickly as possible, so that when he returns the party has disappeared as if by magic. This always causes fun.

Stalking and Reporting

The umpire places himself out in the open and sends each Scout or pair of Scouts away in different directions about half a mile off. When he waves a flag as the signal to begin, they all hide, and then proceed to stalk him, creeping up and watching all he does. When he waves the flag again, they rise, come in, and report each in turn all that he did, either by handing in a written report or verbally, as may be ordered.

The umpire meantime has kept a look-out in each direction, and, every time he sees a Scout, he takes two points off that Scout's score. He, on his part, performs small actions, such as sitting down, kneeling, looking through glasses, using handkerchief, taking hat off for a bit, walking round in a circle a few times, to give Scouts something to note and report about him. Scouts are given three points for each act reported correctly.

It saves time if the umpire makes out a scoring card beforehand, giving the name of each Scout, and a number of columns showing each act of his, also a column for minus marks for Scouts who expose themselves.

Spider and Fly

A bit of country or section of the town about a mile square with its boundaries described is selected as the web, and an hour fixed at which operations are to cease.

One Patrol (or half-Patrol) is the "spider", which goes out and selects a place to hide itself. The other Patrol (or half-Patrol) starts a quarter of an hour later as the "fly" to look for the "spider". They can spread themselves about as they like, but must tell their leader anything that they discover.

An umpire goes with each party.

It takes much time and patience to stalk close enough to wild animals to be able to study their habits without disturbing them.

If within the given time (say, about two hours) the fly has not discovered the spider, the spider wins. The spiders write down the names of any of the fly Patrol that they may see. Similarly, the flies write down the names of any spiders that they may see, and their exact hiding-place.

Camp Fire Yarn
No. 15

ANIMALS

The Calling of Wild Animals
Animals · Birds · Reptiles · Fishing
Insects

SCOUTS IN MANY PARTS of the world use the calls of wild animals and birds for communicating with each other, especially at night or in thick bush, or in fog. But it is also very useful to be able to imitate the calls if you want to watch the habits of the animals. You can begin by calling chickens or by talking to dogs in dog language, and very soon find you can give the angry growl or the playful growl of a dog. Owls, woodpigeons, and curlews are very easily called.

In India, I have seen a tribe of gipsies who eat jackals. Now jackals are some of the most suspicious animals that live. It is very difficult to catch them in a trap, but these gipsies catch them by calling them in this way.

Several men with dogs hide themselves in the grass and bushes round a small field. In the middle of this open place one gipsy imitates the call of the jackals calling to each other. He gets louder and louder till he sounds like a whole pack of jackals coming together, growling and finally tackling each other with violent snapping, snarling, and yelling. At the same time he shakes a bundle of dried leaves, which sounds like the animals dashing about among grass and reeds. Then he flings himself down on the ground, and throws dust up in the air, so that he is completely hidden in it, still growling and fighting.

If any jackal is within sound of this, it comes tearing out of the jungle, and dashes into the dust to join in the fight. When it finds a man there, it comes out again in a hurry. But meantime the dogs have been loosed from all sides, and they quickly catch the jackal and kill it.

Big Game Hunting

William Long in his very interesting book, *Beasts of the Field*, describes how he once called a moose. The moose is a very huge kind of stag, with an ugly, bulging kind of nose. It lives in the forests of North America and Canada, is very hard to get near, and is pretty dangerous when angry.

Long was in a canoe, fishing, when he heard a bull-moose calling in the forest. So just for fun he went ashore and cut a strip of bark off a birch tree and rolled it up cone or trumpet-shaped into a kind of megaphone about fifteen inches long, five inches wide at the larger end, and about an inch or two at the mouth-piece. With this he proceeded to imitate the roaring grunt of the bull-moose. The effect was tremendous. The old moose came tearing down and even went into the water and tried to get at him—and it was only by hard paddling that he got away.

One of the finest sports is the hunting of big game—that is, going after elephants, lions, rhino, wild boar, deer, and those kinds of animals. A fellow has to be a pretty good scout if he hopes to succeed at it.

You get plenty of excitement and plenty of danger too, and all that I have told you about observation and tracking and hiding yourself comes in here. In addition to these, you must know all about animals and their habits and ways.

I said that "hunting" or "going after big game" is one of the

In India, they hunt jackals in a peculiar way: A man imitates the calls of a whole flock of jackals, and shakes dry leaves . . .

161

finest sports. I did not say shooting or killing the game was the finest part, for, as you get to study animals, you get to like them more and more. You will soon find that you don't want to kill them for the

. . . then he flings himself on the ground and throws dust up in the air. The jackal rushes in to join in the fight and is quickly caught.

mere sake of killing. Also the more you see of them the more you see the wonderful work of God in them.

Adventurous Life of Hunting

All the fun of hunting lies in the adventurous life in the jungle, the chance in many cases of the animal hunting *you* instead of you hunting the animal, the interest of tracking it up, stalking it and watching all that it does and learning its habits. The actual shooting the animal that follows is only a very small part of the excitement.

No Scout should ever kill an animal unless there is some real reason for doing so, and in that case he should kill it quickly and effectively, to give it as little pain as possible.

"Shooting" with a Camera

In fact, many big-game hunters nowadays prefer to shoot their game with the camera instead of with the rifle which gives just as interesting results—except when you are hungry. Then you must, of course, kill your game.

My brother was once big-game shooting in East Africa and had very good sport with the camera, living in the wilds, and tracking and stalking and finally snap-shotting elephants, rhinoceroses, and other big animals.

One day he had crept up near to an elephant and had set up his camera and was focusing it, when his bearer cried, "Look out, sir!"

and started to run. My brother turned around and found a great elephant coming for him, only a few yards off. So he just pressed the button, and ran too. The elephant rushed up to the camera, stopped,

PEEP BO!

When big-game shooting with a camera, you must have eyes in the back of your head. Otherwise your game may surprise you.

and seemed to recognize that it was only a camera after all, and smiling at his own irritability lurched off into the jungle again.

Boars and Panthers

The boar is certainly the bravest of all animals. He is the real "King of the Jungle", and the other animals all know it. If you watch a drinking pool in the jungle at night, you will see the animals that come to it all creeping down nervously, looking out in every direction for hidden enemies. But when the boar comes he simply swaggers down with his great head and its shiny tusks swinging from side to side. He cares for nobody, but everybody cares for him. Even a tiger drinking at the pool will give a snarl and sneak quickly out of sight.

I have often lain out on moonlight nights to watch the animals, especially wild boars, in the jungle.

And I have caught and kept a young wild boar and a young panther, and found them most amusing and interesting little beggars. The boar used to live in my garden. He never became really tame, though I got him as a baby.

He would come to me when I called him—but very warily; he would never come to a stranger.

He used to practise the use of his tusks while turning at full speed round an old tree stump in the garden. He would gallop at it and round it in a figure eight continuously for over five minutes at a time, and then fling himself down on his side panting with his exertions.

163

My panther was also a beautiful and delightfully playful beast, and used to go about with me like a dog. But he was very uncertain in his dealings with strangers.

A young panther can be a beautiful and delightfully playful pet.

I think one gets to know more about animals and to understand them better by keeping them as pets at first, and then going and watching them in their wild natural life.

STUDY ANIMALS AT HOME

But before going to study big game in the jungles you must study all animals, wild and tame, at home.

Every Boy Scout ought to know all about the tame animals which he sees every day. And if you live in the country, you ought to know all about grooming, feeding, and watering a horse, about putting him into harness or taking him out of harness and putting him in the stable, and know when he is going lame and should not therefore be worked.

Your Dog

A good dog is the very best companion for a Scout, who need not think himself a really good Scout till he has trained a young dog to do all he wants of him. It requires great patience and kindness, and genuine sympathy with the dog. Dogs are being used frequently for finding lost men and for carrying messages.

A dog is the most human of all animals, and therefore the best companion for a man. He is always courteous, and always ready for a game—full of humour, and very faithful and loving.

Where to Study Animals

Of course a Scout who lives in the country has much better chances of studying animals and birds than in a town.

Still, if you live in a big city there are lots of different kinds of birds in the parks, and there is almost every animal under the sun to be seen alive in zoological gardens.

In smaller towns it is perhaps a little more difficult, but many of them have their Natural History Museum, where a fellow can learn the appearance and names of many animals, and you can do a lot of observing in the parks or by starting a feeding-box for birds at your own window. But, best of all, is to go out into the country whenever you can get a few hours for it, by train, or bicycle, or on your own flat feet, and there stalk animals and birds, and watch what they do, and get to know different kinds and their names, and also what kind of tracks they make on the ground, and, in the case of the birds, their nests and eggs, and so on.

If you are lucky enough to own a camera, you cannot possibly do better than start making a collection of photos of animals and birds. Such a collection is ten times more interesting than the ordinary boy's collection of stamps, or autographs.

Watching Animals

Every animal is interesting to watch, and it is just as difficult to stalk a weasel as it is to stalk a lion.

We are apt to think that all animals are guided in their conduct by instinct—that is, by a sort of idea that is born in them. For

The mother animal teaches her young. This lioness seems to be telling her cubs how to act if a man should come.

instance, we imagine that a young otter swims naturally, directly he is put into water, or that a young deer runs away from a man from a natural inborn fear of him.

Any naturalist will tell you that animals largely owe their cleverness to their mothers, who teach them while they are young. Thus an otter

165

will carry her young upon her back into the water, and after swimming about for a little while, suddenly dive from under them, and leave them struggling in the water. But she will rise near them and help them to swim back to the shore. In this way she gradually teaches them to swim.

I once saw a lioness in East Africa sitting with her three little cubs all in a row watching me approach her. She looked exactly as though she were teaching her young ones how to act in the case of a man coming.

She was evidently saying to them:

"Now, cubbies, I want you all to notice what a white man is like. Then, one by one, you must jump up and skip away, with a whisk of your tail. The moment you are out of sight in the long grass, you must creep and crawl till you have got to leeward (down-wind) of him. Then follow him, always keeping him to windward, so that you can smell whereabouts he is, and he cannot find you."

BIRDS

A man who studies birds is called an ornithologist. Mark Twain, the amusing yet kind-hearted American writer, said:

"There are fellows who write books about birds and love them so

The crows seem to be everywhere with their loud "Caw-caw".

much that they'll go hungry and tired to find a new kind of bird—and kill it.

"They are called 'ornithologers'.

"I could have been an 'ornithologer' myself, because I always loved birds and creatures. And I started out to learn how to be one. I saw a bird sitting on a dead limb of a high tree, singing away with his head tilted back and his mouth open—and before I thought I fired my gun at him. His song stopped all suddenly, and he fell from the branch, limp like a rag, and I ran and picked him up—and he was dead. His body was warm in my hand, and his head rolled about this way and that, like as if his neck was broke, and there was a white skin over his eyes, and one drop of red blood sparkled on the side of his head—and—laws! I couldn't see nothing for the tears. I haven't ever murdered no creature since then that warn't doing me no harm—and I ain't agoing to neither."

Watching Birds

A good Scout is generally a good "ornithologer", as Mark Twain calls him. That is to say, he likes stalking birds and watching all that they do. He discovers, by watching them, where and how they build their nests.

He does not, like some boys, want to go and rob them of their eggs, but he likes to watch how they hatch out their young and teach them to feed themselves and to fly. He gets to know every species of bird by its call and by its way of flying. He knows which birds remain all the year round and which only come at certain seasons, what kind of food they like best, and how they change their plumage, what sort of nests they build, where they build them, and what the eggs are like.

When a young bird falls out of the nest, its parents come to feed it.

A good deal of natural history can be studied by watching birds in your neighbourhood, especially if you feed them daily in winter. It is interesting to note, for instance, their different ways of singing, how some sing to make love to the hen birds, while others, like the barn-door cock, crow or sing to challenge another to fight. A herring gull makes an awful ass of himself when he tries to sing and to show himself off to the ladies, and an old crow is not much better.

It is also interesting to watch how the young birds hatch out.

Some appear naked, with no feathers, and their eyes shut and their mouths open. Others, with fluffy kinds of feathers all over them, are full of life and energy. Young moorhens, for instance, swim as soon as they come out of the egg, young chickens start running about within a very few minutes, while a young sparrow is useless for days, and has to be fed and coddled by his parents.

William Long, a famous author and naturalist wrote:

"Watch, say, a crow's nest. One day you will see the mother bird standing near the nest and stretching her wings over her little ones. Presently the young stand up and stretch their wings in imitation. That is the first lesson.

"Next day, perhaps, you will see the old bird lifting herself to tip-toe and holding herself there by vigorous flapping. Again the young imitate, and soon learn that their wings are a power to sustain them. Next day you may see both parent birds passing from branch to branch about the nest, aided by their wings in the long jumps. The little ones join and play, and lo! they have learned to fly without even knowing that they were being taught."

A good many birds are almost dying out, because so many boys bag all their eggs when they find their nests.

FISHES AND FISHING

Every Scout ought to be able to fish in order to get food for himself. A tenderfoot who starved on the bank of a river full of fish would look very silly, yet it might happen to one who had never learned to catch fish.

Fishing brings out a lot of the points in Scouting, especially if you fish with a fly. To be successful you must know about the habits and ways of the fish, what kind of haunt he frequents, in what kind of weather he feeds and at what time of day, which kind of food he likes best, how far off he can see you, and so on. Without knowing these, you can fish away until you are blue in the face and never catch one.

A fish generally has his own particular haunt in the stream, and when once you discover a fish at home you can go and creep near and watch what he does.

Then you have to be able to tie very special knots with delicate gut, which is a bit of a puzzler to any boy whose fingers are all thumbs.

I will only give you a few here, but there are many others. These are drawn half tied, just before pulling tight.

Here is the overhand loop:

To join a line to a loop, do it this way:

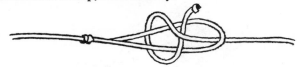

Much the same kind of knot is used to tie a hook to a line:

To join two lengths of line together, even when of different thickness, follow this method:

And you have to have infinite patience. Your line gets caught up in bushes and reeds, or in your clothes—or when it can't find any other body it ties up in a knot round itself. Well, it's no use getting angry with it. There are only two things to do—the first is to grin, and the second is to set to work very leisurely to undo it. Then you will have loads of disappointments in losing fish through the line breaking, or other mishaps. But remember they happen to everybody who begins fishing, and are the troubles that in the end make it so very enjoyable when you get them.

When you catch your fish do as I do—only keep those you specially want for food or as specimens, put back the others the moment you have landed them. The prick of the hook in their leathery mouth does not hurt them for long, and they swim off quite happily to enjoy life in their water again.

If you use a dry fly, that is, keeping your fly sitting on top of the water instead of sunk under the surface, you have really to stalk your fish, just as you would deer or any other game, for a trout is very sharp-eyed and shy.

Trout fishing demands great skill and cunning. A trout can put up a grand fight, and you must be alert to catch him.

You can also catch fish by netting, or as Scouts often have to do, by spearing them with a very sharp three-pronged spear. I have done it many a time, but it requires practice.

REPTILES

Of course a Scout ought to know about snakes, because in almost all wild countries you come across plenty of them and many of them are dangerous.

Snakes sometimes creep into tents and under blankets, or into boots. You will always notice an old hand in snake country look very carefully through his blankets before he turns in at night, and shake out his boots in the morning before putting them on. I even find myself doing it now at home, just from habit.

Snakes don't usually like crawling over anything rough. So in India you often construct a kind of path, made of sharp, jagged stone, all round a house to prevent snakes crawling into it from the garden.

And on the prairie, hunters lay a hair rope on the ground in a circle round their blankets.

A hair rope has so many tiny spikes sticking out of it that it tickles the snake's tummy to such an extent he cannot go over it.

I used to catch snakes when I was at school by using a long stick with a small fork at the end of it. When I saw a snake I stalked him, jammed the fork down on his neck, and then tied him up the stick with strips of old handkerchief, and carried him back to sell to anybody who wanted a pet. But they are not good things to make pets of as a rule, because so many people have a horror of them, and it is not fair, therefore, to have them about in a house where people might get frightened by them.

Poisonous Snakes

Poisonous snakes carry their poison in a small bag inside their mouths. They usually have two fangs or long pointed teeth, which are on a kind of hinge. The fangs lie flat along the snake's gums till he gets angry and wants to kill something, then they stand on end, and he dives his head forward and strikes them into his enemy. As he does so, the poison passes out of the poison bag, or gland, into the two holes in the skin made by the fangs. This poison then gets into the veins of the man who has been bitten and is carried by the blood all over the body in a few seconds, unless steps are at once taken to stop it by binding the veins up and sucking the wound. Snake poison does no harm when swallowed.

INSECTS

Insects are very interesting animals to collect, or to watch, or to photograph.

Also for a Scout who fishes, or studies birds or reptiles, it is most important that he should know a certain amount about the insects which are their favourite foods at different times of the year or different hours of the day.

About bees alone whole books have been written—for they have wonderful powers in making their honeycomb, in finding their way for miles, sometimes as far as six miles, to find the right kind of flowers for giving them the sugary juice for making honey, and getting back with it to the hive. They are quite a model community, for they respect their queen and kill those who won't work.

Then some insects are useful as food. Locusts—a big kind of grasshopper—are eaten in India and South Africa. We were very glad to get a flight or two of them over Mafeking. When they settled on the ground we beat them down, with empty sacks, as they turned to rise. They were then dried in the sun and pounded up and eaten. Ants make a substitute for salt.

Ants as Life Savers

I have known another case of ants being useful—in fact they were not only useful but saved the lives of several men.

These men were a party of scientific professors who were hiking in the wilds of Australia, searching for rare plants and animals, reptiles and bugs.

Out in the desert they ran out of water. For hours they struggled on, maddened with thirst and weak with exhaustion. It looked as though, like many explorers before them, they would collapse and die. Luckily, to their great relief, a small aborigine girl appeared.

A small aborigine girl came to the aid of the scientific professors who ran out of water when hiking in the wilds of Australia.

They made a sign to her that they were dying of thirst and wanted her to go and fetch water.

In reply she pointed to a string of ants which were climbing up a baobab tree. (This tree has a great fat hollow trunk which thus forms a sort of water tank.)

The little girl picked a long stalk of dried grass and climbed up to a little hole in the trunk which the ants were running into. She put one end of the straw down this hole and the other end into her mouth and sucked up water.

In this way the wild little imp of the desert taught the learned gentlemen a valuable bit of knowledge which with all their school and college education they did not possess.

I hope that had a Scout been with them he would have been wise to the idea, or at any rate would have used his eyes and wits and would have noticed the ants at their work and guessed why they were using that hole in the tree.

Watching Insects

It doesn't sound very exciting to watch insects, but the great French naturalist, Henri Fabre, the son of peasants, spent days in studying the lives and habits of insects, and found out all kinds of curious things about them. He became world famous for his studies.

Some insects are our friends—such as the silkworm and the ladybird or "ladybug"—but others are our enemies. They destroy vegetables and attack flowers. You all know how the mosquito spreads such dangerous diseases as malaria and yellow fever. And I need not remind you of how the house-fly can carry disease germs— that is why, in camp as well as at home, all food should be kept carefully covered, and no dirt or rubbish be allowed to lie about.

PATROL PRACTICES IN ANIMAL OBSERVATION

In the country, send out the Scouts to find out by observation, and to report on such points as these:

How does a wild rabbit dig its hole? When a lot of rabbits are alarmed, does a rabbit merely run because the others do, or does he look around to see what is the danger before he goes?

Does a woodpecker break the bark away to get at insects on a tree trunk, or does he pick them out of holes, or how does he get at them?

Does a trout when disturbed by people passing along the bank go up or down stream? Does he go away altogether or return to his place?

If in a large town, take the Scouts to the Zoological Garden or to the Natural History Museum. About half a dozen animals would be quite enough to study for one day.

Get Patrols to find out all about their Patrol animals. Learn their calls. Discover their haunts, tracks and habits. If they are not local animals, study them in a museum or zoo.

Get each Patrol to keep an outdoors log for a month, then compare results. Each Scout should contribute something to the log, such as a note of something seen or a sketch of a bird or animal. Or have a nature scrap book, with cuttings from newspapers and magazines of nature photographs, notes on outdoor life, nature calendars, etc.

Encourage the taking of photographs. Even the cheapest camera can be used for showing the surroundings in which each kind of bird makes its nest.

Bird-feeding can be practised both in town and country, particularly in the winter. A window-sill feeding-tray in town can

In the country you can make a "club" for the birds, with a "dining-room", a basin of fresh water, and branches to lounge on.

attract many different birds. The provision of water in summer is also important.

———

Build up a Patrol library of well-illustrated books for recognizing animals, birds, reptiles, fish and insects.

———

Try to get a pair of good field glasses for the Patrol so that the Scouts can learn the fun of watching birds and animals. Also introduce the Scouts to the use of the magnifying glass, and, if possible, the microscope. Any instrument attracts a boy, and the new world it opens up will fascinate many of the Scouts.

Camp Fire Yarn

No. 16

PLANTS

Trees and Their Leaves
Edible Plants · Plant Observation

A BACKWOODSMAN WHO LIVES FAR AWAY from human habitations in the deep forests must know about useful trees and other plants.

A Scout often has to describe the country he has been through. If he reports that it is "well wooded", it might be of great importance for the reader of his report to know what kind of trees the woods were composed of.

For instance, if the wood were of fir or larch trees it would mean you could get poles for building bridges. If it were coco palm trees, you know you could get nuts for eating and "milk" for drinking. Willow trees mean water close by. Pine or sugar bush or gum trees means lots of good fuel.

A Scout should therefore make a point of learning the names and appearances of the trees in his country.

He should get hold of a leaf of each kind and compare it with the leaf on the tree, and then get to know the general shape and appearance of each kind of tree, so he can recognize it at a distance—not only in summer, but also in winter. Some trees have typical shapes—as the Oak, Elm and Poplar in the sketches. See if you can find others, say of Pine, Birch, Willow, and so on.

Guardian of the Woods

As a Scout, you are the guardian of the woods. A Scout never damages a tree by hacking it with his knife or axe. It does not take long to fell a tree, but it takes many years to grow one, so a Scout cuts down a tree for a good reason only—not just for the sake of using his axe. For every tree felled, two should be planted.

Learn to sketch the leaves and outline of trees, such as this Oak.

Firewood

It is seldom necessary to chop trees even for firewood, as usually there is plenty of dead wood lying about on the ground. Or a dead branch can be broken off a tree. Dead wood burns far more easily than green wood.

Generally speaking, *soft woods*—Pine, Fir, Spruce and Larch—make good kindling and give quick fires for short jobs such as boiling water. *Hard woods*—Oak, Beech, Maples and others—give lasting fires with many embers for longer jobs such as roasting, stewing and baking.

In America they say, "One tree may make a million matches—one match may destroy a million trees." A Scout is very careful about fires. When he uses one he sees that it is completely out before he leaves the place, by dousing the last spark with water.

OTHER PLANTS

You ought to know what plants are useful to you in providing you with food.

Supposing you were out in a jungle without any food and knew nothing about plants—you might die of starvation or of poisoning, from not knowing which fruits or roots were wholesome and which were dangerous to eat.

Edible Plants

There are numbers of berries, nuts, roots, barks, and leaves that

176

make good eating. Find out which of these are found near your camp site, and try to make a camp meal of them.

Crops of different kinds of corn and seed, vegetable roots, and many grasses are also edible. Certain kinds of moss are used for food. Some types of seaweed can also be eaten.

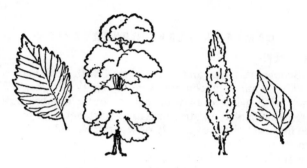

European Elm has a distinctive form. So has Lombardy Poplar.

You will want to be able to recognize the common flowers of the field and wood. Some of these are related to our garden flowers, and have some of the same beauty. Others are herbs which are useful for flavouring in cooking and for medicine.

PATROL PRACTICES IN PLANT OBSERVATION

Take out the Scouts to get specimens of leaves, fruits, or blossoms of various trees and shrubs, and observe the shape and nature of trees both in summer and in winter.

Collect leaves of different trees. Let Scouts make tracings of them and write the name of the tree on each.

In the country have Scouts examine crops in all stages of their growth, so that they know pretty well by sight what kind of crop is coming up.

Find all the local wild plants that may be used for food.

Make a collection of leaf impressions: get some carbon copying paper, lay the leaf, vein side downwards, on the carbon, place a piece of thin paper on top and rub the whole firmly. Remove the paper and pick up the leaf. Now lay it, again vein side downwards, on the paper you are using for the impressions; again place a piece of paper on top and rub firmly. This should give a very clear impression of the leaf.

GAMES IN PLANT OBSERVATION

What Is It?

Two Scouts start out and make a trail with trail marks. They have decided upon an uncommon sign to signify "What is it?", such as a circle with a line drawn through it, and a number next to it.

The remainder of the Patrol or Troop start out, say, ten minutes after the first two, either as a body or separately, and take notebooks and pencils with them.

The game consists of entering in their notebooks the "What is it?"s that have been noticed and write down the nature of the article closest to the sign, such as "Oak", "Dandelion", etc.

Marks should be given according to the number of signs observed and for the correct answers to the "What is it?"s.

Besides being very interesting, this game develops observation, strengthens the memory and is good botany instruction.

Plant Race

The Patrol Leader starts off with his Scouts, either cycling or on foot, to go in any direction they like, to get a specimen of any ordered plant. This may be a sprig of yew, a shoot of holly, a horseshoe mark from a horse chestnut tree, a briar rose, or something similar that will tax their knowledge of plants, test their memory as to where they noticed one of the kind required, and make them quick in getting there and back.

ENDURANCE FOR SCOUTS

Camp Fire Yarn
No. 17

HOW TO GROW STRONG

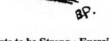

BP.

**Need for Scouts to be Strong · Exercises
Care of Body · Nose · Ears · Eyes
Teeth · Nails · Practices**

A SCOUT LAY SICK IN HOSPITAL in India with that dangerous disease called cholera. The doctor told the servant attending him that the only chance of saving his life was to warm up his feet and keep the blood moving in his body by constantly rubbing him.

The moment the doctor's back was turned, the servant gave up rubbing and squatted down to have a quiet smoke.

The poor patient, though he could not speak, understood all that was going on, and he was so enraged at the conduct of the attendant that he resolved then and there that he would get well if only to give the servant a lesson. Having made up his mind to get well he *got* well.

A Scout saying is "Never say die till you're dead"—and if he acts up to this, it will pull him out of many a bad place when everything seems to be going wrong for him. It means a mixture of pluck, patience, and strength, which we call "endurance".

A Sample of Endurance
The great South African hunter and scout, F. C. Selous, gave a good example of scouts' endurance on a hunting expedition in

G   179

Barotseland, north of the Zambesi River, some years ago. In the middle of the night his camp was suddenly attacked by a hostile tribe, that fired into it at close range and charged in.

He and his small party scattered at once into the darkness and hid themselves away in the long grass. Selous himself had snatched up his rifle and a few cartridges and got safely into the grass. But he could not find any of his men, and, seeing that the enemy had taken possession of his camp, and that there were still a few hours

Animals know how to exercise to keep strong. A horse left to itself seems to do its jumping for the love of the sport.

of darkness before him in which to make his escape, he started off southward, using the stars of the Southern Cross as his guide.

He crept past an outpost of the enemy whom he overheard talking, then swam across a river and finally got well away, only dressed in a shirt, shorts, and shoes. For the next few days and nights he kept walking southward, frequently hiding to avoid the enemy. He shot deer for food.

But one night, going into what he thought was a friendly village, he had his rifle stolen from him, and was again a fugitive, without any means of protecting himself or of getting food. However, he was not one to give in while there was a change of life left, and he pushed on and on till at length he reached a place where he met some of his men who had also escaped. After further tramping they got safely back into friendly country.

But what a terrible time they must have had!

Three weeks had passed since the attack, and the great part of that time Selous had been alone—hunted, starving, bitterly cold at night, and in sweltering heat by day.

None but a scout with extraordinary endurance could have lived through it, but then Selous was a man who as a lad had made himself strong by care and exercise. And he kept up his pluck all the time.

It shows you that if you want to get through such adventures safely when you are a man and not be a "slopper," you must train yourself to be strong, healthy, and active as a lad.

The Wrong Way to Endurance

A man told me recently with great pride that he was teaching his son endurance by making him do long marches and bicycle runs. I told the man that he was likely to do just the opposite for his boy —that the way for a lad to gain endurance was not by trying to perform feats, *as these would very probably injure his heart and break him down*, but by making himself strong and healthy, by good feeding and moderate exercise, so that when he became a man and his muscles were all "set" he could *then* go through hardships and strains where another weaker man would fail.

EXERCISES AND THEIR OBJECTS

There is a great deal of nonsense done in the way of bodily exercises —so many people seem to think that their only object is to make huge muscle. But to make yourself strong and healthy it is necessary to begin with your inside and to get the blood into good order and the heart to work well. That is the secret of the whole thing, and exercises of the body do it for you. This is the way:

(a) MAKE THE HEART STRONG to pump the blood properly to every part of the body, and so to build up flesh, bone, and muscle.
Exercise: "Wrist Pushing" and "The Struggle". See pages 193 and 194.

(b) MAKE THE LUNGS STRONG to provide the blood with fresh air.
Exercise: "Deep Breathing". See page 183.

(c) MAKE THE SKIN PERSPIRE to get rid of the dirt from the blood.
Exercise: Bath, or *dry* rub with a *damp* towel every day.

181

(d) MAKE THE STOMACH WORK to feed the blood.
Exercise: "Cone", or "Body Bending", and "Twisting".
See pages 184 and 185.

(e) MAKE THE BOWELS ACTIVE to remove the remains of
food and dirt from the body.
Exercise: "Body Bending" and "Kneading the Abdomen".
Drink plenty of good water. Regular daily "rear".

(f) WORK MUSCLES IN EACH PART OF THE BODY to
make the blood circulate to that part, and so increase your
strength.
Exercise: Running and Walking, and special exercises of
special muscles, such as "Wrist Pushing" (page 193), etc.

The secret of keeping well and healthy is to keep your blood
clean and active. These different exercises will do that if you will
use them every day.

The blood thrives on simple good food, plenty of exercise, plenty
of fresh air, cleanliness of the body both *inside* and out, and proper
rest of body and mind at intervals.

SIX EXERCISES FOR HEALTH

It is possible for almost any boy, even though he may be small and
weak, to make himself into a strong and healthy man if he takes the
trouble to do a few body exercises every day. They only take about
ten minutes, and do not require any kind of apparatus.

They should be practised every morning, the first thing on getting
up, and every evening before going to bed. It is best to do them with
little or no clothing on, and in the open air, or close to an open
window. The value of these exercises is much increased if you think
of the object of each move while you are doing it, and if you are very
particular to breathe the air in through your nose and to breathe out
through your mouth.

Here are some good exercises. It strengthens the toes and feet to
do them barefooted.

1. **For Head and Neck**—Rub the head, face, and neck firmly
over several times with the palms and fingers of both hands. Thumb
the muscles of the neck and throat.

Brush your hair, clean your teeth, wash out your mouth and
nose, drink a cup of cold water, and then go on with the following
exercises.

The movements should all be done as slowly as possible.

2. **For Chest**—From upright position bend to the front, arms stretched downwards, with back of the hands together in front of the knees. Breathe out.

Raise the hands gradually over the head and lean back as far as possible, drawing a deep breath *through the nose* as you do—that is,

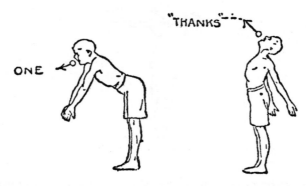

In the pictures, an arrow means drawing in the breath through the nose; an arrow with a circle means breathing out through the mouth.

drinking God's air into your lungs and blood. Lower the arms gradually to the sides, breathing out the word "Thanks" (to God) through the mouth.

Lastly, bend forward again, breathing out the last bit of breath in you, and saying the number of times you have done it, in order to keep count.

Repeat this exercise twelve times.

Remember while carrying it out that the object of the exercise is to develop shoulders, chest, heart, and breathing apparatus inside you.

Deep breathing is important for bringing fresh air into the lungs to be put into the blood, and for developing the size of the chest, but it should be done carefully, and not overdone. It is done by sucking air in through the nose until it swells out your ribs as far as possible, especially at the back; then, after a pause, you breathe out the air slowly and gradually through the mouth until you have not a scrap of air left in you, then after a pause draw in your breath again through the nose as before.

Singing develops simultaneously proper breathing and development of heart, lungs, chest, and throat, together with dramatic feeling in rendering the song.

3. **For Stomach**—Standing upright, send out both arms, fingers

extended, straight to the front, then slowly swing round to the right from the hips without moving the feet, and point the right arm as far round behind you as you can, keeping both arms level with, or a little higher than, the shoulders. Then, after a pause, swing slowly round as far as you can to the left. Repeat this a dozen times.

This exercise is to move the inside organs such as liver and intestines, and help their work, as well as to strengthen the outside muscles round the ribs and stomach.

While carrying out this exercise, the breathing should be carefully regulated. Breathe in through the nose (not through the mouth), while pointing to the right rear; breathe out through the mouth as you come round and point to the left rear, and at the same time count aloud the number of the swing—or, what is better, thinking of it as part of your morning prayer with God, say aloud: "Bless Tim", "Bless Father", and any of your family or friends in turn.

When you have done this six times to the right, change the breathing to the other side: breathe in when pointing to the left rear, and breathe out to the right.

4. **For Trunk**—"Cone Exercise".—Standing at the "Alert", raise both hands as high as possible over the head, and link fingers. Lean backwards, then sway the arms very slowly round in the direction of a cone, so that the hands make a wide circle above and around

the body, the body turning from the hips, and leaning over to one side, then to the front, then to the other side, and then back. This is to exercise the muscles of the waist and stomach.

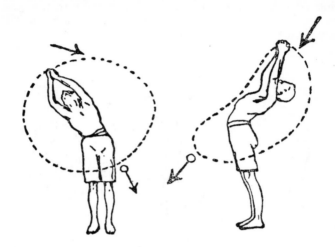

Repeat, say, six times to either hand. With the eyes you should be trying to see all that goes on behind you during the movement.

A meaning attached to this exercise, which you should think of while carrying it out, is this. The clasping hands mean that you are knit together with friends—that is, other Scouts—all round you as you sway round to the right, left, before, and behind you; in every direction you are bound to friends. Love and friendship are the gift of God, so when you are making the upward move you look to heaven and drink in the air and the good feeling, which you then breathe out to your comrades all round.

5. **For Lower Body and Back of Legs**—Like every one of the exercises, this is, at the same time, a breathing exercise by which the lungs and heart are developed, and the blood made strong and healthy. You simply stand up and reach as high as you can sky-wards, and backwards, and then bend forward and downward till your fingers touch your toes, *without bending your knees*.

Stand with the feet slightly apart, touch your head with both hands, and look up into the sky, leaning back as far as you can, as in Fig. 1 on page 186.

If you mingle prayer with your exercises, as I described to you before, you can, while looking up in this way, say to God: "I am yours from top to toe", and drink in God's air (through your nose, not through the mouth). Then reach both hands upwards as far as possible (Fig. 2), breathe out the number of the turn that you are doing, and bend slowly forward and downward, knees stiff, till you reach your toes with your finger-tips (Fig. 3).

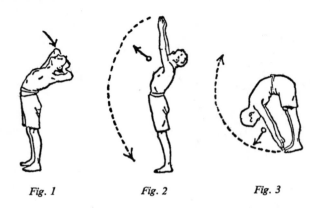

Fig. 1   *Fig. 2*   *Fig. 3*

Tuck in the small of your back while on the downward bend.

Then, keeping arms and knees still stiff, gradually raise the body to the first position again, and repeat the exercise a dozen times.

The object of this exercise is, however, not to touch the toes, but to massage the stomach. If you find you cannot touch your toes do not force yourself to do it, and, more especially, do not jerk yourself or allow anyone else to force you down. The value of the exercise lies in the upward stroke as against the downward stroke.

6. **For Legs, Feet and Toes**—Stand barefooted, at the position of "Alert". Put the hands on the hips, stand on tip-toe, turn the knees outwards, and bend them slowly till you gradually sink down to a squatting position, keeping the heels off the ground the whole time.

Then gradually raise the body and come to the first position again.

Repeat this a dozen times.

The small of the back must be tucked in. The breath should be drawn in through the nose as the body rises, and counted out, through the mouth, as the body sinks. The weight of the body must be on the toes all the time, and the knees turned outwards to make you balance more easily. While performing the practice you should remember that its object is to strengthen the thighs, calves, and toe-sinews, as well as to exercise the stomach, so if you practice it several times during the day, at any odd moments, it will do you all the more good.

And you can connect with this exercise, since it makes you alternately stand up and squat down, that whether you are standing or sitting, at work or resting, you will hold yourself together (as your hands on your hips are doing), and make yourself do what is right.

These exercises are not merely intended as a way of passing time, but really to help a fellow to grow big as well as to grow strong.

CLIMBING

Every boy likes climbing, and if you stick to it and become really good at it, you will go on at it forever.

Most of the great mountain-climbers began as boys climbing up ropes and poles, and then trees. After that, a long way after—because if you haven't had lots of practice and strengthened your muscles you probably would tumble, and attend a funeral as the chief performer—you take up rock climbing, and so on to mountain climbing.

It is glorious sport teeming with adventure, but it needs strength in all your limbs, pluck, determination, and endurance. But these all come with practice.

It is most important for mountain climbing to be able to keep your balance and to place your feet nimbly and quickly where you want them. For this there is nothing like the game of "Walking the Plank" along a plank set up on edge, or "stepping stones" laid about on the ground at varying distances and angles to each other.

*Tree climbing is great exercise. Fasten a thick rope over a strong branch,
and try different ways of climbing it.*

When I was a fairly active young bounder I went in for the vigorous kind of folk dancing. It amused people at our regimental theatricals and it was good exercise for me. But I came to realize a new value in it later on when I had to carry out some scouting in service against the Matabele in South Africa.

I had climbed into their mountain fastnesses in the Matopo Hills and was discovered by them. I had to run for it. Their great aim was to catch me alive as they wanted to give me something more special in the execution line than a mere shot through the head—they had

*This is a home-made camp gymnasium. Build it from strong poles and ropes
for the lashings—and there you are! There are no regular exercises; you make
up your own stunts.*

some form of unpleasant torture in view for me. So when I ran, I ran heartily.

The mountain consisted largely of huge granite boulders piled one on another. My running consisted mostly in leaping down from one boulder to another, and then it was that the balance and foot management gained in folk dancing came to my aid. As I skipped down the mountain I found myself out-distancing my pursuers with the greatest of ease. These, being plains men, did not understand rock-trotting and were laboriously slithering and clambering down the boulders after me. So I got away. And with the confidence thus

Training in folk dancing was of great help in evading the Matabele.

engendered, I paid many successful visits to the mountains after this.

NOSE

A Scout must be able to smell well, in order to find his enemy by night. If he always breathes through the nose, and not through the mouth, this helps him considerably. But there are other reasons more important than that for always breathing through the nose. An American once wrote a book called *Shut your Mouth and Save your Life*, and he showed how the Red Indians for a long time had adopted that method with their children to the extent of tying up their jaws at night, to ensure their breathing through the nose only.

Breathing through the nose prevents many disease germs from getting from the air into the throat and lungs.

For a Scout, nose-breathing is also specially useful. By keeping the mouth shut you prevent yourself from getting thirsty when you are doing hard work. And also at night, breathing through the nose prevents snoring, and snoring is a dangerous thing if you are sleeping anywhere in enemy country. Therefore practise keeping your mouth shut and breathing through your nose at all times.

EARS

A Scout must be able to hear well. Generally the ears are very delicate, and if they are once damaged you may become incurably deaf.

People are too apt to fiddle about with their ears in cleaning them, by putting the corners of handkerchiefs, hairpins, and so on into them, and also stuffing them up with hard cotton wool. All of this is dangerous because the drum of the ear is a very sensitive tightly-stretched skin which is easily damaged. Many children have had the drums of their ears permanently injured by getting a box on the ear.

EYES

A Scout, of course, must have particularly good eyesight—he must be able to see a long way off. By practising your eyes in looking at things at a great distance, they will grow stronger. While you are young you should save your eyes as much as possible. Avoid reading by poor light, and sit with your side to the light when doing any work during the day. If you sit facing the light it strains your eyes.

Eye strain is a common failure with growing boys, although very often they do not know it. Headaches come frequently from the eyes being strained. If a boy frowns, it is generally a sign of eye strain.

A Scout, besides having good eyesight, must be able to tell the colour of things which he sees. Colour blindness is a trouble from which some boys suffer. It takes away a pleasure from them, and it makes them almost useless for certain trades and professions. For instance, a railway signalman or engine-driver or a sailor would not be much good if he couldn't tell the difference between red and green.

It can sometimes be overcome. A way of doing this, if you find you are rather colour blind, is to get a collection of little bits of wool, or paper, of different colours, and pick out which you think is red, blue, yellow, green, and so on, and then get someone to tell you where you were right and where wrong. Then go at it again, and in time you will find yourself improving, until you have no difficulty in recognizing the colours.

TEETH

A would-be recruit came up to an Army recruiting officer to be enlisted. He was found to be a sufficiently strong and well-made man, but when the doctors examined his teeth they found that these were

A bushman makes a simple tooth brush by fraying the end of a dry stick, about six inches long.

in bad condition, and he was told that he could not be accepted as a soldier. To this he replied: "But, sir, that seems hard lines. Surely we don't have to eat the enemy when we've killed them, do we?"

Good teeth depend upon how much you look after them when you are young, which means that you should keep them carefully clean. Brush them at least twice a day—when you get up in the morning and when you go to bed, both inside and out, with a tooth-brush and tooth paste. Rinse them with water, if possible, after every meal.

Scouts in the jungle cannot always find tooth-brushes, but they make substitutes out of dry sticks, which they fray out at the end, and make an imitation of a brush.

NAILS

Soldiers, as well as other people, often suffer great pain and lameness from the nail of their big toe growing down into the toe at the side. This is generally caused by permitting the nail to grow too long, until by pressure of the shoe it is driven to grow sideways into the toe. So every Scout will be careful to cut his toenails frequently, every week or ten days. They should be cut square across the top, not rounded, and with sharp scissors.

Finger-nails should also be cut about once a week with sharp scissors, to keep them in good order. Biting the nails is not good for them.

PATROL PRACTICES IN HEALTH

Example will teach much—not just the Patrol Leader's personal actions but the example given by having open windows when meeting indoors, and open tent doors when camping.

Health can best be taught in camp where there is time and opportunity to give close attention to cleanliness and sound habits.

In camp, remember the importance of rest and plenty of sound sleep. There should be an hour's rest after the main meal.

Teach the six exercises given in the Yarn, but don't use them as a drill. Encourage the Scouts to do them daily.

Give each Scout a card on which he can keep a record of his physical measurements. Make arrangements for these measurements to be taken every three months.

GAMES TO DEVELOP STRENGTH

Boxing, wrestling, rowing, swimming, skipping, cock-fighting, are all valuable health aids to developing strength, but climbing is best of all.

Wrist Pushing

Stand with both your arms to the front about level with the waist, cross your wrists so that one hand has knuckles up, the other knuckles down. Clench the fists.

Now make the lower hand press upwards and make the upper hand press downwards.

Press as hard as you can with both wrists gradually, and only after great resistance let the lower push the upper one upwards till opposite your forehead, then let the upper press the lower down, the lower one resisting all the time.

These two exercises, although they sound small and simple, develop most muscles in your body if carried out with all your might. They should not be carried on too long at a time, but should be done at frequent intervals during the day for a minute or so.

Wrist Pushing by Two Boys

Two boys face each other. Each puts out the wrist nearest to his opponent, at arm's length, presses it against the other's wrist, and tries to turn him round backwards.

Staff Tossing

With your right hand grasp your staff near the butt and hold it upright. Then toss it straight up in the air a short distance at first, and catch it with the left hand near the butt as it comes down. Toss it straight up again with the left and catch it with the right, and so on, till you can do it one hundred times without dropping it.

Follow the Leader

The leader goes ahead, doing different exercises. The others follow him, doing everything he does.

Leg pushing between two boys helps to strengthen the leg muscles.

The Struggle

Two players face each other about a yard apart, stretch arms out sideways, lock fingers of both hands, and lean towards each other till their chests touch, push chest to chest and see who can drive the other back to the wall of the room or on to a goal line.

"The Struggle"

Camp Fire Yarn
No. 18

HEALTH-GIVING HABITS

**Keep Clean · Don't Smoke · Don't Drink
Keep Pure · Rise Early · Smile**

ALL THE GREAT PEACE SCOUTS who have succeeded in exploring or hunting expeditions in wild countries have only been able to get on by knowing how to keep themselves and others healthy. They had to, because diseases, accidents, and wounds might be suffered by them or their men, and they couldn't find doctors in the jungles to cure them. A Scout who does not know something about taking care of himself would never get on at all; he might just as well stay at home for all the good he will be.

Therefore practise keeping healthy yourself, and then you will be able to show others how to keep themselves healthy too. In this way you can do many good turns.

Also, if you know how to look after yourself you need never have to take medicines. The great English poet, Dryden, in his poem, *Cymon and Iphigenia*, wrote that it was better to trust to fresh air and exercise than to pay doctors' bills to keep yourself healthy:

> *"Better to hunt in fields for health unbought*
> *Than fee the doctor for a nauseous draught:*
> *The wise, for cure, on exercise depend;*
> *God never made his work for man to mend."*

KEEP YOURSELF CLEAN

If you cut your hand when it is dirty, it is very likely to fester, and to become very sore. But if your hand is quite clean and freshly washed, no harm will come of it—it heals quickly.

Cleaning your skin helps to clean your blood. Doctors say that half the good of exercise is lost if you do not have a bath immediately after it.

It may not be always possible for you to get a bath every day, but you can at any rate rub yourself over with a wet towel, or scrub yourself with a dry one, and you ought not to miss a single day in doing this if you want to keep fit and well.

You should also keep clean in your clothing—your underclothing as well as that which shows.

TOMMY THE TENDERFOOT No. 9   TOMMY TRIES SMOKING
Tommy thought smoking would give him some fun.
But he quickly wished he had never begun.

And to be healthy and strong, you *must* keep your blood healthy and clean inside you. This is done by breathing in lots of pure, fresh air, by deep breathing, and by clearing out all dirty matter from inside your stomach, which is done by having a "rear" daily, without fail; many people are the better for having it twice a day. If there is any difficulty about it one day, drink plenty of good water, especially before and just after breakfast, and practise body-twisting exercises, and all should be well. Never start work in the morning without some sort of food inside you.

SMOKING

Every Scout knows the Scout Law. But there is an extra point to that Law which is not written but is understood by every Scout. It is this: "A Scout is not a fool", and that is why Scouts do not smoke while they are still growing boys.

Any boy can smoke—it is not such a very wonderful thing to do. But a Scout will not do it because he is not such a fool. He knows that when a lad smokes before he is fully grown up it may weaken his heart, and the heart is the most important organ in a lad's body. It pumps the blood all over him to form flesh, bone, and muscle. If the heart does not do its work the boy cannot grow to be healthy. Any Scout knows that smoking spoils his sense of smell, which is of greatest importance to him for scouting on active service.

A large number of the best sportsmen, soldiers, sailors, and others, do not smoke—they find they can do better without it.

No boy ever began smoking because he liked it, but generally because either he feared being chaffed by the other boys as afraid to smoke, or because he thought that by smoking he would look like a great man—when all the time he only looks like a little ass.

So just make up your mind for yourself that you don't mean to smoke till you are grown up, and stick to it. That will show you to be a man much more than any slobbering about with a half-smoked cigarette between your lips. The other fellows will in the end respect you much more, and will probably in many cases secretly follow your lead.

DRINKING

A soldierly-looking man came up to me one night and brought out his discharge certificates, showing that he had served with me in South Africa. He said he could get no work, and he was starving— every man's hand was against him, apparently because he was a soldier. My nose and eyes told me in a moment another tale, and that was the real cause of his distress.

A stale smell of tobacco and beer hung about his clothes, his finger-tips were yellow with cigarette smoke, he had even taken some kind of scented lozenge to try to hide the whisky smell in his breath. No wonder nobody would employ him, or give him more money to drink with, for that was all that he would do with money if he got it.

Much of the poverty and distress in the world is brought about by men getting into the habit of wasting their money and time on drink.

And a great deal of crime, and also of illness, and even madness, is due to the habit of drinking too much.

The old saying, "Strong drink makes weak men", is a very true one.

It would be simply impossible for a man who drinks to be a Scout. Keep off liquor from the very first, and make up your mind to have nothing to do with it. Water, tea, or coffee are quite good enough drinks for quenching your thirst or for picking you up at any time, or, if it is very hot, lemonade or a squeeze of lemon are much better refreshment.

On the Hike

A good Scout trains himself pretty well to do without liquid. It is very much a matter of habit. If you keep your mouth shut when walking or running, or keep a pebble in your mouth (which also makes you keep your mouth shut), you do not get thirsty as you do when you go along with your mouth open, sucking in the air and dry dust. But you must also be in good hard condition. If you are fat from want of exercise, you are sure to get thirsty and want to drink every mile. If you do not let yourself drink, the thirst wears off after a short time. If you keep drinking water on the line of march, or while playing games, it helps to tire you and spoils your wind.

"Standing Treat"

It is often difficult to avoid taking strong drinks when you meet friends who want to treat you, but they generally like you all the better if you say you don't want anything, as then they don't have to pay for it. If they insist you can take something quite harmless. Wasters like to stand about a bar talking and sipping—generally at the other fellow's expense—but they are wasters, and it is as well to keep out of their company, if you want to get on and have a good time.

Remember that drink never yet cured a single trouble—it only makes troubles grow worse and worse the more you go on with it. It makes a man forget for a few hours what exactly his trouble is, but it also makes him forget everything else. If he has wife and children, it makes him forget that his duty is to work and help them out of their difficulties, instead of making himself all the more unfit to work.

Some men drink because they like the feeling of getting half stupid, but they are fools, because once they take to drink no employer will trust them, and they soon become unemployed and easily

Men who get into the habit of drinking often ruin their own health and the happiness of themselves and their families. The old saying, "Strong drink makes weak men", is a very true one.

get ill. There is nothing manly about getting drunk. Once a man gives way to drink it ruins his health, his career, and his happiness, as well as that of his family. There is only one cure for this disease, and that is—never to get it.

CONTINENCE

Smoking and drinking are things that tempt some fellows and not others, but there is one temptation that is pretty sure to come to you at one time or another, and I want just to warn you against it.

You would probably be surprised if you knew how many boys have written to me thanking me for what I have written on this subject, so I expect there are more who will be glad of a word of advice against the secret vice which gets hold of so many fellows. Smoking and drinking and gambling are men's vices and therefore attract some boys, but this secret vice is not a man's vice—men have nothing but contempt for a fellow who gives way to it.

Some boys, like those who start smoking, think it is a very fine and manly thing to tell or listen to dirty stories, but it only shows them to be little fools.

Yet such talk and the reading of trashy books or looking at lewd pictures are very apt to lead a thoughtless boy into the temptation of masturbation. This tends to lower both health and spirits.

But if you have any manliness in you, you will throw off such temptation at once. You will stop looking at the books and listening to the stories, and will give yourself something else to think about.

Sometimes the desire is brought on by eating food that is too rich,

199

or from sleeping in too warm a bed with too many blankets. It is a help at times such as these to take a cold bath or shower, or exercise the upper part of the body by arm exercises, boxing, etc.

It may seem difficult to overcome the temptation the first time, but when you have done so once it will be easier afterwards.

A Scout is "clean in thought, word and deed". He knows what to do to the fellow who talks smut.

If you still have trouble about it, do not make a secret of it, but go to your father, or your Scoutmaster, and talk it over with him, and all will come right.

EARLY RISING

The Scout's time for being most active is in the early morning, because that is the time when wild animals do their feeding and moving about.

So a Scout trains himself to the habit of getting up early. When once he is in the habit it is no trouble at all to him, as it is to some fat fellows who lie asleep after the daylight has come.

The Duke of Wellington, who preferred to sleep on a little camp bed, used to say, "When it is time to turn over in bed it is time to turn out."

Many men who manage to get through more work than others in a day, do so by getting up an hour or two earlier. By getting up early you also can get more time for play.

If you get up one hour earlier than other people, you get thirty hours a month more of life than they do. While they have twelve months in the year, you get 365 extra daylight hours, or thirty more days—that is, thirteen months to their twelve.

The old rhyme has a lot of truth in it when it says—
> "*Early to bed and early to rise,*
> *Makes a man healthy, and wealthy, and wise.*"

SMILE

Want of laughter means want of health. Laugh as much as you can—it does you good. So whenever you can get a good laugh, laugh on. And make other people laugh, too, when possible, as it does them good.

If you are in pain or trouble, make yourself smile at it. If you remember to do this, and force yourself, you will find it really does make a difference.

Throwing the assegai, or a simple spear, gives good exercise for the arms.
The aborigine in Australia uses a piece of wood as an extension to his arm,
to send off the spear with greater force.

If you read about great scouts like Captain John Smith, the "Pathfinder", and others, you will generally find that they were pretty cheery old fellows.

The ordinary boy is apt to frown when working hard at physical exercises, but the Boy Scout is required to smile all the time. He drops a mark off his score whenever he frowns.

GAMES

Relay Races

One Patrol pitted against another to see who can get a message sent a long distance in the shortest time by means of relays of runners (or cyclists).

The Patrol is ordered out to send in three successive notes or tokens (such as sprigs of certain plants), from a point, say two miles distant or more.

The leader in taking his Patrol out, drops Scouts at convenient distances, who will then act as runners from one post to the next and back.

If relays are posted in pairs, messages can be passed both ways.

Throwing the Assegai

Target, a thin sack, lightly stuffed with straw, or a sheet of cardboard, or canvas stretched on a frame.

Assegais (spears) to be made of wands, with weighted ends pointed, or with iron arrow-heads on them.

Camp Fire Yarn
No. 19

PREVENTION OF DISEASE

Germs, and How to Fight Them
Proper Food · Clothing
Troop Formations

SOME years ago, when I was in Kashmir, some local inhabitants brought to me a young man on a stretcher, who they said had fallen off a high rock, and had broken his back and was dying. I soon found that he had only dislocated his shoulder and had got a few bruises, and seemed to think that he ought to die.

So I pulled off my shoe, sat down alongside of him facing his head, put my heel in his arm-pit, got hold of his arm, and pulled with all my force till the bone jumped into its socket. The pain made him faint, and his friends thought I had really killed him. But in a few minutes he recovered and found his arm was all right. Then they thought I must be no end of a doctor, so they sent round the country for all the sick to be brought in to be cured; and I had an awful time of it for the next two days. Cases of every kind of disease were carried in, and I had scarcely any drugs with which to treat them, but I did the best I could, and I really believe that some of the poor creatures got better from simply *believing* that I was doing them a lot of good.

But most of them were ill from being dirty and letting their wounds get poisoned with filth; and many were ill from bad drainage, and from drinking foul water, and so on.

This I explained to the headmen of the villages, and I hope that I did some good for their future health.

At any rate, they were most grateful, and gave me a lot of help ever afterwards in getting good bear-hunting and also food, etc.

If I had not known a little doctoring I could have done nothing for these poor creatures.

While talking about doctoring I want to warn you against the excessive use of patent medicines and drugs. You will find advertisements for these in many magazines and they sound like cures for all ills. Whilst some may be quite beneficial, others can be very harmful, especially if they are taken in large quantities. So if you are ill go to a qualified doctor rather than buy some remedy which the advertisement says will cure whatever you may think is wrong with you.

GERMS AND HOW TO FIGHT THEM

Disease is carried about in the air and in water by tiny invisible "germs" or "microbes". You are very apt to breathe them in through the mouth or to get them in your drink or food and to swallow them, and then they breed disease inside you. If your blood is in really good order, it generally does not matter, no harm results. But if your blood is out of order, these germs may make you ill.

A great point is, therefore, to abolish the germs, if possible. They like living in dark, damp, and dirty places. And they come from bad drains, old dustbins, rotting refuse, etc. Therefore, keep your room, or your camp, and your clothes clean, dry, and as sunny as possible, and well aired; and keep away from places that smell badly.

Before your meals you should always wash your hands and fingernails, for they are very apt to harbour microbes which have come from anything that you may have been handling in the day.

Sleeping in Fresh Air

A Scout has to sleep a great deal in the open air anyway, therefore, when he is in a house he sleeps with the windows as wide open as possible. If he is accustomed to sleep in a warm atmosphere he might catch cold when he goes into camp, and nothing could be more ridiculous or more like a "tenderfoot" than a Scout with a cold in his head. When once he is accustomed to having his windows open, he will not catch cold.

Many persons who are pale and seedy, are often made so by living in rooms where the windows are seldom opened and the air is full of unwholesome gases or germs. Open your windows every day to let the foul air out.

FOOD

A good many illnesses come from over-eating or eating the wrong kind of food.

A Scout must know how to keep himself fit and active. Once he has got the right kind of muscles, he can remain fit without further special exercising of those muscles, provided that he eats the right kind of food.

In the siege of Mafeking, when we were put on short rations, those of the garrison who were accustomed to eat little at their meals, did not suffer like some people, who had been accustomed to stuff themselves well in peace time and who became weak and irritable. Our food there towards the end was limited to a hunk of pounded-up oats, about the size of a penny bun, which was our whole bread supply for the day, and about a pound of meat and two pints of "sowens", a kind of stuff like paper-hangers' paste that had gone wrong.

The cheapest foods are dried peas, flour, oatmeal, potatoes, rice, macaroni, and cheese. Other good foods are fruits, vegetables, fish, eggs, nuts, and milk, and one can live on these perfectly well with little or no meat.

If you have lots of fresh air, food keeps you healthy. If, on the other hand, you are sitting indoors all day, much food makes you fat and sleepy. In either case you are better for eating moderately. Still, growing boys should not starve themselves but, at the same time, they need not be like that little hog at the school feast, who when asked, "Can't you eat any more?" replied, "Yes, I could *eat* more, but I've no room to *swallow* it."

A great weakness nowadays is the amount of medicine which fellows dose themselves with when there is no reason for taking any medicine at all.

The best medicine is open air and exercise and a big cup of water in the early morning if you are constipated, and a pint of hot water on going to bed.

FOOTWEAR

One great point that a Scout should take care about, to ensure his endurance and being able to go on the march for a long time, is his shoes or boots. I like shoes better than boots, because they let more air in for the feet.

A Scout who gets sore feet with much walking becomes useless.

You should, therefore, take great care to have good, well-fitting, roomy boots, and fairly stout ones, and as like the natural shape of your bare feet as possible, with a straight edge on the inside. Keep your boots soft with lots of grease, mutton fat, dubbin, saddle soap or castor oil.

If feet are allowed to get wet, from perspiration or from outside moisture, the skin is softened, and very soon gets blistered and rubbed raw where there is a little pressure of the boot.

Here is a shoe laced in the Scout's way: one end of the lace is knotted under the lowest hole. The lace is brought through and threaded through the opposite hole; it is then taken up to the top and laced down. The blackened part of the lace is not visible.

Therefore, the feet should be kept as dry as possible. To do this it is necessary to wear good woollen socks. If a man wears thin cotton or silk socks, you can tell at once that he is no walker. A fellow who goes on a long walking trip for the first time is called a "tenderfoot", because he generally gets sore feet until by experience he learns how to keep his feet in good order.

If your feet always perspire a good deal, it is a useful thing to powder them with powder made of boric acid, starch, and oxide of zinc in equal parts. This powder should be rubbed in between the toes, to prevent soft corns forming there. Your feet can be hardened to some extent by soaking them in alum and water, or salt and water. Wash the feet every day.

DRILL FOR SCOUTS

Troop Movements

Scouts use drill to enable them to move quickly from one point to another in good order.

When done right, drill also sets them up, and makes them smart and quick. It strengthens the muscles which support the body, and by keeping the body upright the lungs and heart get plenty of room to work, and the inside organs are kept in the proper position for proper digestion of food.

A slouching position, on the other hand, depresses all the other

"S" stands for Sloucher, and "I" stands for you, if you are upright. Ask yourself the question, "Am I 'S', or am I 'I' ?"

organs, and prevents them doing their work properly, so that a man in that position is generally weak and often ill.

Growing lads are very apt to slouch, and should therefore do all they can to get out of the habit by plenty of physical exercises and drill.

Stand upright when you are standing, and when you are sitting down sit upright, with your back well into the back part of the chair Alertness of the body, whether you are moving, standing, or sitting. means alertness of mind, and it is a paying thing to have, because many an employer will select an alert-looking boy for work and pass over a sloucher. When you have to stoop over writing at a table, or even tying a boot-lace, do not round your back, but tuck in the small of your back, which helps to strengthen your body.

On the word "Alert", the Scout stands upright looking straight to his front, with both feet together, hands hanging naturally at the sides, fingers straight.

On the word "At ease", or "Easy" he carries his left foot away six inches, and clasps his hands behind his back and can turn his head about. At the word "Sit easy", he squats down on the ground in any position he likes. "Sit easy" should usually be given whenever you don't want the boys to be at the "Alert", provided that the ground is dry.

On the command "Quick march"—boys move off with the left

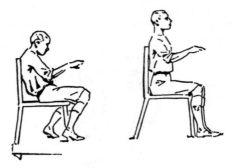

When you sit in a chair, sit upright and don't let your body slide down into the "S" shape.

foot leading at a smart pace, swinging the arms freely, as this gives good exercise to the body and muscles and inside organs.

On the command "Double"—boys run at a jog-trot with short, easy steps, hands swinging loosely, not tucked up at the side.

On the command "Scout Pace"—the boys march at the quick march for twenty paces, then double twenty paces, and so on, alternately running and walking, until the word is given "Quick march" or "Halt".

"Right turn"—each boy turns to the right.

"Follow your leader, leader right turn"—the leading man turns to his right, the remainder move up to the place where he turned, and then follow after him.

"Front form line" (when "Following the leader")—those in rear run up and form in line alongside the leader on his left.

Troop Formations

Line (means parties side by side)—Each Patrol has its Scouts in line, Patrol Leader on the right, Second on the left, the others in their order from right to left, Scoutmaster in front of centre.

Open Column (means parties one behind the other)—Give the word "Patrols right wheel" (form line). "Halt" (when exactly behind each other at their proper distance, such as will enable them to wheel either to right or left into line).

Close Column—Rear Patrols moved up to leading Patrols for taking up less room on parade, or for being addressed by a leader.

Line can be formed from "open column", to the right or left by wheeling the Patrols to that hand; or to the front by the leading Patrol standing fast (or advancing), the second Patrol inclining and moving up on its right, the third Patrol moving up into line on its

Don't slouch along looking at the ground, as if ashamed of yourself.
Straighten up and flash a Scout smile.

left, and so on with other Patrols in rear, even numbers going up on the right, odd numbers on the left of the leading Patrol. The Patrols which move up always do so at the "double".

Line can be formed to the rear from "open column" by "about turn" for everybody (always turn about to the right hand), and then proceeding to form line as above.

Formations by Silent Signals

With an alert Troop these formations can easily be made without any word of command; all that is needed is for the Scoutmaster to give a signal and every Scout immediately doubles to his proper place in his Patrol, the whole formation facing the Scoutmaster.

For instance, for "Line" he might extend both arms outwards to the sides from the shoulder; for "Open column" extend both arms outwards but bend them upward at the elbow; for "Close column" the signal might be like that for "Open column" but with the arms held forward instead of outward from the shoulders.

"Horseshoe formation" is the ordinary one for Troop parades.

The signal for this is usually to swing the arms to and fro with a semi-circular motion in front of the body.

For inter-Patrol games "Rows" is used. This means that the Patrols are in Indian file, behind their Patrol Leaders with their Seconds at the back, facing the Scoutmaster, and in their usual Patrol order from right to left. The usual signal is both arms stretched forward from the shoulders.

Movements by signal are always made at the run and in dead silence.

CHIVALRY

Camp Fire Yarn
No. 20

CHIVALRY TO OTHERS

Knights Errant · Helpfulness to Others
Courtesy to Women

"IN DAYS OF OLD, when knights were bold", it must have been a fine sight to see one of these steel-clad horsemen come riding through the dark green woods in his shining armour, with shield and lance and waving plumes, bestriding his gallant war-horse, strong to bear its load, and full of fire to charge upon an enemy. And near him rode his squire—a young man, his assistant and companion, who would some day become a knight.

Behind him rode his group, or patrol, of men-at-arms—stout, hearty warriors, ready to follow their knight to the gates of death if need be. They were the tough yeomen of the old days, who won so many fine fights for their country through their pluck and loyal devotion to their knights.

In peace time, when there was no fighting to be done, the knight would daily ride about looking for a chance of doing a good turn to any needing help, especially a woman or child who might be in distress. When engaged in thus doing good turns, he was called a "Knight Errant". The men of his patrol naturally acted in the same way as their leader, and a man-at-arms was always equally ready to help the distressed with his strong right arm.

The knights of old were the Patrol Leaders of the nation, and the men-at-arms were the Scouts.

You Patrol Leaders and Scouts are therefore very like the knights and their retainers, especially if you keep your honour ever before you, and do your best to help other people who are in trouble or who want assistance. Your motto is, "Be Prepared" to do this, and the motto of the knights was a similar one, "Be Always Ready".

CHIVALRY

Chivalry—that is, the order of the knights—was started in England some 1500 years ago by King Arthur.

On the death of his father, King Uther Pendragon, he was living with his uncle, and nobody knew who was to be King. He did not himself know that he was the son of the late King.

Then a great stone was found in the churchyard, into which a sword was sticking, and on the stone was written:

"Whosoever pulleth this sword out of this stone is the rightwise King born of all England."

All the chief lords had a try at pulling it out, but none could move it.

That day there was a tournament at which Arthur's cousin was to fight, but when he got to the ground he found he had left his sword at home, and he sent Arthur to fetch it. Arthur could not find it, but remembering the sword in the churchyard he went there and pulled at it. It came out of the stone at once, and he took it to his cousin. After the sports he put it back again into the stone; and then they all tried to pull it out, but could not move it. But when Arthur tried he drew it out quite easily. So he was proclaimed King.

He afterwards got together a number of knights, and used to sit with them at a great round table, and so they were called the "Knights of the Round Table".

ST. GEORGE

They had as their patron saint St. George, because he was the only one of all the saints who was a horseman. He is the Patron Saint of cavalry from which the word Chivalry is derived, and the special saint of England.

He is also the Patron Saint of Boy Scouts everywhere. Therefore, all Scouts should know his story.

St. George was born in Cappadocia in the year A.D. 303. He enlisted as a cavalry soldier when he was seventeen, and soon became renowned for his bravery.

On one occasion he came to a city named Selem, near which lived

212

a dragon who had to be fed daily with one of the citizens, drawn by lot.

The day St. George came there, the lot had fallen upon the king's daughter, Cleolinda. St. George resolved that she should not die, and so he went out and attacked the dragon, who lived in a swamp close by, and killed him.

Prepared and alert a Scout follows the lead.
Of our Patron Saint George and his spirited steed.

St. George was typical of what a Scout should be:

When he was faced by a difficulty or danger, however great it appeared—even in the shape of a dragon—he did not avoid it or fear it, but went at it with all the power he could put into himself and his horse. Although inadequately armed for such an encounter, having merely a spear, he charged in, did his best, and finally succeeded in overcoming a difficulty which nobody had dared to tackle.

That is exactly the way in which a Scout should face a difficulty or danger, no matter how great or terrifying it may appear to him or how ill-equipped he may be for the struggle.

He should go at it boldly and confidently, using every power that he can to try to overcome it, and the probability is that he will succeed.

St. George's Day is April 23rd, and on that day all Scouts remind themselves of their Promise and of the Scout Law. Not that a Scout every forgets either, but on St. George's Day he makes a special point of thinking about them. Remember this when April 23rd comes round again.

213

THE KNIGHTS' CODE

The laws of the knights were these:

"Be Always Ready, with your armour on, except when you are taking your rest at night.

Defend the poor and weak; help them that cannot defend themselves.

Do nothing to hurt or offend anyone else.

Be prepared to fight in the defence of your country.

At whatever you are working try to win honour and a name for honesty.

Never break your promise.

Maintain the honour of your country with your life.

Rather die honest than live shamelessly.

Chivalry requireth that youth should be trained to perform the most laborious and humble offices with cheerfulness and grace; and to do good unto others."

These are the first rules with which the old knights started, and from which the Scout Law of today comes.

A knight (or Scout) is at all times a gentleman. So many people seem to think that a gentleman must have lots of money. Money does not make a gentleman. A gentleman is anyone who carries out the rules of chivalry of the knights.

UNSELFISHNESS

Captain John Smith, the old English adventurer of three hundred years ago, was a pretty tough customer to deal with, as he had fought in every part of the world and had been wounded over and over again; but he also had a good, kind heart within him.

He was as good a type of scout as you could find anywhere. One of his favourite expressions was, "We were born, not for ourselves, but to do good to others", and he carried this out very much in his life, for he was the most unselfish of men.

SELF-SACRIFICE

One of the finest examples of self-sacrifice was the action of Captain Lawrence Oates, who was on Scott's Last Expedition to the South Pole.

The little party of men had reached the Pole on January 18th, 1912, to find to their bitter disappointment that the Norwegian explorer, Roald Amundsen, had been there ahead of them, only a few weeks before.

On the return journey the party suffered great hardships from intense cold and terrible weather. The men became weaker and weaker. One of them, Petty Officer Evans, died.

Then Oates became badly frost-bitten in hands and feet, and he realized that he was becoming a burden on the others.

This is what Captain Scott wrote of him, "He has borne intense suffering for weeks without complaint, and to the very last was able and willing to discuss outside subjects. He did not—would not —give up hope till the very end. He was a brave soul. This was the end. He slept through the night before last, hoping not to wake; but he woke in the morning—yesterday. It was blowing a blizzard, He said, 'I am just going outside and may be some time.' He went out into the blizzard and we have not seen him since. . . . We knew that Oates was walking to his death, but though we tried to dissuade him, we knew it was the act of a brave man and an English gentleman."

Captain Lawrence Oates proved himself a man of great courage on Scott's Last Expedition to the South Pole. He sacrificed himself so that his comrades might live.

Boys, too, can show just the same spirit.

A lad of eighteen named Currie saw a little girl playing on a railway line at Clydebank in front of an approaching train. He tried to rescue her, but he was lame from an injury he had suffered at football, and it delayed him in getting her clear. The train knocked both of them over, and both were killed.

But Currie's gallant attempt is a true example of chivalry. It was sacrifice of himself in the attempt to save a child.

Thousands of cases of gallantry in saving life by Scouts have occurred.

KINDNESS

"Kindness and gentleness are great virtues", says an old Spanish proverb. And another says, "Oblige without regarding whom you oblige", which means be kind to anyone, great or small, rich or poor.

The great point about a knight was that he was always doing kindnesses or good turns to people. His idea was that everyone must die, but you should make up your mind that before your time comes

A Scout does everything he can to help others, especially old people and children. He does at least one Good Turn a day.

you will do something good. Therefore do it at once, for you never know when you may be going off.

So, with the Scouts, it has been made one of our promises that we help other people at all times. It does not matter how small that good turn may be, if it only be to help an old woman lift her bundle, or to guide a child across a crowded street, or to put a coin in the poor-box.

Something good ought to be done each day of your life. Start today to carry out this rule, and never forget it during the remaining days of your life. Remember the knot in your neckerchief and on your Scout Badge—they are reminders to you to do a Good Turn. And do your good turn not only to your friends, but to strangers as well.

GENEROSITY

Some people are fond of hoarding their money and never spending it. It is well to be thrifty, but it is also well to give away money where it is needed—in fact, that is part of the object of saving up your money.

In being charitable, be careful that you do not fall into the mistake of false charity. That is to say, it is very easy and comforting to you to give a penny to a beggar in the street, but you ought not to do it. That beggar in ninety-nine times out of a hundred is an arrant old fraud, and by giving your penny you are encouraging him and others to go on with that trade. There may be, probably are, hundreds of really poor and miserable people hiding away, whom you never see and to whom that penny would be a godsend. The charity organizations know where they are, and who they are, and if you give your penny to them they will put it into the right hands for you.

You need not be rich to be charitable. Many of the knights were poor men. At one time some of them wore, as their crest, two knights riding on one horse, which meant they were too poor to afford a horse apiece.

TIPS

Then "tips" are a bad thing.

Wherever you go, people want to be "tipped" for doing the slightest thing which they ought to do out of common good feeling. A Scout will never accept a "tip", unless it is to pay for work done. It is often difficult to refuse, when it is offered, but for a Scout it is easy. He has only to say, "Thank you very much, but I am a Scout, and our rules don't allow us to accept anything for doing a good turn."

"Tips" put you on a wrong footing with everyone.

You cannot work in a friendly way with a man if you are thinking how much "tip" you are going to get out of him, or he is thinking how much he'll have to "tip" you. And all Scout's work for another ought to be done in a friendly way.

I have had a number of letters of admiration for the Scouts on account of their doing good acts and then declining to be tipped for them. I am very glad to hear it, Scouts.

Remember, that it was because a Scout refused a tip for helping an American in London that Scouting went to the United States. At Gilwell Park, our Training and Camping Ground in Epping Forest, there is a statuette of a bison given to us by the Boy Scouts of America to commemorate that Good Turn.

Of course, proper pay that is earned by your work is another thing, and you will be right to accept it.

FRIENDLINESS

The great difference between bushmen and a stay-at-home city-dweller is, that the first is in shirt-sleeves while the other is buttoned up in his coat. The bushman is open and cheery with everybody at once, while the city person is rather inclined to shut himself up from his neighbours inside his coat, and takes a deal of drawing out before he becomes friendly. The free, open-air, shirt-sleeve habits of the man of the woods or the open spaces do away with this, and life becomes much more pleasant to everybody all round.

A Boy Scout should remember that he is like Kim, the "friend of all the world". But don't let your friendliness lead you into the foolery of throwing away your hard-earned savings in standing treat to your friends.

Our Scout Law says: "A Scout is a friend to all and a brother to every other Scout." This has shown itself very much when our Jamborees have brought thousands of Scouts together from many

A Scout is a "friend of all the world" and "a brother to every other Scout". "The way to have a friend is to be one."

different nations. The boys have found out that though they come from different countries they are after all very much alike in their tastes and amusements and that they can be jolly good friends with each other.

I want you Scouts to keep up that friendship and to make it wider and stronger. You can do this by writing to your Brother Scouts abroad and visiting them or by getting them to visit you in camp.

It will be fun for you and fun for them. But better than that it will be making friendships between you, so that if difficulties should arise later on between the different countries they will not at once want to go to war, but will talk things over as friends and see how to come to agreement without the cruel and unfair test of fighting.

POLITENESS

One of the stories that the knights used to tell as an example of politeness was about Julius Caesar. Once when he was entertained for supper by a poor peasant, the man gave him a dish of pickles to eat, thinking that they were the sort of vegetables that a highborn officer would like. Caesar showed his politeness by eating the whole dish of pickles and pretended to like them, although they burnt his mouth and disagreed with him considerably.

In Spain, you ask a man the way—he does not merely point it out, but takes off his hat, bows, and says that it will be a great pleasure to him to show it, and walks with you till he has set you properly upon it. He will take no reward.

A Frenchman will take off his hat when he addresses a stranger, even when he asks a policeman the way.

The Dutch fishermen, big and brawny as they are, take up the whole street when walking down it. But when strangers come along they stand to one side, and smilingly take off their caps as he passes.

A lady told me that when in one of the far west Canadian townships she met a group of wild-looking cowboys walking down the street, she felt quite alarmed. But as they got near they stood to one side, and took off their hats with the greatest respect, and made way for her.

COURTESY TO WOMEN

The knights of old were particularly attentive in respect and courtesy to women.

Sir Nigel Loring in Conan Doyle's *The White Company* is a type of chivalrous knight of the old times. Although very small, and half blind from some lime which an enemy had thrown in his eyes very early in his career, he was an exceedingly brave man, and at the same time very humble, and very helpful to others.

But, above all things, he reverenced women. He had a big, plain lady as his wife, but he always upheld her beauty and virtue, and was ready to fight anybody who doubted him. Then with poor women, old or young, he was always courteous and helpful. And that is how a Scout should act.

King Arthur, who made the rules of chivalry, was himself chivalrous to women. One day a girl rushed into his hall crying for help. Her hair was streaming and smeared with mud, her arms were torn with brambles, and she was dressed in rags. She had been ill-treated by a band of robbers who roved the country, doing all the harm they could. When he heard her tale, King Arthur sprang to his horse and rode off himself to the robbers' cave, and, even at the risk of his own life, he fought and defeated them, so that they could no more trouble his people.

When walking with a lady or a child, a Scout should always have her on his left side, so that his right is free to protect her. This rule is altered when walking in the streets—then a man will walk on the side of her nearest to the traffic, to protect her against accident or mud-splashes, etc.

In meeting a woman or a child a man should, as a matter of course, always make way for her, even if he has to step off the pavement into the gutter.

So also in riding in a crowded bus or railway carriage, no man worthy of the name will allow a woman to stand up if he has a seat. He will at once give it up to the woman and stand himself. As a Scout, you should set an example in this by being the first man in the carriage to do it. And in doing so do it cheerfully, with a smile, so that she may not think you are annoyed at having to do it.

When in the street, always be on the look-out to help women and children. A good opportunity is when they want to cross a street, or to find the way, or to hail a taxi or bus. If you see them, go and help them at once—and don't accept any reward.

The other day I saw a boy help a lady out of a car, and as he shut the door after her she turned to give him some money, but he touched his cap and smilingly said, "No, thank you, ma'am; it's my duty", and walked off. So I shook hands with him, for I felt that although he had not been taught, he was a Scout by nature.

This is the kind of courtesy one wants to see more amongst boys.

Of course, in accidents men and boys will always see that the women and children are safely out of danger before they think of going themselves. In shipwrecks, it is very noticeable how carefully arrangements are made for saving the women and children and old people before men are rescued.

You should carry on your courtesy to ladies at all times. If you are sitting down and a lady comes into the room, stand up, and see if you can help her in any way before you sit down.

Don't spend time on a girl whom you would not like your mother or sister to see you with. Don't marry a girl unless you are in a position to support her and to support some children.

THANKS!

And, look here! Here is a very important bit of courtesy that is too often forgotten, but which a true Scout will never omit, and that is to *thank* for any kindness you receive. A *present is not yours till you have thanked for it.* You have not finished your camp, even if you have packed up your kit and cleaned up the ground, until you have thanked the owner for the use of it and have thanked God for giving you a good time.

PATROL PRACTICES IN CHIVALRY

The Patrol Leader can do much to encourage the Good Turn by referring to it at opportune moments (don't overdo it!), and by occasionally asking the Scouts what Good Turns they have done lately. When out with his Patrol, he can suggest opportunities for individual and Patrol Good Turns. But remember: IT IS THE PATROL LEADER'S OWN EXAMPLE THAT COUNTS MOST.

———

Make each Scout tie a knot in his neckerchief every morning as a reminder to carry out his idea of doing a good turn every day, till it becomes a habit with him.

———

Talk over some of the many good turns a boy can do in his daily life: sprinkle sand on a frozen road where someone is liable to slip —remove orange or banana skins from the pavement, as they are apt to throw people down—help old people—help to keep the streets clean by removing scraps of paper. THEN DO SOME OF THEM!

———

Have a Scout bring in a boy who is a total stranger, as his guest for the evening to play games, hear camp yarns, and so on.

GAMES

"Knight Errantry"

Scouts go out singly, or in pairs, or as a Patrol. If in a town, to find women or children in need of help, and to return and report, on their honour, what they have done. If in the country, to call at any farms or cottages and ask to do odd jobs—for nothing. The same can be made into a race called a Good Turn Race.

Camp Fire Yarn No. 21

SELF-DISCIPLINE

Honour · Obedience
Courage · Cheeriness

THE TRUE KNIGHT placed his honour before all things. It was sacred. A man who is honourable is always to be trusted. He will never do a dishonourable action, such as telling an untruth or deceiving his superiors or employers, or those under his orders, and always commands the respect of his fellow-men.

A captain sticks to the ship till the last. Why? She is only a lump of iron and wood and his life is as valuable as that of any of the women and children on board. But he makes everybody get away safely before he attempts to save his more valuable life. Why? Because the ship is his ship, and he has been taught that it is his duty to stick to it, and he considers it would be dishonourable of him to do otherwise—so he puts honour before safety.

So also a Scout should value his honour most of anything.

Lord Kitchener said to the Boy Scouts: "There is one thought I would like to impress upon you all—ONCE A SCOUT, ALWAYS A SCOUT." By this he meant that when you are grown up you must still carry out what you learned as a Scout—and especially that you will go on being honourable and trustworthy.

223

FAIR PLAY

Play fair yourself and insist on fair play in others.

If you see a big bully going for a small or weak boy, you stop him because it is not "fair play". If a prize fighter, in fighting another, knocks him down, he must not hit him while he is down.

The point is that "fair play" is an old idea of chivalry that has come down to us from the knights of old, and we must always keep up that idea.

HONESTY

Honesty is a form of honour. An honourable man can be trusted with any amount of money or other valuables with the certainty that he will not steal it.

Cheating at any time is a sneaking, underhand thing to do.

When you feel inclined to cheat in order to win a game, or feel very distressed when a game in which you are playing is going against you, just say to yourself, "After all, it is only a game. It won't kill me if I do lose. One can't win always, though I will stick to it in case of a chance coming."

If you keep your head in this way, you will very often find that you win after all from not being over anxious or despairing. And don't forget, whenever you *do* lose a game, if you are a true Scout, you will at once cheer the winning team or shake hands with and congratulate the fellow who has beaten you.

This rule is carried out in *all* games and competitions among Boy Scouts.

"O God, help me to win, but if I can't win, make me a good loser."

LOYALTY

Our highest loyalty is to God; we can show that by carrying out our duties to the Church to which we belong, and by keeping our Promise as Scouts.

Loyalty was, above all, one of the distinguishing points about the knights. They were always devotedly loyal to their King and to their country, and were always ready and eager to die in their defence. In the same way a follower of the knights should be loyal to his country and to every one who is above him, whether his officers or employers, and he should stick to them through thick and thin as part of his duty. If he does not intend to be loyal, he will, if he has any honour and manliness in him, resign his place.

He should also be equally loyal to his family and his friends and should support them in evil times as well as in good times.

Loyalty to duty was shown by the Roman soldier of old who stuck to his post when the city of Pompeii was overwhelmed with ashes and lava from the volcano Vesuvius. His remains are still there, his hand covering his mouth and nose to prevent the suffocation which in the end overcame him.

DUTY BEFORE ALL

The name and fame of Jack Cornwell are known to every boy in Britain as the lad who in the great sea fight off Jutland in 1916 stuck

Jack Cornwell was just a boy. But he proved in the sea fight off Jutland that he could take a man's place.

to his gun aboard the *Chester* when all the gun's crew were killed or wounded and he might have got away under cover.

He was badly wounded himself—but in the responsible work of sight-setter his duty was to be at his post by the gun, and there he stayed for twenty minutes under heavy fire, in case he should be wanted.

At the end of the fight, after the *Chester* had come successfully through her tremendous contest with three German cruisers, the only unwounded man of the gun's crew said to him, "Well done, lad. You stuck it out well. Lucky you weren't wounded."

"Well! I am wounded—here in the chest. But did we win?"

"Yes, my lad."

The boy sank down fainting. He lingered a few days in a hospital

225

and died of his wound, but satisfied—knowing that he had done his duty. He had "stuck to it", as every Scout should.

DISCIPLINE AND OBEDIENCE

Discipline and obedience are as important as bravery for Scouts and for soldiers.

The *Birkenhead* was a transport ship carrying troops. She had on board 630 soldiers with their families and 130 seamen. Near the Cape of Good Hope one night she ran on to some rocks, and began to break up.

The soldiers were at once paraded on deck. Some were ordered to get out the boats, and to put the women and children into them, and others were told to get the horses up out of the hold, and to lower them overboard into the sea, so that they might have a chance to swim ashore. When this had all been done, it was found that there were not enough boats to take the men, and so the men were ordered to remain in their ranks.

Then the ship broke in half and began to go down. The captain shouted to the men to jump over and save themselves, but the officer in charge, Colonel Seaton, said, "No, keep your ranks." For he saw that if they swam to the boats, and tried to get in, they would probably sink them too.

So the men kept their ranks, and as the ship rolled over and sank, they gave a cheer and went down with her. Out of the whole 760 on board, only 192 were saved, but even those would probably have been lost had it not been for the discipline and self-sacrifice of the others.

A British training ship, the *Fort Jackson*, full of boy-sailors, was run into by a steamer, but just as in the *Birkenhead* there was no panic or crying out. The boys fell in quickly on parade, put on their life-belts, and faced the danger calmly and well. And not a life was lost.

HUMILITY

Humility, or being humble, was one of the things which was practised by the knights. Although they were generally superior to other people in fighting or campaigning, they never allowed themselves to swagger about it. So don't swagger.

And don't imagine that you have rights in this world except those that you earn for yourself. You have the right to be believed, if you earn it by always telling the truth, and you have the right to go to prison if you earn it by thieving.

There are lots of men who go about howling about their rights

The Red Indians had to be courageous to survive. They depended on buffalo meat for food, and buffalo hunting was dangerous.

who have never done anything to earn any rights. Do your duty first, and you will get your rights afterwards.

COURAGE

Very few men are born brave, but any man can make himself brave if he tries—and especially if he begins trying when he is a boy.

The brave man dashes into danger without hesitation, when a less brave man is inclined to hang back. It is very like bathing. A lot of boys will come to a river to bathe, and will cower shivering on the bank, wondering how deep the water is, and whether it is very cold —but the brave one will run through them and take his header into the water, and will be swimming about happily a few seconds later.

The thing is, when there is danger before you, don't stop and look at it—the more you look at it the less you will like it—but take the plunge, go boldly in at it, and it won't be half as bad as it looked, when you are once in it.

FORTITUDE

The knights were men who never said "die" until they were dead. They were always ready to stick it out till the end. But it is a very common fault with men to give in to trouble or fear long before there is any necessity. Many of them give up working hard because they don't get success all at once; probably if they stuck to it a little

227

longer, success would come. A man must expect hard work at first to have success later.

Some of you may have heard the story of the two frogs. If you have not, here it is:

Two frogs were out for a walk one day, and they came to a big bowl of cream. In looking into it they both fell in.

One said: "This is a new kind of water to me. How can a fellow swim in stuff like this? It is no use trying." So he sank to the bottom and was drowned because he had no pluck.

But the other was a more manly frog, and he struggled to swim, using his arms and legs as hard as he could to keep himself afloat. Whenever he felt he was sinking he struggled harder than ever, and never gave up hope.

At last, just as he was getting so tired that he thought he must give it up, a curious thing happened. By his hard work with his arms and legs he had churned up the cream so much that he suddenly found himself sitting all safe on a pat of butter!

So when things look bad, just smile and sing to yourself, as the thrush sings: "Stick to it, stick to it, stick to it," and you will come through all right.

A very great step to success is to be able to stand disappointments.

CHEERINESS

The knights laid great stress on never being out of temper. They thought it bad form to lose their temper and to show anger.

Captain John Smith was himself a cheerful man. In fact, towards the end of his life two boys to whom he told his adventures, wrote them down in a book, but said that they found great difficulty in hearing all that he said, because he roared with laughter at his own descriptions of his troubles. But it is very certain that had he not been a cheery man, he never could have come through half the dangers with which he was faced at different times in his career.

Over and over again he was made prisoner by his enemies— sometimes savage enemies—but he managed always to captivate them with his pleasant manner, and become friends with them, so that they let him go, or did not trouble to catch him when he made his escape.

If you do your work cheerfully, your work becomes much more of a pleasure to you. And also, if you are cheerful it makes other people cheerful as well, which is part of your duty as a Scout. Sir J. M. Barrie wrote: "Those who bring sunshine to the lives of others cannot keep happiness from themselves." If you make other people happy, you make yourself happy.

And I'll tell you a secret about making your work easy, whatever it is. If your work is lessons in school, or doing jobs for an employer, or in a workshop, or an office, you can, if you like, get very bored and tired of it. If you keep thinking of what you will do to enjoy yourself when you get out and how much better off other fellows are who don't have to work, then you will get to hate your work—it will hang on you all the time, you will do it badly, and you won't get on. But if you take the other line and see what your work will lead to in

Captain John Smith once fell in a bog with his Indian guide tied to his wrist. When captured, his cheerfulness helped him to escape.

the end and the good it will bring to yourself or others for whom you are making things, then you will go at it eagerly, and very soon you will find that instead of hating it you will love it, and keep doing it better and better all the time.

If you are in the habit of taking things cheerfully, you will very seldom find yourself in serious trouble, because if a difficulty or annoyance or danger seems great, you will, if you are wise, force yourself to laugh at it—although I will allow it is very difficult to do so at first. Still, the moment you do laugh, most of the difficulty seems to disappear at once, and you can tackle it quite easily.

GOOD TEMPER

Good temper can be attained by a boy who wants to have it. It will help him in every game under the sun, and more especially in difficulty and danger, and will often keep him in a situation where a short-tempered fellow gets turned out, or leaves in a huff.

Bad language and swearing are used, like smoking, by boys who want to try to show off how manly they are, but it only makes them look like fools. Generally, a man who swears is a man easily upset, who loses his head in a difficult situation. He is not, therefore, to be depended upon.

You want to be quite undisturbed under the greatest difficulties; so when you find yourself particularly anxious, or excited, or angry, don't swear—force yourself to smile, and it will set you right in a moment.

Captain John Smith, who neither smoked nor swore, had a way of dealing with swearers, which is also adopted by Scouts. He says in his diary that when his men were cutting down trees, the axes blistered their tender fingers, so that at about every third blow a loud oath would drown the echo of the axe.

To remedy this he devised a plan of having every man's oath noted down, and at night, for every oath, he had a can of water poured down the wearer's sleeve, "with which an offender was so washed that a man would scarce hear an oath for a week".

Camp Fire Yarn
No. 22

SELF-IMPROVEMENT

Religion · Thrift
How Scouts Earn Money
How to Get On

RELIGION

THE OLD KNIGHTS WERE very religious. They were always careful to attend religious services, especially before going into battle or undertaking any serious difficulty. They considered it the right thing always to be prepared for death. Besides worshipping God in church, the knights always recognized His work in the things which He made, such as animals, plants, and all scenery.

And so it is with peace scouts today. Wherever they go they love the woodlands, the mountains, and the prairies, and they like to watch and know about the animals that inhabit them, and the wonders of the flowers and plants.

No man is much good unless he believes in God and obeys His laws. So every Scout should have a religion.

Religion seems a very simple thing:

First: *Love and serve God.* Second: *Love and serve your neighbour.*

In doing your duty to God always be grateful to Him. Whenever you enjoy a pleasure or a good game, or succeed in doing a good thing, thank Him for it, if only with a word or two, just as you say grace at a meal. And it is a good thing to bless other people. For instance, if you see a train starting off, just pray for God's blessing on all that are in the train.

In doing your duty towards man, be helpful and generous, and also always be grateful for any kindness done to you, and be careful to show that you are grateful. Remember again that a present given to you is not yours until you have thanked the giver for it.

While you are living your life on this earth, try to do something good which may remain after you.

One writer says: "I often think that when the sun goes down the world is hidden by a big blanket from the light of heaven, but the stars are little holes pierced in that blanket by those who have done good deeds in this world. The stars are not all the same size;

A Scout is active in DOING GOOD, not passive in BEING GOOD.
It is his duty to be helpful and generous to other people.

some are big, some are little, and some men have done great deeds and others have done small deeds, but they have made their hole in the blanket by doing good before they went to heaven."

Try and make your hole in the blanket by good work while you are on the earth.

It is something to *be* good, but it is far better to *do* good.

THRIFT

It is a funny thing that out of you boys who now read these words, some are certain to become rich men, and some may die in poverty and misery. It pretty well depends on your own selves which you are going to do.

And you can very soon tell which your future is going to be.

The fellow who begins making money as a boy will go on making it as a man. You may find it difficult to do at first, but it will come easier later on. If you begin and go on, remember, you are pretty certain to succeed in the end—especially if you get your money by hard work.

If you only try to make it by easy means—that is by betting, say on a horse race—you are bound to lose after a time. Nobody who makes bets ever wins in the end; it is the bookmaker, the man who

There are many ways in which a boy can earn money—from painting a fence and tending a garden to running errands.

receives the bets, who scores. Yet there are thousands of fools who go on putting their money on, because they won a bit once or hope to win some day.

Any number of poor boys have become rich men. But in nearly every case it was because they meant to do so from the first. They worked for it, and put every penny they could make into the bank to begin with.

So each one of you has the chance, if you like to take it.

The knights of old were ordered by their rules to be thrifty, not to expend large sums on their enjoyment, but to save it in order that they might keep themselves, and not be a burden to others, and also so that they might have more to give away in charity. If they had no money of their own, they were not allowed to beg for it, but had to work and make it in one way or another. Thus money-making goes with manliness, hard work, and sobriety.

HOW SCOUTS EARN MONEY

There are many ways by which a Scout, or a Patrol working together, can make money.

Repairing and re-covering old furniture is a very paying trade.

A Patrol can earn money by collecting old metal and waste paper.

Picture frames, bird boxes, toys, can easily be sold. Breeding canaries, chickens, or rabbits pay well. So does beekeeping.

Collect old packing-cases and boxes, and chop them into bundles of firewood. Keeping goats and selling their milk will pay in some places. Basket-making, pottery, book-binding, etc., all bring money.

Or a Patrol working together can form a corps of messenger boys in a country town, or start a garden and work it for selling vegetables and flowers, or make a minstrel troupe, or perform Scouting displays or pageants.

These are only a few suggestions. There are loads of other ways of making money which you can think out for yourself, according to the place you are in.

But in order to get money you must expect to work.

The actor, Ted Payne, used to say in one of his plays, "I don't know what is wrong with me. I eat well, I drink well, and I sleep well; but somehow whenever anybody mentions the word 'work' to me, I get a cold shudder all over me." There are a good many other chicken-hearted fellows, who, when any work faces them, "get a cold shudder all over them".

Start a money box, put any money you can make into that, and when you have got a fair amount in it, hand it over to a bank, and start an account for yourself.

HOW TO GET ON

A good many years ago the United States was at war on the island of Cuba.

The American President McKinley wanted to send a letter to Garcia, the Cuban leader, but did not know how to get it to him, as the rebels were fighting with the Americans in wild and difficult country.

When he was talking it over with his advisers, someone said:

On this map of Central America and the Caribbean Sea you will find the island of Cuba through which Rowan travelled to find Garcia.

"There's a young man called Rowan who seems to be able to get anything done that you ask him. Why not try him?"

So Rowan was sent for, and when he came in, the President explained why he had sent for him and, putting the letter in his hand, said, "Now, I want that letter taken to Garcia."

Rowan simply smiled and accepted the letter. He walked out of the room and set out.

Some weeks passed, and Rowan appeared again before the Presi-

235

dent and said, "I gave your letter to Garcia, sir." Of course McKinley made him explain how he had done it.

It turned out that Rowan had taken a boat, had landed on the coast of Cuba, and had disappeared into the jungle. In three weeks' time he reappeared on the other side of the island, having gone through the enemy, found Garcia, and given him the letter.

Rowan was a true scout. The way he acted is the way a Scout

Rowan did his duty, kicking the IM out of the word IMPOSSIBLE.
Any fellow who acts like that is certain to get on.

should carry out an order when he gets it. No matter how difficult it may seem, he should tackle it, with a smile. The more difficult it is, the more interesting it will be to carry out.

Most fellows would have asked a lot of questions—how they were to set about it, how they could get to the place, where they were to get food from, and so on. But not so Rowan. He merely learned what duty was wanted of him, and then did the rest without a word, kicking the IM out of the word IMPOSSIBLE. Any fellow who acts like that is certain to get on.

A lot of Scouts do special messenger service. These lads, from having difficult jobs frequently given them and being expected to carry them out successfully, take them on with the greatest confidence, and, without asking a lot of silly questions, they start off in a businesslike way, and do them.

That is the way to deal with any difficulty in life. If you get a job or have trouble that seems to you to be too big for you, don't shirk it. Smile, think out a way by which you might get successfully through with it, and then go at it.

Remember that "a difficulty is no longer a difficulty when once you laugh at it—and tackle it".

Don't be afraid of making a mistake. Napoleon said, "Nobody ever made anything who never made a mistake."

A boy learning what he can as a Scout has a good chance in the world.

MEMORY

Then practise remembering things. A fellow who has a good memory will get on because so many other people have poor memories from not practising them.

A great coral island is built up of tiny sea animals blocking themselves together. So also great knowledge in a man is built up by his noticing all sorts of little details and blocking them together in his mind by remembering them.

LUCK

If you want to catch a bus you don't sit down and let it run past you, and then say, "How unlucky I am." You run to it and jump on. It is just the same with what some people call "luck"; they complain that luck never comes to them. Well, luck is really the chance of getting something good or of doing something great. The thing is to look out for every chance and seize it—run at it and jump on—don't sit down and wait for it to pass. Opportunity is a bus which has very few stopping places.

CHOOSE A CAREER

"Be Prepared" for what is going to happen to you in the future. If you are in a situation where you are earning money as a boy, what are you going to do when you finish that job? You ought to be learning some proper trade, and save your pay in the meantime, to keep you going till you get employment in your future trade.

And try to learn something of a second trade, in case the first one fails you at any time, as so very often happens.

An employer told me once that he never engaged a lad who had yellow finger-tips (from smoking), or who carried his mouth open (boys who breathe through the mouth have a stupid look). Any man

Don't be an idler. Follow a useful trade if you want Success.

is sure of employment who has money in the bank, keeps away from drink, and is cheery.

Lots of wasters or weaklings have gone out into the world and many of them have failed to make good, but I have never come across a failure among young fellows who have gone out *with a real desire to work and with the ability to stick to their job, to act straight, and to keep sober.*

238

SAVING LIFE

Camp Fire Yarn
No. 23

**BE PREPARED
FOR ACCIDENTS**

The Knights Hospitallers of St. John
Accidents · Boy Heroes
Life-Saving Medals

THE KNIGHTS OF OLD DAYS were called "Knights Hospitallers" because they had hospitals for the treatment of the sick, poor, and those injured in accidents or in war. They used to save up their money and keep these hospitals going, and although they were brave fighting men they used also to act as nurses and doctors themselves.

The Knights of St. John of Jerusalem especially devoted themselves to this work eight hundred years ago. The British St. John Ambulance Brigade and the Red Cross today represent those knights.

Explorers and hunters and other scouts in out-of-the-way parts of the world have to know what to do in case of accident or sickness, either to themselves or their followers, as they are often hundreds of miles away from any doctors. For these reasons Boy Scouts should, of course, learn all they can about looking after sick people and dealing with accidents.

My brother was once camping with a friend away in the bush in Australia. His friend was drawing a cork, holding the bottle between his knees to get a better purchase. The bottle burst and the jagged edge of it ran deeply into his thigh, cutting an artery. My brother quickly got a stone, wrapped it in a handkerchief to act as a pad, and tied the handkerchief round the limb above the wound, so that the stone pressed on the artery. He then got a stick, and, passing it through the loop of the handkerchief, twisted it round until the bandage was drawn so tight that it stopped the flow of blood. Had

239

he not known what to do the man would have bled to death in a few minutes. As it was he saved his life by knowing what to do and doing it at once.

ACCIDENTS

Accidents are continually happening, and Boy Scouts will continually have a chance of giving assistance at First Aid.

We all think a great deal of any man who, at the risk of his own life, saves someone else's. He is a hero.

TOMMY THE TENDERFOOT No. 10   TOMMY ON THE ROAD
Tommy's a "Road Fool". He steps off a bus
Without looking round and then there's a fuss.

Boys especially think him so, because he seems to them to be a being altogether different from themselves. But he isn't. Every boy has just as much a chance of being a life-saving hero if he chooses to prepare himself for it.

It is pretty certain that nearly every one of you Scouts will some day or another be present at an accident where, if you know what to do, and do it promptly, you may win for yourself the lifelong satisfaction of having rescued or helped a fellow-creature.

Be Prepared

Remember your motto, BE PREPARED. Be prepared for acci-

240

dents by learning beforehand what you ought to do in the different kinds that are likely to occur.

Be prepared to do that thing the moment the accident does occur.

I will explain to you what ought to be done in different kinds of accidents, and you must practise them as far as possible. But the great thing for you Scouts to bear in mind is that wherever you are, and whatever you are doing, you should think to yourself, "What accident might occur here?" and, "What is my duty if it occurs?"

You are then prepared to act.

And when an accident does occur remember always that as a Scout it is your business to be the first man to go to the rescue. Don't let an outsider be ahead of you.

Think It Out in Advance

Suppose, for instance, that you are standing on a crowded platform at a station, waiting for the train.

You think to yourself, "Now, supposing someone falls off this platform on to the rails just as the train is coming in, what shall I do? I must jump down and jerk him off the track on to the far side —there would be no time to get him up to the platform again. Or if the train was very close, the only way would be to lie flat and make him lie flat too, between the rails, and let the train go over us both."

Then, if this accident happened, you would at once jump down and carry out your idea, while everybody else would be running about screaming and excited and doing nothing, not knowing what to do.

Such a case actually happened. A lady fell off the platform at Finsbury Park Station in London just as the train was coming in. A man named Albert Hardwick jumped down and lay flat, and held her down, too, between the rails, while the train passed over both of them without touching them.

On the other hand there was a disgraceful scene which occurred at Hampstead, where a woman drowned herself before a whole lot of people in a shallow pond, and took half an hour doing it, while not one of them had the pluck to go in and bring her out. One would not have thought it possible that a lot of men could only stand on the bank and chatter—but so it was, to their eternal disgrace. The first man to arrive on the scene did not like to go in, and merely called another. More came up, but finding that those already there did not go in, they got a sort of fear of something uncanny, and would not go in themselves, and so let the poor woman drown before their eyes.

What a Scout Can Do

Had one Boy Scout been there, there would, I hope, have been a very different tale to tell. It was just the opportunity for a Boy Scout to distinguish himself. He would have remembered his training.

Do your duty.

Help your fellow-creature, especially if it be a woman.

Don't mind if other people are shirking.

Plunge in boldly and look to the object you are trying to attain, and don't consider your own safety first.

Boys have an idea that they are too young and too small to take any but an outside part in saving life. But this is a great mistake.

Since I wrote this book many thousands of cases have occurred of Boy Scouts plunging in to save drowning people where the crowd was afraid to help.

In the Scouts, we have medals for gallantry, which are granted for acts of heroism and life saving.

Let every Boy Scout prepare himself for emergencies. Some day you may see an accident happen; if you have learned beforehand what to do, you can step forward at once and do the right thing. In any case, you will have the satisfaction of having helped a fellow-creature.

242

Camp Fire Yarn
No. 24

ACCIDENTS AND HOW TO DEAL WITH THEM

Panic · Fire · Drowning
Runaway Horse · Miscellaneous

PANIC

EVERY YEAR NUMBERS OF LIVES are lost by panics, which very often are due to the smallest causes, and which might be stopped if only one or two men would keep their heads.

One evening some years ago, on board a ferry-boat in New York harbour, a man who had been catching some crabs thought it would be a good joke to let one of them loose on board the boat. One crab caught hold of the ship's cat and made it squeal, and it jumped into the middle of a crowd of schoolgirls, who at once scattered, screaming. This started a panic among the hundreds of passengers on board. They rushed in every direction, and in a moment the railings broke and eight people fell overboard. Before anything could be done they were swept away by the tide and drowned.

Some years back a man in a town in Russia, on opening his shop in the morning, saw a big black bomb lying on the counter. He rushed out into the street to get away from it, and a policeman seeing him running mistook him for a thief, and when he would not stop he fired at him. The bullet missed him, but hit another man; panic broke out and many lives were lost. After it was over the man went back to his shop and found the bomb still on his counter—but it was not a bomb, it was only a black watermelon!

Some years ago occurred a case of crush and panic among children in a theatre at Barnsley, from no cause at all except overcrowding, and eight children were crushed to death. More lives would certainly have been lost had not two men kept their heads and done the right thing. One man, named Gray, called to a number of the children in a cheery voice to come another way, while the man who was working the show threw a picture on the screen and so diverted the attention

243

of the rest, and prevented a panic. If only one or two people keep their heads and do the right thing on the spur of the moment, they can often calm hundreds of people, and thus save many lives.

When there is a panic among those around you, you may get a sudden desire to do as the others are doing. Perhaps it is to run away, perhaps it is to stand still and cry "Oh!" Well, you should check yourself when you have this feeling. Don't catch the panic, as you see others do—keep your head and think what is the right thing to do, and do it at once.

RESCUE FROM FIRE

Instances of gallant rescues of people from burning houses are frequent. One sees them every day in the newspapers. You should study each of these cases as they occur, and imagine to yourself what you would have done under the circumstances. In this way you begin to learn how to deal with the different accidents.

An instance occurred some years ago where a young sailor, George Obeney, stationed at Chatham in H.M.S. *Andromeda*, was walking along the Kingsland Road, when he suddenly saw a house on fire. A woman several storeys up was screaming that she had some children there who could not get out. The sailor rushed from his friends and somehow scrambled up the face of the wall till he reached the window below the woman, and broke in the glass so that he could obtain room to stand. The woman at the window above was then able to lower a child so that he could catch it, and in turn pass it down to the ground. Child after child was thus handed down till he had passed six of them to the ground, and finally two women. Then the sailor, overcome by smoke himself, fell insensible, but was caught by the people below. His was an example to you of how to do your duty AT ONCE, without thinking of dangers or difficulties.

A few years ago a house caught fire at Shoreham Beach, and the local Boy Scout Troop was quickly on the scene. They did their work as true Scouts, not only in acting as firemen and getting the fire under control, but also as life-savers in rescuing two ladies and a child, and then in rendering first aid to them and dressing their injuries.

HOUSE ON FIRE!

If you discover a house on fire you should—

1st—Alarm the people inside.

2nd—Warn the nearest policeman or fire station.

3rd—Rouse neighbours to bring ladders, mattresses, carpets, to catch people jumping.

After the arrival of the fire engines the best thing boys can do is to help the police in keeping back the crowd out of the way of the firemen.

If it is necessary to go into a house to search for feeble or insen-

It is not pleasant to be rolled on the floor in a rug or carpet, but that is the way to help a person with his clothes on fire. Take care that your own clothes do not catch fire.

sible people, the thing is to place a wet handkerchief or cloth over your nose and mouth and walk in a stooping position, or crawl along on your hands and knees quite near the floor, as it is here that there is least smoke or gas. Also, for passing through fire and sparks, get hold of a blanket, if you can, and wet it, and cut a hole in the middle through which to put your head; it forms a kind of spark-proof mantle with which you can push through flames and sparks.

When a fire occurs anywhere near, Scouts should assemble their Patrols as quickly as possible and go off at Scout's Pace guided by the glare or the smoke. Then the Patrol Leader should report to the police or firemen, and offer the help of his Patrol either to form a line to keep the crowd back, or to run messages, or guard property, or to help in any way.

If you find a person with his clothes on fire, you should throw him flat on the floor, because flames only burn upwards, then roll him up in a rug or carpet, coat or blanket. Take care in doing so that you don't catch fire yourself. The reason for doing this is that fire cannot continue to burn where it has no air.

When you find an insensible person (in his fright he may have hidden himself under a bed or table), you should either carry him out on your shoulder, or, what is often more practicable in the case of heavy smoke or gas fumes, harness yourself on to him with sheets or cords and drag him out of the room along the floor, crawling on all fours yourself.

To do this you make a bowline at each end of your rope; one you put over the patient's chest and under his arms, and the other over your own neck. Then with your back to his head you start on all fours to pull him along head first. If the bowline is the right length it will keep his head up off the ground, as the picture on page 258 shows.

RESCUE FROM DROWNING

The list of Boy Scout heroes shows you what a large proportion of accidents are due to not knowing how to swim. It is therefore most important that everybody should learn to swim, and, having done so, to learn how to save others from drowning.

A great Channel swimmer, writing in "The Boys' Own Paper", pointed out that a boy, when learning to swim, should learn first how to get in and out of a boat, i.e., by climbing in over the stern. Secondly, how to support himself on an oar or plank, i.e., by riding astride on it, or by catching hold of one end, and pushing it before him and swimming with his legs. Thirdly, how to get into a floating lifebuoy, i.e., by shoving the nearest side of it down under water and capsizing it over his head and shoulders, so that he is inside it when it floats. Fourthly, how to save life.

A moderate swimmer can save a drowning man if he knows how, and has practised it a few times with his friends.

The popular idea that a drowning person rises three times before he finally sinks is all nonsense. He may drown at once, unless someone is quick to help him.

The important point is not to let the drowning person catch hold of you when you get to him, or he may drown you too. *Keep behind him always.*

Put an arm across his chest and your hand under his armpit, telling him to keep quiet and not to struggle. If he obeys, you can easily keep him afloat. But otherwise be careful that in his terror he does not turn over and catch hold of you. If he should seize you by the neck place your arm round his waist, and the other hand, palm upwards, under his chin, with your finger-tips under his nose. Pull and push, and he must let go. If you find yourself clutched by the wrist, turn your wrist against his thumb and force yourself free. But you will never remember this unless you practise it frequently with other boys first, each taking turns in being the drowning man or the rescuer.

Any of you who cannot swim as yet, and who fall into the water out of your depth, remember that you need not sink if you take care to do the following things. First, keep your mouth upwards by throwing the head well back. Secondly, keep your lungs full of air by taking in long breaths, but breathe out very little. Thirdly, keep your arms under water. To do this you should not begin to shout, which will only empty your lungs, and you should not throw your arms about or beckon for help, because this will make you sink.

If you see a person fall into the water and begin to drown, and you

To rescue someone fallen through the ice push a ladder to him.

yourself are unable to swim, throw a rope, or an oar or plank right to him, so that he may clutch at it and hold it. If a person falls through ice, and is unable to get out again because of the edges breaking, throw him a rope and tell him not to struggle. This may give him confidence until you can get a long ladder or pole across the hole, which will enable him to crawl out, or will allow you to crawl out to catch hold of him.

THROWING A LIFELINE

It is often much more use to be able to throw a rope within the reach of a drowning person than to jump in after him and make two to be pulled out.

A good length for a throwing or heaving line is 7 fathoms (42 feet). If you are making up a special throwing line, it should be of nice pliable braided or stranded rope about $\frac{1}{4}$ in. in diameter. For long throws it's usually the practice to make a heavy knot in the throwing end.

Now decide which hand is going to do the throwing. Most people naturally use their right. On that hand coil up your throwing line very carefully, *clockwise*, making the coils, say, 18 ins. from top to bottom. When about half is coiled on, turn up a finger to separate those coils and coil the rest on to the remaining fingers of your hand.

It takes practice to learn to throw a life line correctly, so that you do not get yourself snarled up in it.

When you come to the end of the rope, hold it firmly in your left hand with the last three fingers, or, better, have a loop in the end that will fit down over your wrist so you don't lose the end in throwing. Then pass back the second set of coils from your right to the first two fingers of your left hand. Now you have a coil in each hand.

The right-hand coil is the one you throw first, and you follow it instantly with the left coil, *not letting go of the end*. Thrown out like this, the line won't tangle up, and it's possible to throw the whole line out straight, so that it will reach the farthest. Sending it out in one coil nearly always results in the coil not opening properly, and a short reach in consequence.

Throwing can be underhand or overhand. The latter is better exercise and almost essential if the line has to be thrown from behind an obstruction, such as a bulwark or wall, or has to be thrown to people in an upper storey in case of fire.

RESCUE FROM RUNAWAY HORSES

Accidents sometimes occur from runaway horses running down people. It is well that everybody should know how to stop a runaway horse, and thus to prevent injuries.

The way to stop a runaway horse is not to run out in front of it and wave your arms, as so many people do. Instead race alongside it, catch hold of the shaft to keep yourself from falling, seize the reins with the other hand and drag the horse's head round towards you, turning the horse until you can bring it up against a wall or house, or otherwise compel it to stop. But, of course, for a boy, with his light weight, this is a very difficult thing to do. The share he would have in such an accident would probably be to look after the people injured by the runaway horse.

MISCELLANEOUS ACCIDENTS

One cannot go through the whole list of accidents that might come to your notice, but the point is that a Scout should always remember to keep his head, and think what is the right thing to do at the moment, and be the man to do it, even under the most unexpected circumstances.

Scout J. C. Davel, 1st Bloemfontein Troop (South Africa), saw a little girl entangled in some electric-light wires on the roof of a house. Although he was warned not to go to her, as he might be killed too, he climbed up and got her down. Unfortunately, the child was dead.

Scout Lockley, 1st Atherstone Troop, was at a fair looking on at a roundabout (merry-go-round) which was being worked by electricity from a steam engine. The driver of the engine in leaning over got his clothes caught in the machinery, and was being dragged into it when Lockley sprang on to the engine, and, knowing something of mechanics, pulled over the lever, and stopped it just in time to save the man's life.

There is an example of a fellow Being Prepared, knowing what to do, and doing it without a moment's waiting.

PATROL PRACTICES IN LIFE SAVING

Practise forming a "fence" with staffs, for keeping back a crowd. This can be made a game by dividing the Troop into "crowd" and "Scouts".

Instruct Scouts to know the position of fire plugs and hydrants, police points, fire alarms, fire stations, ambulances, hospitals, etc., in the neighbourhood.

Practise tying bowlines in rope and dragging an insensible person.

Do everything possible to get Scouts taught how to swim. In a town with a swimming bath this should offer no difficulty. In the country, the best chance for Scouts to learn swimming is by arranging summer camp near the sea or a lake or river where it is safe to swim.

Practise the various methods of rescue of a drowning person.

GAMES IN FIRE RESCUE

Prepare a heavy smoke fire in a neighbouring room or building, while you are in the club room. Secretly arrange with two or three boys that if an alarm of fire is given they should run about frightened and try to start a panic.

Have the alarm given either by getting someone to rush in and tell you of the fire, or by having some noisy fireworks fired. Then let a Patrol or two Patrols tackle the fire under the direction of their Patrol Leaders. They should shut windows and doors, and send Scouts into different parts of the building to see if the fire is spreading, and to search for people in need of rescue.

These Scouts should have wet handkerchiefs over their mouths and noses. "Insensible" people (or sack dummies) should be hidden under tables, etc. Scouts rescue them by shouldering them or dragging them out and getting them down to the ground. Use jumping sheet, chute, etc.

Other parties make lines for passing fire buckets.

Another party revive the rescued. Another party form a "fence" to help the police and fire brigade by keeping the crowd back.

Camp Fire Yarn
No. 25

HELPING OTHERS

Rendering First Aid · Shock
Bleeding · Artificial Respiration
Other First Aid
How to Carry a Patient

IF YOU SHOULD COME UPON an accident, remember this: *You are not a doctor.* As a first aider you should send for a doctor at once except for minor injuries. Your job is to keep the patient from getting worse until medical attention can arrive, by preventing shock, stopping bleeding, giving artificial respiration, or doing whatever else is necessary.

In an accident when you are alone with an injured person who is unconscious, lay him on his back with his head a little raised and on one side so that he does not choke, and so that any vomit can run out of his mouth. Loosen the clothing about his neck and chest. Cover him up to keep him warm. See where he is injured, and care for him according to what you are taught in first aid.

If you have found the man lying insensible, you should carefully examine the ground round him for any "signs", and take note of them and of his position in case it should afterwards appear that he had been attacked by others.

If you are out with a Patrol and an accident happens, or you find an injured man, the Patrol Leader should send one Scout for a doctor; he himself will attend to the patient with one Scout to help him. The Second will use the other Scouts in assisting by getting water or blankets, or making a stretcher or keeping the crowd back if one is forming by making a fence with their staves.

As a rule it is best to keep a patient quiet at first. Do not try to move him unless it is necessary, and don't bother him with questions until he recovers a bit.

SHOCK

Shock is a dangerous condition that comes with almost all injuries. You should always be on the watch for it, or, better, take for granted that it is there and do what you can to prevent it from becoming serious.

The patient gets faint, his face pale. He may become unconscious. Don't let that happen. Lay him down immediately, flat on his back, with head to one side. Keep him warm by putting blankets or coats around him.

BLEEDING

When a man is bleeding badly from a wound, press the wound or the flesh just above it—that is, between the wound and the heart—press it hard with your thumb to stop the blood running in the artery. Then make a pad with something like a flat rounded pebble and bind it over the wound. Keep the wounded part raised above the rest of the body if possible. Get a doctor as soon as possible.

On a small wound apply an antiseptic and cover with a clean (sterile) dressing. Hold this in place with a bandage.

Bleeding from the ears and insensibility after a fall indicate injury to the skull. The patient should not be moved at all, if possible. It is best to keep him lying on the spot, put cold water or ice to his head and keep him quiet till a doctor comes.

Spitting or throwing up blood means internal injury or bursting of a small blood-vessel inside the patient. If the blood is light red in colour and mixed with froth it means injury to the lungs. In either case keep the patient quiet and give ice to suck or cold water to sip. Send for a doctor.

ARTIFICIAL RESPIRATION

To restore anyone who is apparently drowned, or someone who is not breathing from having been overcome by smoke or fumes, you need to apply artificial respiration. It consists of forcing air into his lungs and out again. Several methods of doing this have been invented. Every Scout should know at least one good way; the St. John Ambulance Brigade or Red Cross can tell you the most effective methods.

As soon as the patient is breathing, you can leave off—but watch him, and if he fails you must start again till he can breathe for himself. It may be necessary to have relays of helpers.

Then let him lie in a natural position, and set to work to get him warm by putting hot flannels or hot water bottles between his thighs and under the arms and against the soles of his feet.

Wet clothing should be taken off, and hot blankets rolled round him. The patient should be disturbed as little as possible, and encouraged to sleep, while carefully watched for at least an hour afterwards.

Now just practise artificial respiration, so that you understand exactly how to do it, and so BE PREPARED to do it one day to some poor fellow in need of it.

OTHER FIRST AID

Acid Burning

A case occurred of a woman throwing vitriol over a man's face. This is an awful acid, which burns and eats away the flesh wherever it touches. Fortunately a policeman happened to be on the spot at the time, and knew what to do. He at once applied lots of water to which some soda has been added to wash off the acid, then cared for the wound as a regular burn.

Appendicitis

This catches some people rather suddenly, though generally it is preceded by feeling out of sorts. It gives a sharp pain in the abdomen two inches to the right and below the navel. Send for doctor.

Bandages

For binding a broken limb you want a good large three-cornered bandage, such as your Scout neckerchief. Its two sides should each be about forty inches long.

To make a sling for a broken arm or collar-bone, hang the bandage round the patient's neck, tying the two ends together in a reef-knot (square knot) with the point of the bandage towards the damaged arm. Rest the arm in this sling and bring the point round the back of the arm and pin it to hold the elbow in the sling.

The head bandage is used for keeping a dressing on a scalp wound.

Open out your triangular bandage, and fold the base up about two inches. Place the middle of this on the patient's forehead, just at the eyebrows, so that the point hangs down over his neck. Now take the two ends and cross them firmly at the base of the patient's skull, and bring them up round and tie in a reef-knot on the forehead. Turn

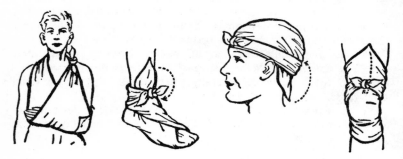

A Scout neckerchief can be used for making a sling and a bandage. Make the bandage neat by tucking in the end as shown by the arrows.

the point up and pin on the top of the head. Be careful that the folds are neat at the side of the head, and that the two ends are tucked away.

Bleeding from the Nose

This does not usually do much harm or prove dangerous. But the bleeding sometimes refuses to stop, which means the patient is losing a lot of blood. To stop it, sit the patient on a chair and tell him to lean his head forward and breathe entirely through his mouth. Applying cold to the back of his neck may prove beneficial.

Blood Poisoning

This results from dirt being allowed to get into a wound. Swelling, pain, red veins appear. Fomenting with hot water is the best relief. Get the patient to a doctor.

Broken Bones

You can generally tell that an arm or a leg is broken by a swelling and pain about the place where the break is. Sometimes the limb is bent in an unnatural way and the patient cannot use it. Get a doctor. Treat for shock.

The broken limb should not be moved about at all. If it is absolutely

254

necessary to transport the patient, bind the broken limb to something stiff, a *splint* that will keep it stiff and straight while the patient is being moved to hospital.

A splint may be a wooden batten, Scout staff, tightly-rolled newspaper, etc. It should be long enough to go beyond the joints above and below the break. You should put a splint on each side of the limb if possible. Then bind the splints firmly from end to end with handkerchiefs, neckerchiefs, or strips of linen or cloth, but not so tightly as to stop the blood circulating or to press into the swelling.

The collar bone may sometimes be broken in a fall. No splint is needed. Bend the forearm on the injured side diagonally across the chest and place it in a sling. Tie a narrow bandage around the body, over the sling.

Burns and Scalds

When anyone gets accidentally burnt or scalded with hot water, and the skin gets red, the thing to do at once, is to put some sort of grease over it, such as vaseline, and then bandage gently. A paste made from baking soda and water gives relief for a light burn. SUNBURN is treated as any other burn.

If any part of the dress sticks to the burn, do not tear it away, but cut the cloth around it with a SHARP knife or scissors, then as quickly as possible protect burnt parts from the air.

In a case of severe burning (blisters or even charring), send for a doctor and treat the patient for shock. Never break blisters.

Choking

To dislodge the obstruction, lean the patient forward and thump the back hard between the shoulder blades. A child may be turned upside down and thumped on the back. If this is unsuccessful, open the mouth, forcibly if need be, pass two fingers along the tongue right to the back of the throat and try to pull up the foreign body. If vomiting results, immediately turn the head on one side.

Choking sometimes comes from a sudden swelling inside the throat. In this case put hot steaming flannel fomentations to the neck and give the patient ice to suck, or cold water to sip.

Concussion or Stunning

This is a common result of a fall or bang on the head. Keep the patient quite still and warm. Get a doctor as quickly as possible. The worst thing you can do is to give spirits or stimulants and to move the patient.

Electric Shock

Men frequently get knocked insensible by touching an electric cable or rail. The patient should be moved from the rail, but you have to be careful in doing this that you don't get the electric shock also. If possible switch off electric current. Otherwise insulate yourself by standing on glass, or dry wood if glass is not obtainable, or put on rubber boots. Also put on rubber gloves before touching the patient. If you have none, wrap your hands in several thicknesses of *dry* cloth, and pull the patient away with a *dry* stick. Artificial respiration may be necessary; when breathing is restored, treat for regular shock.

A boy was hunting butterflies at St. Ouen, in France, when he fell on the "live" rail of the electric railway and was instantly killed. A passer-by, in trying to lift him off, fell dead beside him. A brickmaker ran up and tried to rescue them and was himself struck dead in the same way. The two would-be rescuers were killed through not having learned beforehand what was the right thing to do.

Fainting

If your patient faints and is pale—fainting comes from too little blood in the head—make him sit down and push his head down between his knees. Bathe the face with cold water. If his face is flushed, raise the head—there is too much blood in it, as in apoplexy or sunstroke.

Fish Hook in the Skin

I got a fish-hook into my finger once. I got a knife and cut off all the fly which was on the hook, then pushed the hook farther into my finger till the point began to push against the skin from inside. With a sharp knife I cut a little slit in the skin so that the point came easily through, and I was then able to get hold of it and to pull the whole hook through. Of course you cannot get a hook out backwards, as the barb holds tight in the flesh all the time.

Clean the wound.

Fits

If a man cries out and falls, and twitches and jerks his limbs about, froths at the mouth; he is in a fit. It is no good to do anything to him but to put a bit of wood or cork between his jaws, so that he does not bite his tongue. Let him sleep well after a fit.

256

Grit in the Eye

Do not let your patient rub the eye; it will only cause inflammation and swelling, and so make the difficulty of removing the grit all the greater.

If the grit is in the lower eyelid, draw down the lid as far as you can, and gently brush it out with the corner of a moistened handkerchief.

If it is under the upper lid, pull the lid away from the eyeball, down over the lower lid. In this way the eyelashes of the lower lid will generally clean the inside of the upper one.

Another way, which every Scout must practise, is to seat your patient and stand behind him yourself with the back of his head against your chest. Lay a match on the upper part of the upper eyelid, and then catch hold of the edge of the eyelid and draw it upwards over the match so that it turns inside out. Gently remove the grit with the corner of a wet handkerchief, and roll the eyelid down again.

If the eye is inflamed, bathe it with lukewarm water.

If the grit is firmly imbedded in the eye, drop a little oil (olive or castor oil) into the lower lid. Close the eye, cover it with a soft wet pad and bandage, and get a doctor to see it.

Hysterics

Nervous people, especially women, sometimes get hysterics when excited, crying, laughing, and screaming. The best treatment is to shut the patient into a room and leave him entirely alone till he gets over it. Don't try to soothe him, it only makes him worse.

Poisoning

If a person suddenly falls very ill after taking food, or is known to have taken poison, the first thing to do is to send for a doctor. Then, if the mouth is not stained or burnt by the poison, make him sick by giving him salt and warm water or mustard and warm water, and try tickling the inside of his throat with a feather. If the poison is an acid that burns, the patient should not be made to vomit, but given magnesia or baking soda in water to destroy the acid. The patient should be kept awake if he gets drowsy.

Smoke, Fumes or Gas

Accidents are continually occurring from escapes of gas in mines, sewers, and houses.

In endeavouring to rescue a person, keep your nose and mouth well covered with a wet handkerchief, get your head as close to the floor as possible, and drag the insensible person out as I have suggested in the case of a fire. Drag your patient as quickly as possible into the fresh air—(I say as quickly as possible, because if you delay about it you are very apt to be overcome by the noxious gas yourself)—then loosen all his clothing about the neck and chest and dash

Tie bowlines in the rope for dragging an insensible person.

cold water in his face. If you find that he is no longer breathing, then treat him as you would a drowned person, and try to work back the breath into his body with artificial respiration.

Snake Bite

Remember that poison from a snake bite gets into your blood, and goes all through your body in a very few beats of your pulse. Therefore, whatever you do must be done immediately. The great thing is to stop the poison rushing up the veins into the body. To do this bind a cord or handkerchief immediately round the limb *above* the place where the patient has been bitten, so as to stop the blood flowing back to the heart with the poison from the wound, and cut the wound still more, to make it bleed, and run the poison out. The poison, when sucked into the mouth, does no harm unless you have a wound in your mouth.

The patient should also be given stimulants, such as coffee, and should not be allowed to become drowsy, but walked about and pricked and smacked in order to keep his senses alive until a doctor takes him over.

Sprained Ankle

Apply a tight bandage. Keep the patient from trying to walk, or put any weight on the foot. Fetch help and have the patient carried home. Keep the foot raised; remove the shoe carefully. Apply cold compresses, to relieve the pain and stop the swelling. This is done by wringing out a piece of material or a small towel, folded in several thicknesses, in very cold water, and wrapping the ankle in it.

If cold fails to relieve the pain hot applications may be a comfort. These are called hot fomentations, and there are several things to remember about them: Pour boiling water upon the folded material, which should then be wrapped in a thin towel or cloth so that you may be able to wring it out. Be sure to wring *as dry as possible*, otherwise you may scald the patient. Shake the fomentation out, and apply quickly while very hot. When the pain is relieved, leave off the fomentations. Keep the foot firmly bandaged, and make the patient rest for a few days.

Stings

The best antidote for most stings is ammonia. You can remember this by the front letters of the alphabet: (A)mmonia for (B)ee sting. Baking soda is also good. Remove the sting from the patient with a clean needle. Vinegar is the best antidote for wasp stings and this can also be remembered from the alphabet (V)inegar—(W)asps.

Suicides

Where a man has gone so far as to attempt suicide, a Scout should know what to do with him.

In the case of a man cutting his throat, the point is to stop the bleeding from the artery, if it is cut. The artery runs from where the collar-bone and breast-bone join up, to the corner of the jaw, and the way to stop bleeding is to press hard with the thumb on the side of the wound nearest to the heart, and to keep up the pressure until assistance arrives.

In a case where the would-be suicide has taken poison, give him first aid for poison (see page 257).

In the case of hanging, cut down the person at once, taking care to support him with one arm while cutting the cord. Cut the noose, loosen all tight clothing about the neck and chest. Let the patient have as much fresh air as possible, throw cold water on the face and chest, or cold and hot water alternately. Perform artificial respiration, as in the case of apparently drowned people.

A "tenderfoot" is sometimes inclined to be timid about handling an insensible man or a dead man, or even of seeing blood. Well, he won't be much use till he gets over such nonsense. The poor insensible fellow can't hurt him, and he must force himself to control himself. When once he has done this his fears will pass off.

HOW TO CARRY A PATIENT

A four-handed seat can be made by two Scouts each grasping his own left wrist with his right hand and in the same way grasping the the right wrist of the other Scout with his left hand. If a back is required a three-handed seat is made in much the same way, except that one Scout makes a back by grasping the shoulder of the other.

Stretchers may be arranged in some of the following ways:

(a) A door or gate, covered well with straw, hay, clothing, sacking.

(b) A piece of carpet, blanket, sacking, tarpaulin, spread out, and two stout poles rolled up in the sides. Put clothes for a pillow.

(c) Two coats, with the sleeves turned inside out. Pass two poles through the sleeves; button the coats over them.

(d) Two poles passed through a couple of sacks, through holes at the bottom corners of each.

In carrying a patient on a stretcher be careful that he is made quite comfortable before you start. Let both bearers rise together; they must walk *out of step* and take short paces. It should be the duty of the rear bearer to keep a careful watch on the patient.

If the poles are short, four bearers will be necessary, one at each corner of the stretcher.

PATROL PRACTICES IN FIRST AID

Training in first aid should be very thorough as the public expects much of Scouts.

———

Arrange surprise "accidents" during Patrol or Troop meetings, and let different Scouts take charge.

———

Introduce at odd moments such practices as: improvised stretchers, four-handed seat, artificial respiration, making splints for an injured limb.

GAMES IN FIRST AID

Missionaries

Each Scout in turn acts as an explorer or missionary, with a few simple remedies. Three patients are brought to him in succession to be treated, each having a different disease or injury. He has to advise or show what treatment should be carried out.

Displays

Life-saving displays are very popular both with performers and with the audience.

Bicycle Accident—Boys returning from camp. A rash cyclist. Misfortune. Injuries attended to and patients carried away to hospital on improvised stretchers.

Gas Explosion—Mrs. Coddles and family take a walk. On her way home, Mrs. Coddles meets a friend. Maria is sent on to light the gas stove and prepare father's tea. Father gets back from work and finds the house full of gas. Ambulance squad comes to the rescue. Maria is dragged out and given artificial respiration. Constable Ado arrives on the scene. How not to look for a gas escape. Sad end of a gallant but thoughtless policeman.

Fire Display—Evening at No. 5 Suburban Villas. Fire alarm. Inmates aroused. Fence formed to keep back the crowd. Arrival of fire party with jumping-sheet, life-lines and ladders. Rescue of remaining occupants.

Factory Fire—The workmen are engaged in their daily occupation when an explosion occurs, causing a fire inside the building and an exterior wall to collapse, which injures a man who happens to be passing at the time. The uninjured workmen attend to their unfortunate comrade, while others rush off for help and return with the ambulance and fire apparatus. Some of the men are rescued from the burning building by jumping from the tower into the jumping-sheet.

OUR DUTIES AS CITIZENS

Camp Fire Yarn No. 26

CITIZENSHIP

Duties of Scouts as Citizens
Citizens of the World

EVERY SCOUT OUGHT TO PREPARE himself to be a good citizen of his country and of the World.

For this you must begin, as boys, to look on all boys as your friends. Remember, whether rich or poor, from town or from country, you have to stand shoulder to shoulder for your country. If you are divided among yourselves you are doing harm to your country. You must sink your differences.

If you despise other boys because they belong to a poorer home than yourself you are a snob. If you hate other boys because they happen to be born richer than you, you are a fool.

We must, each one of us, take our place as we find it in this world and make the best of it, and pull together with the others around us.

We are very much like bricks in a wall, we each have our place, though it may seem a small one in so big a wall. But if one brick crumbles or slips out of place, it begins to throw an undue strain on others, cracks appear, and the wall totters.

Don't be too anxious to push yourself on. You will get disappointments without end if you start that way.

Work for the good of your country, or of the business in which you are employed, and you will find that as you do this you will be getting all the promotion and all the success that you want.

Try and prepare yourself for this by seriously taking up the subjects they teach you at school, not because it amuses you, but because it is your duty to your country to improve yourself. Take up your mathematics, your history, and your language learning in that spirit, and you'll get on.

Don't think of yourself, but think of your country and the good that your work is going to do to other people.

WHEN YOU GROW UP

Then, when you grow up, you will become a voter and have a share in governing your country.

And you will, many of you, be inclined to belong automatically to the political party your father or friends belong to. I should not, if I were you. I should hear what each party has to say. If you listen to one party you will certainly agree that that is the only right one,

The elephants of Burma can teach a lesson to the nations of the world. By working together they can carry their heaviest load.

the rest must all be wrong. But if you go and listen to another you may find that after all *that* one is quite right, and the first one wrong.

The thing is to listen to them all, and don't be persuaded by any particular one. And then be a man, make up your mind and decide for yourself which you think is best for the whole country—not for some little local question—and vote for that one so long as it works the right way, namely, for the good of the country.

Many people get led away by some new politician with some new extreme idea. Never believe in one man's idea till it has been well considered from all points of view. Extreme ideas are seldom much good; if you look them up in history you will see almost always that they have been tried somewhere and have failed.

Your forefathers worked hard, fought hard, and died hard, to make your country for you. Don't let them look down from heaven and see you loafing about with your hands in your pockets, doing nothing to keep it up.

Play up! Each man in his place, and play the game!

"A FRIEND TO ALL THE WORLD"

Remember, too, that a Scout is not only a friend to the people round him, but "a friend to all the world". Friends don't fight each other. If we make friends with our neighbours across the sea in foreign countries, and if they keep friends with us, we shan't want to fight. And that is by far the best way of preventing future wars and of making sure of lasting peace.

One thing which brings about wars is the fact that people of the different countries know very little about each other personally, but are told by their governments that the right thing is to fight. So they fight and are all jolly sorry for it afterwards.

If they had been good friends in peace time they would have understood each other better and would never have come to blows.

Nowadays travelling has become so much easier and distances have become so much smaller through motor transport, aeroplanes, and radio that people of different countries have a better chance of getting to know each other more closely.

Then the Boy Scout and Girl Guide (Girl Scout) Movements have spread among the nations. As Scouts we can visit many different countries about the world and find Brother Scouts in each of them, all acting under the same Law and Promise and doing the same Scout work as ourselves. Already thousands of Scouts of different nations are making trips to each other's countries regularly on interchange visits. In this way they have the fun of seeing what other countries are like, and what is more important, they are getting to know one another as friends and not as mere "foreigners".

THE WORLD BROTHERHOOD OF SCOUTING

As a Scout you join a great host of boys of many nationalities and you will have friends in every continent.

This Brotherhood of Scouting is in many respects similar to a Crusade. Scouts from all parts of the world are ambassadors of good will, making friends, breaking down barriers of colour, of creed, and of class. That surely is a great Crusade. I advise you to do your best in that work, for soon you will be a man, and if quarrels should arise between any nations it is upon you that the burden of responsibility will fall.

Wars have taught us that if one nation tries to impose its particular will upon others, cruel reaction is bound to follow. A series of Scout World Jamborees and other meetings of Scouts from many countries has taught us that if we exercise mutual forbearance and give-and-take, then there is sympathy and harmony. These Jamborees have showed what a firm link the Scout Law is between boys of all nations. We can camp together, go hiking together, and enjoy all the fun of outdoor life, and so help to forge a chain of friendship.

The Scout Movement is a world-wide brotherhood. You may have a chance some time, at a Jamboree, to meet Scouts from many nations.

If we are friends we will not want to be in dispute, and by cultivating these friendships such as have been cemented at our great Jamborees, we are preparing the way for solutions of international problems by discussion of a peaceful character. This will have a vital and very far-reaching effect throughout the world in the cause of peace. Therefore, let us pledge ourselves to do our absolute utmost to establish friendship among Scouts of all nations and to help to develop peace and happiness in the world and good will among men.

In all of this, it is the spirit that matters. Our Scout Law and Promise, when we really put them into practice, take away all occasion for wars and strife between nations.

DO YOUR PART

So let us all do our part. Those who are Scouts now should determine to be better Scouts, not only in backwoodsmanship and camping, but in sticking to the Law and carrying it out. If you are not a Scout, come along and join this happy Brotherhood. There are great times ahead, and we shall need you!

FINALLY

I hope I have been able in this book to show you something of the appeal that lies in Scouting for all of us.

I want you to feel that you are really Scouts out in the wilds, able to work things out for yourselves, and not just Scouts in a Troop carefully looked after by Patrol Leaders and Scouters.

I know that you want to be up and doing things for yourselves; that these old explorers and frontiersmen appeal to the spirit of adventure in you; that, despite all the modern inventions, you want to get out on your own, fending for yourselves, enjoying the freedom of the open air.

I have just tried to suggest to you some ways of doing this and of helping you to become real men.

Scouting is a fine game, if we put our backs into it and tackle it well, with real enthusiasm. As with other games, too, we will find that we gain strength of body, mind, and spirit from the playing of it. But remember! it is *a game for the open air*, so whenever the opportunity occurs get out into the open, and **Good Luck and Good Camping** go with you!

THE STORY OF "B.-P."

Lord Baden-Powell of Gilwell 1857-1941
Founder of the Boy Scout Movement
Chief Scout of the World

IF YOU WANT TO UNDERSTAND Scouting completely, you must know something about the man who founded the Boy Scout Movement, one of the most real "boy-men" who has ever lived—Lord Baden-Powell of Gilwell, Chief Scout of the World, affectionately known to all Scouts as "B.-P."

Robert Stephenson Smyth Baden-Powell was born in London, England, on February 22, 1857. His father was the Reverend Baden Powell, Professor at Oxford. His mother was the daughter of Admiral W. H. Smyth. His great-grandfather, Joseph Brewer Smyth, was born in America but joined the British forces during the American Revolution and eventually settled in England. Baden-Powell was thus the descendant of a minister on one side, and of an adventurous colonist of the New World on the other.

B.-P. as a Boy

His father died when Robert was about three years old, leaving his mother with seven children under fourteen years of age. There were often hard times for the large family, but the mutual love of the mother for her children and of the children for their mother always carried them through. Robert lived a glorious outdoor life with his four brothers, hiking and camping with them in many parts of England.

267

In 1870 B.-P. gained a scholarship to Charterhouse School, which shortly after his arrival moved from London to Godalming, Surrey in the heart of the country. He was not an especially outstanding scholar—but he was one of the liveliest. He was always in the thick

The stalking tricks which B.-P. learned in the woodlands around Charterhouse School became of benefit to him in India and Africa.

of it when something was going on in the schoolyard, and soon became known for his ability as a goal-keeper in the Charterhouse soccer team. His dramatic abilities were highly appreciated by his fellow students. Whenever called upon, he would put on a performance that would have the whole school in fits of laughter.

He was also musically inclined, and his gift for sketching later made it possible for him to illustrate his own writings.

B.-P. in India

At 19, B.-P. passed the Army examination and immediately accepted a chance to go to India as a sub-lieutenant, to join the 13th Hussars, the regiment which had formed the right of the cavalry line in the famous "Charge of the Light Brigade" in the Crimean War.

Besides performing excellent military service—he was a Captain at the age of twenty-six—he won the most desired sports trophy in all India—that for "pig-sticking", wild boar hunting on horseback with a short lance as the only weapon. You will realize how dangerous this sport is when you know that the wild boar is often spoken of as "the only animal that dares drink at the same water hole with a tiger".

Fighting in Africa

In 1887 we find B.-P. in Africa, taking part in the campaigns against the Zulus, and later against the tribes of Ashanti and the Matabele warriors. The tribesmen respected him so much that they gave him the the name of "Impeesa", the "wolf-that-

268

never-sleeps", because of his courage, his scouting skills and his amazing tracking abilities.

Baden-Powell's advancement in rank was almost automatic, so regularly did it occur—until suddenly he stepped into fame.

It was the year 1899, and B.-P. had risen to Colonel.

In India, B.-P. won the famous sports trophy for wild boar hunting. He became the accepted authority on "pig-sticking".

Trouble was brewing in South Africa. The relations between the British and the government of the Transvaal republic had reached the breaking point. Baden-Powell was directed to raise two battalions of mounted rifles and proceed to Mafeking, a town in the heart of South Africa. "Who holds Mafeking, holds the reins of South Africa" was a popular belief which proved to be true.

The Siege of Mafeking

War came, and for 217 days—from October 11, 1899—B.-P. held Mafeking in a siege against overwhelming numbers of the enemy, until relief forces finally fought their way to his help on the seventeenth day of May, 1900.

Great Britain had been holding its breath through these long months. When finally the news came: "Mafeking has been relieved", it went mad with joy. Look up "Mafeking" in your English dictionary, and you will find next to it a word created on that wild day from the name of the African town: "maffick"—meaning "riot-like celebration".

B.-P., now raised to the rank of Major-General, found himself a hero in the eyes of his countrymen.

Scouting is Born

It was as a hero of men and boys that he returned to England from South Africa in 1901, to be showered with honours and to

269

discover, to his amazement, that his personal popularity had given popularity to his book for army men—*Aids to Scouting*. It was being used as a textbook in boys' schools.

B.-P. saw a great challenge in this. He realized that here was his

The cover of the first part of "Scouting for Boys", January 1908.

opportunity to help the boys of his country to grow into strong manhood. If a book for men on scouting practices could appeal to boys and inspire them, how much more would a book written for boys themselves!

He set to work adapting his experiences in India, and in Africa

Brownsea Island saw the world's first Scout camp in the summer of 1907.

and many other parts of the world. He gathered a special library of books and read of the training of boys through all ages—from the Spartan boys, the ancient British, the Red Indians, to our own day.

Slowly and carefully B.-P. developed the Scouting idea. He wanted to be sure that it would work, so in the summer of 1907 he took a group of twenty boys with him to *Brownsea Island* in Poole Harbour for the first Boy Scout camp the world had ever seen. The camp was a great success.

"Scouting for Boys"

And then, in the early months of 1908, he brought out in six fortnightly parts, illustrated by himself, his handbook for training, *Scouting for Boys*—without dreaming that this book would set in motion a Movement which was to affect the boyhood of the entire world.

Scouting for Boys had hardly started to appear in the book shops before Scout Patrols and Troops began to spring up—not just in England, but in numerous other countries.

B.-P.'s Second Life

The Movement grew and grew and had in 1910 reached such proportions that B.-P. realized that Scouting was to be his life job. He had the vision and faith to recognize that he could do more for his country by training the rising generation to be good citizens than by training a few men for possible future fighting.

And so he resigned from the army where he had become a Lieutenant-General and embarked upon his "second life", as he called it—his life of service to the world through Scouting.

He reaped his reward in the growth of the Scout Movement and in the love and respect of boys around the globe.

World Brotherhood

In 1912 he set out on a trip around the world to meet Scouts in many countries. This was the earliest beginning of Scouting as a World Brotherhood. World War I came and interrupted this work for a while, but with the end of hostilities it was resumed, and in 1920 Scouts from all parts of the world met in London for the first international Scout gathering—the first World Jamboree.

On the last night of this Jamboree, on August 7, B.-P. was proclaimed "Chief Scout of the World" by the cheering crowd of boys.

The Scout Movement continued its growth. The day it reached its twenty-first birthday and thus became "of age", it had mounted to more than two million members in practically all civilized countries of the earth. On that occasion, B.-P. was honoured by King George V, by being made a baron under the name of Lord Baden-Powell of Gilwell . . . Yet, to every Scout he will always remain: "B.-P.", Chief Scout of the World.

*B.-P.'s first life, as a great leader of men, was tied together with
SCOUTING to his second life, as an even greater leader of boys.*

The original World Jamboree was followed by others—in 1924 in Denmark, 1929 in England, 1933 in Hungary, 1937 in Holland. At each of these Jamborees, Baden-Powell was the main figure, greeted tumultuously by "his" boys wherever he went.

*B.-P. was caught up completely by the Scout Movement which he founded.
His Scouts pulled him into all corners of the world.*

272

But the Jamborees were only a part of the effort for a World Brotherhood of Scouting. B.-P. travelled extensively in the interest of Scouting, he kept up a correspondence with Scout leaders in numerous countries and continued to write on Scouting subjects, illustrating his articles and books with his own sketches.

B.-P.'s Last Years

When finally, after reaching the age of eighty, his strength began to wane, he returned to his beloved Africa with his wife, Lady Baden-Powell, who had been his enthusiastic helper in all his efforts and

Acorns grow into mighty trees. The Scout Acorn which Baden-Powell sowed on Brownsea Island has spread its branches over the world.

who herself was World Chief Guide—a Movement also started by Baden-Powell.

They settled in Kenya, in a peaceful spot, with a glorious view across miles of forest towards snow-covered Mount Kenya.

There B.-P. died on January 8th, 1941—a little more than a month before his eighty-fourth birthday.

B.P.'s LAST MESSAGE

Dear Scouts:

If you have ever seen the play "Peter Pan" you will remember how the pirate chief was always making his dying speech because he was afraid that possibly when the time came for him to die he might not have time to get it off his chest. It is much the same with me, and so, although I am not at this moment dying, I shall be doing so one of these days and I want to send you a parting word of good-bye.

Remember, it is the last you will ever hear from me, so think it over.

I have had a most happy life and I want each one of you to have as happy a life too.

I believe that God put us in this jolly world to be happy and enjoy life. Happiness doesn't come from being rich, nor merely from being successful in your career, nor by self-indulgence. One step towards happiness is to make yourself healthy and strong while you are a boy, so that you can be useful and so can enjoy life when you are a man.

Nature study will show you how full of beautiful and wonderful things God has made the world for you to enjoy. Be contented with what you have got and make the best of it. Look on the bright side of things instead of the gloomy one.

But the real way to get happiness is by giving out happiness to other people. Try to leave this world a little better than you found it and when your turn comes to die, you can die happy in feeling that at any rate you have not wasted your time but have done your best. "Be Prepared" in this way, to live happy and to die happy—stick to your Scout Promise always—even after you have ceased to be a boy—and God help you to do it.

Your friend,

Baden-Powell of Gilwell

(*Found among Baden-Powell's papers after his death, January 8th,* 1941)

APPENDIX

The Scout Movement resulted, first in our own country and soon afterwards in many other countries, from the ideas and ideals in this book *Scouting for Boys* by Robert Baden-Powell. It was not the Founder's intention then, or at any other time during his life, that the Movement should remain fossilised in its origins. The background and thought-pictures and horizons of Edwardian young persons lingered only a little while: certainly today they are largely irrelevant to a generation that finds nothing unusual in men visiting the moon. Baden-Powell often pointed out that a Movement ceases to be a Movement if it doesn't move. As a result every so often to its credit Scouting has taken a good look at itself, not at its purpose or its ethos which do not alter, but at all else—its appearance, its administration, its activities—and has done so particularly on three occasions.

After the Coming-of-Age celebrations in 1929, the Founder himself set up what he significantly called a "Development Committee". In 1941 his successor, Lord Somers, appointed a "Post-War Commission" to emphasise the Movement's awareness that different ways might be needed for the coming different days. And in 1964, the year of Scouting's Diamond Jubilee, under the inspired leadership of Sir Charles (now Lord) Maclean an "Advance Party" was selected to examine what must be done to make Scouting relevant to the nineteen-seventies and nineteen-eighties. From these investigations in depth have come all the changes, all the extensions and all the activities which, while not specifically mentioned in *Scouting for Boys*, stem directly from it.

This book was, in the beginning, written for young teenagers like those who accompanied its author to that first historic camp on Brownsea Island in 1907. But even in the months following the book's publication it became clear that the Movement must extend its frontiers to include both younger and older boys; the clamour from the boys themselves allowed no denial.

In 1916 the eight-to-eleven-year-olds were officially welcomed in and called Wolf Cubs. Today they are known as Cub Scouts and there is less emphasis on Rudyard Kipling's *The Jungle Book* which once permeated their world. But like their older brothers, they have a uniform, make a simple Promise and have a simple Law to help them, have in their "Six" a comparable unit to the Scout "Patrol" and can earn insignia—now Bronze, Silver and Gold Arrows—and various Proficiency Badges as they progress in the interests and hobbies of young boyhood. As for the Scout, the original "Boy Scout", he wears a different uniform; his grades of progress and Proficiency Badges have different shapes and designs and names— but their purpose remains the same: to show a skill learnt, a standard of achievement won, a further horizon reached. His training, as it always was, is based on the skills of camping and (in the widest sense of the word) exploring, to help him to grow in self-reliance. He is still one of half-a-dozen boys in a Patrol under a boy Patrol Leader. But unlike his predecessors, the Scout of today is more and more fortunate in the facilities available to him. Not only is there a wonderful range of modern gear and equipment for him to choose from, but there are innumerable National, County and District Camp Sites for his use and beyond this various Activity Centres, owned by the Association, exist which are surely the answer to any Scout's dreams. For example, at Lasham in Hampshire he can indulge in gliding and power-flying; at Longridge in Buckinghamshire he can enjoy sailing, canoeing, and the like: at Whernside in Yorkshire the Caving Centre offers training and opportunities for the spelaeologically-minded Scout; at centres in Wales and Scotland he can learn his mountain-craft. At all camp sites, in the Scout's weekend camps and expeditions and in his annual camp, higher standards of achievement in the traditional Scouting skills—camp cooking, mapping, pioneering, tree and weather lore, first aid—are ever apparent. He has all this, and, of course, the interests and comradeship of his weekly Troop Meeting, very often nowadays in a spacious, well-planned, modern Headquarters which the hardworking enthusiasm of parents and friends has provided.

Sea Scouts (since 1911) and Air Scouts (since 1941) have always had their own different uniforms, training activities and opportunities and unlimited enthusiasm; and (since 1926) the Movement can be justly proud that for those boys wishing to be Scouts whose physical handicaps did not permit them fully to cope with the normal badge and other requirements, "special tests" have been authorised. Where their circumstances allow, these young people belong to the same Cub Scout Packs and Scout Troops as other boys, but often of necessity they are members of hospital or special-school Packs or Troops. Extension activities (as they are called) continue to be devised for Scouts with a handicap. They, too, have their camps and expeditions.

As for the older boys, as far back as 1910 Baden-Powell was pondering on how best their needs could be served. In 1917, during the First World War, an experimental Senior Scout Section was introduced. Fourteen months later their name was changed to Rover Scouts, but the omission of an upper age limit, the needs of the times and some confusion of purpose, led to Rover Scouting becoming a service and activities Section for adults rather than a Training Section for older boys. The problem was not easily solved. Indeed, it was not until 1944 that suggestions were made for experiment along certain defined lines, and not until 1946 that a new Senior Scout Section began. Today they are an established third Section called Venture Scouts: maturing early in an ever rapidly-changing society, more sophisticated, better informed, physically stronger, they enjoy self-government, and can determine their own programme. Like the other two Sections they have a goal of achievement: the Queen's Scout Award demands the very highest standards of responsibility in emergency training, community service and personal initiative.

Scouting is a voluntary commitment: no boy is compelled to be a Scout. But all who join make a simple Promise, which in a secular age does not ignore religion, and try, in a permissive age, to live up to the standards set by the Scout Law.

As for the adults in the Movement, there they are still—utterly essential (and one might add dedicated and self-sacrificing) as they were in the beginning and as they have been throughout the years. As Commissioners at Headquarters or in Counties or Districts, as trained Leaders of the various Sections, as members of Service Teams (especially on Camp Sites), as old-Scout members of the B.-P. Scout Guild ready to help in any way as occasion arises, as Instructors, as Badge Examiners, as Secretaries and Treasurers, as members of Group Councils and other committees—without these enthusiastic men (and women, too, especially in the Cub Scout Packs), all volunteers, the Movement would cease to function. And in their turn these men and women would function less ably and indeed with diminishing effect were they not aided and advised by a small number of very hardworking professionals staffing various essential Departments—Uniform and Equipment (from Lancing in Sussex), Editorial, Publicity, Legal, International, Training, etc. (from the Movement's Offices in London) and Adult Leader Training (from Gilwell Park in Essex); or, as Field Commissioners, directly assisting County Commissioners and their Counties.

Today our own country has a boy-membership of over half a million, organised into some 12,000 Groups (a Group consisting of a Cub Scout Pack of several Sixes and a Scout Troop of several Patrols; and, in many cases, a Venture Scout Unit as well). Today Scouting has a world membership of over thirteen million. All Scouting countries are associated in a World Scout Conference. Scouts throughout the world try to follow the same essential Law, to keep the same essential Promise and to consider all other Scouts, regardless of creed or colour or race, as brothers. The great international Scout camps known as Jamborees, held when humanly possible every fourth year, are the outward symbol of this inner truth as is our country's memorial to the Founder, Baden-Powell House in London's South Kensington, an imaginatively-designed modern hostel where Scouts and Scout Leaders from as many as forty different countries may stay in the course of a single year.

The boy of today may be more sophisticated and better informed; he may be healthier, better off, have more worldly goods of his own, more attainable ambitions—at least in many parts of the world— than the boy who first bought this book when it appeared so long ago, but so paramount is Scouting's appeal, so true is it to the dreams and innate aspirations of boyhood, that year by year the Movement continues to grow in quantity and quality.

Who would have imagined that a book written for boys could have achieved so much?

INDEX

279